Econometric Modelling of Stock Market Intraday Activity

Advanced Studies in Theoretical and Applied Econometrics

Volume 38

The titles published in this series are listed at the end of this volume.

Econometric Modelling of Stock Market Intraday Activity

by

Luc Bauwens
Université Catholique de Louvain (CORE), Belgium

and

Pierre Giot
University of Maastricht, The Netherlands and
Université Catholique de Louvain (CORE), Belgium

KLUWER ACADEMIC PUBLISHERS
BOSTON / DORDRECHT / LONDON

Library of Congress Cataloging-in-Piblication Data

Bauwens, Luc, 1952-
Econometric modelling of stock market intraday activity / Luc Bauwens, Pierre Giot.
p. cm. -- (Advanced studies in theoretical and applied econometrics ; 38)
Includes index.
ISBN 0-7923-7424-X (alk. paper)
1. Stocks--Prices--Econometric models. 2. Stock exchanges--Econometric models. 3. Day trading (Securities)--Econometric models. I. Giot, Pierre-Roland, 1919- II. Title. III. Series.

HG4515.2 .B384 2001
332.63'222--dc21

2001038183

ISBN 0-7923-7424-X

Published by Kluwer Academic Publishers,
P.O. Box 17, 3300 AA Dordrecht, The Netherlands.

Sold and distributed in North, Central and South America
by Kluwer Academic Publishers,
101 Philip Drive, Norwell, MA 02061, U.S.A.

In all other countries, sold and distributed
by Kluwer Academic Publishers,
P.O. Box 322, 3300 AH Dordrecht, The Netherlands.

Printed on acid-free paper

Printed in the Netherlands.

Contents

Acknowledgments

This book is based on parts of the Ph.D. thesis of Pierre Giot and presents an updated and very much revised version of this work. We have also used results and material from joint work with Joachim Grammig and David Veredas. We are indebted to Ronald Anderson, Bruno Biais, Robert Engle, Christian Gouriéroux, Joachim Grammig, Christian Hafner, Joanna Jasiak, Thierry Kamionka, Gaelle Le Fol, Ailsa Roell, Alain Ruttiens, Mark Salmon, Olivier Scaillet, David Veredas and Steven Wei for helpful discussions and comments on our work. We are grateful to Helena Beltran Lopez, Walid Ben Omrane, Jeroen Rombouts, Fausto Galli, and David Veredas for valuable feedback regarding the first draft of the text and subsequently revised versions. Of course all remaining errors are ours.

This book presents research results of the Belgian Program on Interuniversity Poles of Attraction initiated by the Belgian State, Prime Minister's Office, Science Policy Programming. The scientific responsability is assumed by the authors.

Introduction

Over the past 25 years, applied econometrics has undergone tremendous changes, with active developments in fields of research such as time series, labor econometrics, financial econometrics and simulation based methods. Time series analysis has been an active field of research since the seminal work by Box and Jenkins (1976), who introduced a general framework in which time series can be analyzed. In the world of financial econometrics and the application of time series techniques, the ARCH model of Engle (1982) has shifted the focus from the modelling of the process in itself to the modelling of the volatility of the process. In less than 15 years, it has become one of the most successful fields of applied econometric research with hundreds of published papers.[1] As an alternative to the ARCH modelling of the volatility, Taylor (1986) introduced the stochastic volatility model, whose features are quite similar to the ARCH specification but which involves an unobserved or latent component for the volatility. While being more difficult to estimate than usual GARCH models, stochastic volatility models have found numerous applications in the modelling of volatility and more particularly in the econometric part of option pricing formulas. Although modelling volatility is one of the best known examples of applied financial econometrics, other topics (factor models, present value relationships, term structure models) were also successfully tackled.[2]

Four major factors can be credited to this fast growing body of research. Firstly, the developments of the models themselves, with increasing use of statistical tools and increasing interaction between statistically and economically minded researchers. Secondly, theoretical developments have been spurred by new fields of applied research, where the models could be applied to practical issues in macroeconomics and finance. Dynamical systems, unit root tests and co-integrated models are among the favorite tools used by researchers working with macroeconomic models. In the finance literature, the development of volatility models has led to numerous applications for equities, interest rates, derivative products and risk management. Following the development of the Black and Scholles (1973) option pricing model, applied finance has witnessed a growing need for time series techniques in order to estimate the pricing formulas. Modern risk management techniques make increasingly use of quantitative tools whose inputs are the products of econometric models. Thirdly, this body of applied research was made possible by the increasing availability of computing power, which allowed for fast and efficient estimation of the models. Fourthly, the data, which are the 'raw material' of the empirical researcher, have been actively collected and recorded in all major fields. This is particularly true of the finance world, where data relative to most traded assets (stocks, bonds, derivatives) have become increasingly available.

Most recently, the availability of *intraday* financial databases has had an important impact on research in applied econometrics and financial market microstructure theory. These intraday databases, also called tick-by-tick databases, are now available for most exchanges, such as the New York Stock Exchange (NYSE), Paris Bourse or Frankfurt Stock Exchange. For currency trading, the Swiss consultancy Olsen & Associates collected several years of data, which are available as the HFDF93 and HFDF96 databases. While 'standard' financial databases usually provided information on daily or weekly data (such as the closing prices and traded volume for stocks), the tick-by-tick databases give much finer information. Because intraday data is recorded 'on the fly', the available information usually consists of the time at which the market event took place and its associated characteristics. From a statistical viewpoint, these intraday databases can be viewed as marked point processes, which are characterized by the event times and the marks (associated characteristics). For example, the trade database at the NYSE for a given stock gives the times of the trades (point process) and the associated price and volume (marks). While price and volume information (on an aggregate basis) is also available in daily databases, the event times are by definition a unique feature of the intraday databases.

In the applied econometrics literature, the availability of these new datasets has given birth to the so-called high-frequency models, which attempt to describe characteristics of the price process (for example the volatility or the trading intensity) on an intraday basis. Broadly speaking, two main classes of high-frequency models exist.

Firstly, extensions of the standard time series models (GARCH models for example) that deal with regularly time-spaced data, and which focus on the volatility process during the day (Andersen and Bollerslev, 1997,

1998, 1999; Bollerslev and Domowitz, 1993). Because tick-by-tick data are not regularly spaced, time transformations are needed to convert the original irregularly spaced data into regularly time-spaced data. This usually involves sampling the data at a given frequency. Once the data have been sampled and the intraday seasonality has been taken into account, standard GARCH models can be applied.

Secondly, the so-called high-frequency duration models, following the introduction of the autoregressive conditional duration (ACD) model by Engle and Russell (1998). As the name implies, these models belong to the class of duration models. The ACD model is a duration model with a time series 'flavor', as it combines features of duration models with time series specifications close to the ARCH model. The aim of this model is to characterize and model the time intervals (also called durations) between market events such as the occurrence of a trade or a bid-ask quote in a trading environment. Much of the motivation for this kind of work stems from the market microstructure literature, where time between market events has been found to have a deep impact on the behavior of market agents (such as the traders and market makers) and on the intraday characteristics of the price process. The important role of time has been recently highlighted by Easley and O'Hara (1992) and Easley, Kiefer and O'Hara (1997). These models generalize the seminal paper by Glosten and Milgrom (1985), who first stressed the importance and the different roles played by the liquidity traders and the informed traders when the pricing behavior of a market maker is modelled.

In this book, both class of high-frequency models are characterized. High-frequency duration models are the topic of Chapters 3 and 4, while high-frequency GARCH models are detailed in Chapter 5. Both types of models are applied to the same datasets, which are based on the trade and quote (TAQ) database for several stocks traded on the NYSE. Some of the material presented in these three chapters has been published as research papers, although all models are applied to different datasets in this book (with respect to the datasets used in the research papers). Most models are also extended as new specifications are investigated.

More specifically, Chapter 3 provides a thorough review of the original ACD model of Engle and Russell (1998) and of logarithmic versions of this model, called the Log-ACD models, which retain the main idea of the ACD model while allowing for more flexibility in the specification of the conditional expectation of the duration. The Log-ACD model has been first introduced in Bauwens and Giot (2000). The original model is extended by considering several distributions for the error term. The performance of the models is assessed using density forecast tools, as suggested in Bauwens, Giot, Grammig and Veredas (2000). In the empirical application, the models are applied to intraday data for stocks traded on the NYSE. For several stocks, we model the durations between specific market events using Log-ACD specifications.

In Chapter 4, we model the durations between the bid-ask quotes posted by the specialist on the floor of the NYSE, and we link this updating process to features of the trade process, such as the trading intensity, the average volume per trade and the quoted spread. The empirical evidence is much in favour of the Easley and O'Hara (1992) model, where supposed informed trading leads to faster bid-ask quote revisions by the market maker. As an extension of the ACD model, we introduce the asymmetric ACD model (Bauwens and Giot, 1998), which allows for a joint modelling of the duration process and the direction of the price changes, i.e. if the price is increasing or decreasing. To illustrate a possible practical application of the asymmetric ACD model, we use the forecasting properties (with respect to the direction of the price process) of the model to implement a trading strategy based on the tick-by-tick data for four stocks traded on the NYSE. The forecasting performance of our algorithm is compared to benchmark strategies such as the buy/hold strategy or the pure trend follower.

Regularly time-spaced data and high-frequency GARCH models are detailed in Chapter 5, which is based on Giot (2000a and 2000b). First, we use high-frequency EGARCH and Student GARCH models to characterize the intraday volatility of several stocks traded on the NYSE. As in the papers of Andersen and Bollerslev (1997, 1998, 1999), we first take into account the intraday seasonality in the volatility prior to estimating the GARCH models. We also highlight the impact of characteristics of the trade process (traded volume, number of trades and average volume per trade) on the volatility specifications. Secondly and to illustrate the possible application of Value-at-Risk (VaR) techniques to intraday data, we apply a collection of parametric (normal, normal GARCH, Student GARCH and RiskMetrics) and non-parametric (empirical quantile, Pareto distribution models) VaR techniques to intraday data for two stocks traded on the NYSE. Because of the small time horizon of the intraday returns (10, 15 and 30 minute returns), intraday VaR can be useful to market participants (traders, market makers) involved in frequent trading.

As outlined above, the econometric part of the high-frequency models strongly interacts with market microstructure issues. Indeed, the econometric tools (duration models, high-frequency GARCH models) are applied to data (trades, quotes) which are the result of the interaction of market participants such as traders and market makers. That is the reason why we provide a thorough description of key theoretical and empirical market microstructure issues in Chapter 1. In this introductory chapter, we also detail the main trading mechanisms used in key exchanges around the world (NYSE, NASDAQ, Paris Bourse) and highlight the characteristics of price and order driven markets. Because the econometric part of Chapters 3 to 5 hinges on data supplied by the NYSE, we detail more particularly the trading mechanisms used at this exchange and we review the recent empirical work related to the NYSE. The trade and quote dataset is detailed in Chapter 2, where we also provide a descriptive analysis of several types of durations (trade, quote, price and volume durations) for a couple of stocks traded on the NYSE. This sets the stage for the econometric analysis which is performed in Chapters 3 to 5.

As mentioned above, most of the material presented in this book is based on recent research papers by the two authors. However and owing to the increasing research interest in the field of high-frequency econometrics, other models have been put forward or are currently developed. Regarding high-frequency models of the GARCH type (i.e. models set in a regularly time-spaced framework), most models are similar to those presented in Chapter 5 and rely heavily on the general methodology developed in Andersen and Bollerslev (1997, 1998, 1999) and the work by the Olsen & Associates research group (see Chapter 5 for references). Current research tends to focus more heavily on high-frequency duration models, where most new models extend the original specification of the basic ACD model or introduce new specifications and applications.

For example, as an alternative to the Weibull distribution used in the original ACD model, Grammig and Maurer (2000) introduce an ACD model based on the Burr distribution (which includes the Weibull as a particular case). This extension is discussed in Chapter 3. In the time series literature on volatility, the stochastic volatility model is the counterpart of the GARCH model. Likewise, in high-frequency duration models, Ghysels, Gouriéroux, and Jasiak (1997) propose the stochastic volatility duration model, which introduces stochastic volatility in a duration framework. Similarly, Bauwens and Veredas (1999) put forward the stochastic conditional duration model (SCD), which uses a stochastic volatility type model instead of a GARCH type model to model the durations. Meddahi, Renault and Werker (1998) also propose a stochastic volatility type model for unequally spaced observations, and a generalization of ACD models. In the GARCH literature, long memory dependence in the volatility is sometimes modelled as being driven by a fractionally integrated process (Baillie, Bollerslev and Mikkelsen, 1996). Likewise, Jasiak (1998) considers the fractionally integrated ACD model which allows for long range dependence in the durations. In yet another extension of the ACD model, Zhang, Russell and Tsay (1999) put forward the threshold ACD model to allow for fast and slow transacting periods (or structural breaks in the trading process).

All these models and extensions share a common feature: they only take into account the duration between market events, and do not incorporate information given by the price process (at most they include additional variables suggested by the market microstructure literature). This may be an important drawback, as the information on the price process is of primary importance. Combining information given by the price process and the duration between market events is an important extension. This issue is addressed in Engle (2000), who proposes an ACD-GARCH model: a marginal ACD model is specified for the durations, while the volatility of the returns is modelled by a GARCH process, conditionally on the duration. The ACD-GARCH model is also studied by Ghysels and Jasiak (1998), and Grammig and Wellner (1999).

Other recent papers focus on joint models for the price and duration processes. Darolles, Gouriéroux and Lefol (2000) model the transaction price dynamics by taking into account both the irregularly spacing of the data and the discreteness of the price. Russell and Engle (1998), with the autoregressive conditional multinomial model, combine an ACD model on the durations and a generalized linear model on conditional transition probabilities of the price process. Hafner (1999) specifies an ACD model for the duration, and a non-parametric model for the return conditionally on the current duration, the lagged returns and the lagged volume. Prigent, Renault and Scaillet (1999) focus on option pricing formulas in incomplete markets by making use of the Log-ACD model to describe the dynamics of the price process.

While most studies focus on stocks traded on the NYSE and on currency trading, some recent papers also take a close look at the Paris Bourse; examples are Gouriéroux, Jasiak and Le Fol (1999), and Bisière and Kamionka (2000). Finally, regarding multivariate models, Russell (1999) considers joint modelling of the trade and quote durations which leads to a bivariate intensity function. A similar model is presented in Engle and Lunde (1998). Camacho and Veredas (2001) use the techniques of random aggregation[3] for analyzing price and volume durations as an aggregation of trade durations.

Extensions of the original ACD model considering other distributions for the durations, models belonging to the stochastic volatility class, joint models for durations and marks (price, volume, volatility) or multivariate duration models belong to the current research topics. This active research agenda should ensure that high-frequency econometrics develops in a mature field of finance and econometrics. Of course, this list of research topics is by no means exhaustive. Indeed, as tick-by-tick data become increasingly available to academic researchers, it is to be expected that new models will be put forward and that existing and new models will be used on a broad range of datasets (US stock markets, European and Asian stocks markets, Electronic Communications Networks). Thus, the material given in this book does not aim at providing a full review of all models developed in high-frequency econometrics. In a more modest scope, we detail some of the basic models and provide a general framework for those interested in getting acquainted with this field of research that combines high-frequency econometrics and market microstructure issues.

Notes

1 For an extensive review of ARCH models and related models, see Bera and Higgins (1993), Bollersev, Chou and Kroner (1992), or Bollerslev, Engle and Nelson (1994).

2 Campbell, Lo and MacKinlay (1997) provide a modern review of research topics in financial econometrics.

3 See Jorda and Marcellino (2000).

Chapter 1

MARKET MICROSTRUCTURE, TRADING MECHANISMS AND EXCHANGES

1. INTRODUCTION

In this first chapter, our goal is twofold. First, we present the most important types of market mechanisms that are used to trade shares in key financial exchanges such as the NYSE, the NASDAQ, the Paris Bourse and the FOREX (currency trading). While the list of well-known and important financial exchanges is certainly not limited to these four places, these four markets provide a comprehensive collection of trading mechanisms, most of which are used in other financial centers as well.

The three main theoretical trading mechanisms, Walrasian auction, price driven market and order driven market, are detailed in Section 2 and we highlight in Section 3 how these mechanisms are implemented at these four exchanges. For each exchange, we provide a brief review of key empirical market microstructure studies. Because the econometric part of this work hinges on data supplied by the NYSE, we detail more particularly the trading mechanisms used at this exchange and we give a more thorough list of recent empirical work related to the NYSE.

In a second step (Section 4), we present a brief review of key theoretical and empirical work in market microstructure while focusing on models involving a single market maker. Theoretical issues such as the inventory models, information models and their relationship to asymmetric information, and modelling market liquidity are also reviewed in this introductory chapter.

2. PRICE SETTING IN FINANCIAL MARKETS

2.1 THE WALRASIAN AUCTION

From a theoretical viewpoint, one of the oldest trading schemes in the economics literature is the Walrasian auction supervised by a Walrasian auctioneer. In this simplified trading mechanism, agents wishing to trade an asset (some agents want to buy the asset, others want to sell it) submit their supplies and demands to the auctioneer. The auctioneer aggregates the demands and supplies and then announces a first potential trading price. Knowing this price, agents revise their supplies and demands, which leads to a revision of the price by the auctioneer. At the end of this process, a market clearing price is obtained, which equates aggregate supply and demand. Trades between buyers and sellers only take place when an equilibrium price has been reached.

Some market mechanisms are organized as Walrasian auctions. As explained in O'Hara (1995), the London gold market uses a price setting mechanism that is quasi identical to the Walrasian auction. Other existing trading mechanisms such as the opening procedures for the NYSE and the Paris Bourse (Biais, Foucault and Hillion, 1997) bear a close resemblance to the Walrasian auction, but are somewhat different. During the so-called preopening hours, agents submit their limit buy and sell orders to the computerized system, which is the modern equivalent of the Walrasian auctioneer.[1] At the end of the preopening period, the opening price is determined by the computer (and the specialist at the NYSE) as the price at which the maximum volume among all submitted orders can be traded.[2]

Based on the same idea, in some exchanges and for some infrequently traded stocks, a 'fixing' mechanism (also called automatic periodic single-price auction[3]) is used, which is very similar to the opening procedures highlighted above. At the Paris Bourse and the Brussels Stock Exchange for example, the simple (or double) 'fixing' mechanism is used once (or twice) during the day, when aggregated supplies and demands for infrequently supplied or demanded stocks are **matched**. Some exchanges, for example the Arizona Stock Exchange, use the repeated call auction process as their standard price matching procedure.

2.2 PRICE DRIVEN AND ORDER DRIVEN MARKETS

In the general terminology used in market microstructure (see for example Pagano and Roell, 1992, or Biais, Foucault and Hillion, 1997), markets are usually characterized as being price driven (also called dealership markets or market maker systems) or order driven (also called auction markets or order book markets). In this section, both trading mechanisms are presented from an empirical viewpoint, while the theoretical market microstructure underpinnings are dealt with in Section 4.

2.2.1 PRICE DRIVEN MARKETS

A price driven market relies on the existence of a **market maker**[4] (or several market makers) to buy and sell the traded asset. Thus a trader wishing to sell an asset to another trader must do so through the designated market maker for the asset: the market maker buys the asset from the first trader and then sells it to the second trader.[5] As detailed in the next section, the market maker can either be an exchange official (such as the specialist at the NYSE), or a trader working for a bank (NASDAQ, FOREX).

The market maker provides liquidity to the market by posting firm quotes, standing ready to buy (at the **bid price**) and sell (at the **ask price**) the asset at any time. For example, if a given market maker quotes a \$100 bid for 500 shares and a $\$100\frac{1}{8}$ ask for 1000 shares, a trader wishing to buy up to 1000 shares can actually buy the shares at $\$100\frac{1}{8}$. It should however be noted that the market maker is somehow restricted in the prices he may quote. Because the range of possible prices is discrete (with the minimum spacing between two successive possible prices called the tick[6]), the market maker must select his quotes among a grid of possible prices.

As the market maker buys the asset from a trader and then, at a subsequent time, sells it to another trader, he holds an unwanted inventory position for a certain amount of time, which is a source of potential risk for him. For example, the company for which the market maker makes the market could announce some bad news just after a large buy by the market maker. In this case, the market maker will only be able to sell the stock at a much lower price than the price he paid to buy the stock. To reward the market maker for running this risk (and thus to reward him for providing liquidity to the market), the exchange usually grants advantages to the market maker:

- the **spread**: as the ask price is higher than the bid price, the market maker earns a positive amount of money when buying and selling the stock immediately (or nearly so);
- an informational advantage: the market maker usually has more information regarding the **limit orders** than the traders. This is the case for the specialist at the NYSE as the specialist has a full knowl-

edge of the order book, while traders are only aware of the best bid and ask prices.

Example: Trading shares in a market maker system Suppose we have two traders X and Y, and a market maker Z making the market for the stock of company A. X wishes to sell 100 shares of A and Y wishes to buy 100 shares. In a pure market maker system, Z posts bid-ask quotes which are made available to all market participants, such as traders X and Y. Let us suppose that the current bid price is \$10 and that the current ask price is $\$10\frac{1}{8}$. Thus trader X, who wishes to sell 100 shares, makes the trade at the bid price of \$10. Once the trade has been made, the market maker's inventory has gone up by 100 shares. Trader Y now buys the 100 shares at $\$10\frac{1}{8}$, and the market maker's inventory reverts to its original position, resulting in a net gain of \$12.5 for the market maker.

Suppose now that, after the sell of the shares to the market maker, company A announces some bad news regarding one of its major products, which leads to a downward revision of the share price of A. As this news is public, no trader will be willing to buy the 100 shares at the prevailing ask price of $\$10\frac{1}{8}$. At the same time, market maker Z is left with an excess inventory of shares that he would like to sell. It is not difficult to see that the only solution left is to decrease his ask price (to \$8 say) to attract buy orders. In this case and assuming that trader Y still wishes to buy 100 shares, Z makes a net loss of \$20 on this trade.

Although this example is extremely simple, it highlights some of the main characteristics of trading in a market maker system:

- the market maker has the potential of making profits from the buy and sell of securities, but can be left 'holding the bag' if some bad news hit the share price;

- did trader X have any indication of the future downward revision of the share price of A (as the bad news was released just after the sell), in other words, did he have some private information? Should Z take this possibility into account when he accepts to trade with X or Y?

- because the buys and sells by the market maker occur at different times, how can he manage his inventory of shares in the most efficient way? Is there a relationship between the inventory position of the market maker and the bid-ask quotes?

Market microstructure theory focuses on these problems by introducing economic models describing the interaction between traders and market makers. A review of some important issues in market microstructure is given in Section 4 of this chapter. Example of price driven markets include the Chicago Mercantile Exchange, the NASDAQ, the FOREX and the London Stock Exchange.[7] As the NYSE combines features from price driven and order driven markets, it is called a hybrid market. Both the NYSE and the NASDAQ are detailed later in this chapter.

2.2.2 ORDER DRIVEN MARKETS

In order driven markets, also called automated continuous double auctions, no market makers are involved in the trading process. Traders directly enter limit buy or sell orders in the **order book** maintained by the exchange; the order book is nowadays usually monitored by a centralized computer system. Trades actually occur when orders can be matched. This trading mechanism is used at the Paris Bourse.

Example: Trading shares in an order driven market Let us assume that the current state of the order book is as given by the situation in Table 1.1. In the current state, five limit orders were entered into the system. Three traders are selling shares, with the lowest price at $100 (meaning that this trader will only sell the shares if the price is equal to $100 or higher) and the highest price at $104. Two traders are willing to buy shares: the first trader agrees to buy 750 shares whenever the price drops below (or is equal to) $98 while the second will buy 2000 shares if the price drops below (or is equal to) $96.

At this stage, a trade is not possible as the highest buy order is at $98, while the lowest sell order is at $100. Suppose now that trader X enters a buy order for 1000 shares with a limit price of $100. His order is immediately matched with the existing limit sell order at $100. At the same time, the **depth** of 4000 shares at $100 is decreased to 3000 shares. The final state of the order book is given in Table 1.2. Although this example is very simple, it describes quite accurately how a limit order system works. Further details about the mechanisms of order book systems are given in the section on the Paris Bourse.

Although no market makers are involved in this trading scheme, a spread also exists in this case. In the example given above, a trader wishing to buy can do so at a price of $100; if he decides to sell these shares immediately afterwards, he can only sell them at a price of $98: the spread is equal to $2. As explained previously for price driven markets, order book markets are also characterized by grids of possible prices, with the tick size determining the minimum possible change in price.

As detailed in the example, price priority is a very important feature of order book systems because it ensures that the most favorable trades are always executed first. Thus, for a trader wishing to buy (sell) shares,

Table 1.1. Start state of the order book

Shares	Limit buy ($)	Limit sell ($)	Shares
750	98	100	4000
2000	96	102	800
		104	1000

Start state of the order book. Five limit orders were entered into the system: three traders are selling shares, with the lowest price at $100 and the highest price at $104; two traders are willing to buy shares at $98 and $96.

Table 1.2. End state of the order book

Shares	Limit buy ($)	Limit sell ($)	Shares
750	98	100	3000
2000	96	102	800
		104	1000

End state of the order book after the crossing of a buy order for 1000 shares with the lowest limit sell order.

it ensures that his order will always be matched with the lowest (highest) limit sell (buy) orders. When several orders are competing for execution at similar prices, time priority is usually enforced, meaning that orders first entered into the limit order book will have execution priority.[8]

Examples of order driven markets include the Toronto Stock Exchange, the Paris Bourse, the Brussels Stock Exchange and most European Exchanges.[9] The Paris Bourse is detailed later in this chapter.

2.3 CHARACTERISTICS OF TRADING MECHANISMS

In the preceding discussion, markets are characterized as being market driven or order driven. As discussed at length, this feature has a deep impact on the way shares are traded by market participants. As indicated in Biais, Foucault and Hillion (1997), it is also possible to characterize a given market as operating continuously or at selected times during the day. By definition, a continuous market is characterized by ongoing trading throughout the day, while trading at a fixing market is only allowed at specific times throughout the day. This last trading mechanism, also called batch auction trading, is usually reserved for infrequently supplied and demanded traded stocks, where continuous trading would result in large swings in price as few market participants are active at the same time. It should also be noted that trading in a continuous market can sometimes be brought to a halt, caused by an 'extraordinary' event (for example the release of important news regarding the company or extreme order imbalances). When trading starts anew, opening procedures are generally used as if a new trading day had begun. These suspension of trading procedures are specific to the exchanges (see Hasbrouck, Sofianos and Sosebee, 1993, for the halting procedures used at the NYSE).

Markets can also be defined as being centralized or decentralized. A centralized market requires that the market participants be gathered at a single place, while a decentralized market allows traders and market makers to be in different locations. For example, trading on the NYSE is considered to be centralized as all trading goes through the specialist on the trading floor; trading on the NASDAQ is decentralized as market makers and traders are based at different locations. Finally, Domowitz (1993) provides a much more detailed classification of automatic trading mechanisms by distinguishing three key features of such systems: the priority rules affecting the submitted bids and offers, the degree of automation of price discovery and the allowed information flow to system traders and public investors. This allows for an encompassing classification of all possible trading mechanisms.

2.4 MARKET LIQUIDITY

While markets can easily be classified as being order/price driven, of the continuous/fixing type or centralized/decentralized, it is much more tricky to compare their characteristics and to assess their relative performance. In other words, answering a question such as "Is it better to trade shares on a price driven market than on an order driven market?" raises a rather difficult question. Of paramount importance is a set of criteria allowing to conduct a fair comparison of the different kinds of markets and to assess their performance. In order to do so, the usual notion used in the existing market microstructure literature is to focus on the so-called liquidity of an exchange. In plain words, liquidity can be defined as the ability to quickly buy or sell a large volume of shares with a minimal price impact. Exchanges offering greater liquidity are of course favored by investors as they allow a much more efficient allocation of capital. As indicated by this short intuitive definition, market liquidity has two distinctive components:

- the time dimension: is it possible to trade a given volume of shares in a short amount of time? This is related to the possibility of trading at any given time, the absence of which introduces immediacy costs.

- the price dimension: will a 'fair' price be paid for the asset? More precisely, is it possible to trade a large volume of shares without disrupting the price process, i.e. without getting an unfavorable price? The price dimension of liquidity is thus closely related to the volume that is to be traded, which has led to the introduction of bidimensional liquidity measures (see Pascual, Escribano and Tapia, 2000, and the examples presented below).

The time dimension of liquidity is easy to characterize, as it measures the time needed between the submission of the order and its execution. The ability to trade quickly is important for traders, as yet-to-be executed orders face the risk of unexpected movements in the underlying value of the asset.

The price dimension of liquidity is complicated by the fact that the notion of fair price is vague, and is related to the fundamental value of the asset, which is usually unknown to market participants. A related definition of liquidity is given by Kyle (1985), who characterizes liquidity by three measures: tightness (bid-ask spread), depth (amount of one sided volume that can be absorbed by the market without causing a revision of the bid-ask quotes) and resiliency (speed of return to the equilibrium).

These three measures are similar to the classification presented above, as the resiliency is somewhat related to the ability to trade quickly without disrupting the price process and the tightness and depth notions are linked to the bidimensional nature of the price-volume relationship. Strictly speaking, these measures are meant for price driven markets, but they can easily be extended to order driven markets. While a full discussion of liquidity at exchanges is outside the scope of this introductory chapter[10], some basic facts regarding price and order driven markets can be ascertained.

2.4.1 PRICE DRIVEN AND ORDER DRIVEN MARKETS

In price driven markets, traders do not face execution risk, as a market maker stands ready to buy or sell at all times. However, this comes at a cost, mainly the obligation for the trader to agree with the market maker on the bid-ask quotes.

In order book systems, traders placing limit buy/sell orders face execution risk (when is the order going to be executed? will it be executed in one lot or in multiple lots?) but no price risk.[11] If trading immediacy is required, traders can decide to place a **market order**, which will be executed against the standing orders in the limit order book. In this case however, the price risk is important as the average price depends on the limit orders entered in the order book. With infrequently traded stocks, there may even be a shortage of buy or sell limit orders and the order will not be filled.

One possible solution to this problem (this is the solution hinted at before with the fixing market) is to run batch auctions at regular times (and not in continuous time), which should ensure a sufficient amount of liquidity. Another solution (which is actually implemented in several European exchanges) is to introduce dealership services in the order book system: member firms of the exchange act as market makers by monitoring the order book and entering limit buy and sell orders when liquidity is not sufficient. See Demarchi and Foucault (2000) for more discussion on this topic.

An example is given in Table 1.3, which displays an order book featuring three limit buy orders and three limit sell orders. The sell side is relatively liquid as 8,750 shares can be sold, but the buy side is only able to handle 1,200 shares, 1,000 of which are sold at a price which is 10% away from the the best ask price. Thus, a trader wishing to buy 2,000 shares 'at best' will only be able to buy 1,200 at an average price of $(100 \times 100 + 100 \times 104 + 1000 \times 110)/(100 + 100 + 1000) = \$108.7$. Thus, this order book is characterized by a relatively good depth at the sell side, but features poor depth at the buy side. It is worth noting that appraising liquidity by just looking at the **inside spread** is misleading, as the inside spread of $2 is only valid for 100 shares!

Furthermore, liquidity involves an important dynamic component. In the example given above, the trader could choose to submit a buy order for 100 shares at $100 and then wait. Because the next limit sell order is at $104, the inside spread has increased to $6, which could prompt traders to place other sell orders within the $98 – $104 range, thus bringing more liquidity to the market (this type of behavior is detailed in Biais, Hillion and Spatt, 1995). If large limit sell orders with low ask prices are entered quickly in the order book, liquidity is restored and the buy order for 2,000 shares will be executed at a more favorable price than $108.7.

The recent theoretical and empirical literature seems to suggest that there is no free lunch. While market maker systems are usually associated with higher transaction costs (which can be due to higher bid-ask spreads for example) than order book systems, they also provide an insurance against execution risks: "in a dealer market, traders always pay the bid-ask spread even if a matching order is available. In return, dealers provide a service: by setting quotes in advance they insulate traders from adverse price shocks arising from order flow imbalances. In

Table 1.3. Example of order book

Shares	Limit buy ($)	Limit sell ($)	Shares
750	98	100	100
2000	96	104	100
6000	95	110	1000

Example of order book with poor liquidity at the buy side (right side of table).

other words, dealers insure traders against execution risks." (Pagano and Roell, 1992). This issue is also emphasized by Pagano (1998), who conducts a comparison of European equity markets and who analyzes price driven (London Stock Exchange) and order driven markets (most continental exchanges). Traders wishing to transact small amount of shares will prefer order book systems, as they are less expensive and usually provide sufficient liquidity. When large volumes have to be traded, market maker systems seem to be more adequate.

It should however be noted that pure order book markets usually make use of special trading procedures which can handle very large trades. Indeed, in this type of markets where no market maker stands ready to absorb a large volume, very large trades usually undergo a different trading mechanism called **block trades**, where buyers and sellers are matched thanks to the active participation of traders (i.e. it is not an automatic procedure based on the order book).

2.4.2 THE IMPORTANCE OF STRUCTURAL ARRANGEMENTS

When describing the liquidity of an exchange, we should keep in mind that 'non-economical' reasons sometimes matter. A good example is provided by Bernhardt, Dvoracek, Hughson and Werner (2000), who show that intertemporal competition and ongoing relationships between traders and market makers help explain why traders sometimes transact with the dealers who do NOT quote the best prices. However, these dealers are involved in enduring relationships with the traders, and on average (large) trades are made at favorable prices. Furthermore, in a market maker's system, dealers quote firm bid-ask quotes, but trades are often made within the quoted quotes as the traders call the dealers over the telephone and subsequently agree on the price of the trade. This issue is also highlighted in Biais, Foucault and Hillion (1997), who comment on a previous study by Pagano and Roell (1996) regarding the liquidity of the Paris Bourse and the London SEAQ[12] International trading system for stocks traded on both places.

The influence of structural arrangements on the liquidity of a given market is also stressed in Huang and Stoll (1996), who study execution costs for two different (but matched in terms of characteristics) samples of stocks traded on the NYSE and NASDAQ. This study is interesting as it provides a direct comparison of liquidity (restricted to execution costs, defined as the spread) available on an auction market (NYSE) and on a dealer market (NASDAQ). More precisely, they argue that the observed persistent positive difference between the spread of NASDAQ stocks and the spread of matched NYSE stocks is not due to differences in information structure or fear of dealing with informed traders, but can be explained by the high degree of **preferencing** and **internalization** at NASDAQ, and to a lesser extent by the different treatment of limit orders (up to 1996) and alternative quoting systems. Because of these arrangements between market makers and traders, a large part of the order flow is routed to specific dealers whatever their posted quotes. As a result, these dealers do no have much incentive for bettering their quotes.

Another example of enduring relationships between market agents can be found at the NYSE, when large amount of shares (so-called block trades) are to be traded. Because of the large volume of the trades, these orders can be routed to the so-called **upstairs** market where the trade is prearranged by a block trader. In this case, it has been shown (see Madhavan and Cheng, 1997) that traders with a 'good reputation' get more favorable prices for these large orders than unknown traders or traders using the regular (**downstairs**) trading procedures. These results are detailed more extensively in the section on the empirical research at the NYSE.

3. EXCHANGES

The previous section has highlighted some important features of trading mechanisms stressing the characteristics of price and order driven markets and market liquidity. We now provide a brief review of some key financial exchanges such as the NYSE, the NASDAQ, the FOREX and Paris Bourse.[13]

3.1 THE NEW YORK STOCK EXCHANGE

Officially founded in 1792, the New York Stock Exchange is one of the oldest stock exchange in the world. It was founded more than 200 years ago on Wall Street, and the Bank of New York was the first stock listed on the NYSE. Over the years, the number of companies listed on the NYSE and its total market capitalization have increased tremendously. Today, there are more than 3,000 companies listed (with a total market capitalization of nearly 12 trillion US dollars) and the average volume of shares traded in one day has surged to more than one billion shares. In market capitalization terms, it is by far the largest exchange in the world (the nearest exchanges are the London Stock Exchange and the NASDAQ). After this brief historical review,[14] we now detail the characteristics of the NYSE and its main market participants.

3.1.1 THE TRADING FLOOR

The NYSE trading floor is subdivided into 17 **trading posts**, where all the trading activity[15] for a given stock is centralized. The exchange official in charge of monitoring the trading activity in a given stock is called the specialist. The specialist must fulfill several important tasks regarding the stock he is assigned to, namely:

- act as a market maker, i.e. an agent posting firm bid-ask quotes for a given depth (price driven system feature);
- monitor the order book which contains the limit buy and sell orders for the stock (order driven system feature);
- ensure price continuity, stabilize and ensure an orderly market for the stock. For example, if there is a temporary lack of buyers or sellers, the specialist is required to buy or sell for his own account to stabilize the market.
- disseminate to the trading crowd and the rest of the world the best bid-ask quotes (these quotes can be quotes posted by the specialist or can be bid-ask quotes from the order book) and record the trades that were made at his trading post.

The other main market participants on the trading floor are the floor brokers and the specialist trading assistants. Floor brokers, who are also NYSE members, are traders representing customer orders to buy or sell a given stock. The floor brokers receive buy and sell orders from the member firms (banks, institutional investors, ...) and execute them at the specialist's trading post. As indicated in a recent research report by Sofianos and Werner (2000), floor brokers play a very important role in the NYSE auction market. First, because only the best bid-ask prices (and not the full content of the order book) are reported to the traders, "off-floor traders can find out what is in the limit order book beyond the best bid and ask" using the physical presence of floor brokers. Secondly, floor brokers actively trade the orders they receive by acting like "smart limit order books, walking to the specialist post, assessing the total liquidity available in the limit order book and in the trading crowd and customizing executing strategies accordingly in order to minimize market impact" (Sofianos and Werner, 2000). Last, the specialist trading assistants and clerks usually assist the specialist in managing the order book and reporting the trades and quotes.

With the growing average volume per day, it would be impossible for the floor brokers to deal with all incoming buy or sell orders. Thus at the NYSE as in all other exchanges, computers and telecommunication devices play an increasing role. Today, an increasingly large fraction (in 1992, this fraction was equal to 75%) of orders are transmitted directly to the specialist via telecommunication networks such as Super-DOT.[16] The electronically transmitted limit buy or sell orders are directly fed into the order book. However, these orders represent only about 30% of executed share volume. Thus, while floor brokers transmit fewer orders, the average size of each order is quite large.

3.1.2 TYPES OF ORDERS

As in most exchanges, the two main types of orders submitted by traders are market and limit orders.[17] At the NYSE, both are handled by the specialist, albeit a bit differently. A limit order is transmitted to the specialist electronically or via a floor broker and is entered directly in the order book or with the help of the specialist's assistant. It can then be crossed with an existing limit order. As the specialist manages the order book, the order could also be dealt with by the specialist, or it could be matched by a floor broker.

A market order is transmitted electronically or by a floor broker. In this case however, the specialist has an obligation to expose the market orders to the trading crowd. The order can be matched with an order from the trading crowd, with an order previously entered in the order book or it can be dealt with by the specialist.

Next to plain limit and market orders, many other types of orders exist, of which three can be highlighted:

- block orders: buy or sell orders to trade large blocks of shares, i.e. large trades with a volume in excess of 10,000 shares. Because the volume in play can be much larger than what is usually traded at the specialist's post, these orders may (it is not an obligation as block orders can also be traded at the specialist's post) undergo a different trading procedure. In this case, the trade is prearranged in the upstairs market (in opposition to the floor or downstairs market) by a block trader, who is in charge of locating potential counterparties to the large order. Once this is done, the order is usually split in smaller chunks, resulting in multiple potential trades with the counterparties. However, to enforce time and price priority at the exchange, each of these trades must be exposed to the trading floor (by a floor trader representing the block trader) where the identified counterparties sometimes lose the trade to floor traders or limit orders. If the block order is not routed to the upstairs market, it is sent directly to the specialist's post, where it undergoes standard trading procedures (surprisingly, around 80% of total dollar volume of block trades are executed directly on the floor of the NYSE). See O'Hara (1995) or Madhavan and Cheng (1997) for further information. Block orders are detailed more extensively in the section on empirical research at the NYSE later in this chapter.

- market-on-close orders: orders which are to be executed near the end of the trading session. They require special trading procedures (see Hasbrouck, Sofianos and Sosebee, 1993, or Brock and Kleidon, 1992).

- odd-lot orders: although stocks are typically traded in units of 100 shares (called a round lot), traders can submit orders for a smaller volume (for example 45 shares), or for a larger volume which is not a multiple of 100 (for example 355 shares). At the NYSE, the non-round orders are executed automatically against the specialist's inventory and at specified quote conditions (see Hasbrouck, Sofianos and Sosebee, 1993).

3.1.3 TRADING ON THE NYSE: A HYBRID SYSTEM

In the previous subsection, the trading process at the NYSE was shown to involve a complex procedure which combines the specialist (whose participation is selective), the floor brokers, the orders transmitted electronically and the order book. As indicated by the statistics (25% of all orders, but 70% of share volume), the floor brokers typically handle large orders, which require 'human' handling to get a better price. Indeed, when a floor trader submits a buy or sell order to the specialist, price competition among floor traders is at play.

With respect to the characteristics of the trading mechanisms described previously, the NYSE is thus a truly hybrid system, combining a market maker (price driven market), an order book with the limit buy and sell orders entered by the traders (order driven market) and a trading crowd made up of floor traders. Thus, it is to be stressed that, although all trading in a given stock goes through the specialist assigned to that stock, only a fraction of the trades actually involve the specialist. Furthermore, the degree of participation of the specialist is not constant across stocks and across time (Madhavan and Sofianos, 1998, Chung,

Van Ness and Van Ness, 1999), with specialists dealing more actively for low volume stocks and during early hours of trading. Examples of trades not handled by the specialist include a trade between two floor brokers both present at the trading post. Two floor brokers, one wishing to sell, the other wishing to buy, can agree on a price while both are at the trading post: the trade is made without the intermediation of the specialist. Another possibility is a trade involving the crossing of two limit orders in the order book.

3.1.4 OPENING PROCEDURE

While the continuous trading process during the day features characteristics from order and price driven systems, the opening procedure uses a call auction (see subsection 2.1 in this chapter) supervised by the specialist. Prior to this call auction, market-on-open orders[18] and limit orders are fed to the trading post of the specialist. The OARS (Opening Automated Report Service) matches the buy and sell market-on-open orders. If these orders cannot be perfectly matched, there is a resulting market order imbalance which the specialist has to deal with: he can either decide to buy or sell shares from his own inventory, or he can let the limit orders absorb the excess imbalance. In all cases, he has to maintain price continuity and avoid large price movements (which is one of his main responsibilities as the single market maker for the stock). In extreme cases, the imbalance is so large that the specialist has to delay the opening of continuous trading for the stock.

3.2 THE NASDAQ

The NASDAQ (National Association of Securities Dealers Automated Quotation) system was officially launched on February 8th, 1971. While the NYSE features a trading floor where market participants meet, the NASDAQ is an automated **over-the-counter securities system**. One of the reasons for the creation of the NASDAQ was the poor state of the over-the-counter securities system before 1971. As indicated by reports from the US Security and Exchange Commission (SEC), the over-the-counter securities market was fragmented and obscure at that time. By creating the NASDAQ, one hoped to provide a well established structure for dealing in the over-the-counter securities market.

In the past 25 years, the NASDAQ has achieved a remarkable growth, with a growing number of stocks listed: this exchange has attracted a large number of the so-called high tech stocks involved in computers, telecommunication equipment, software and biotechnology. As the number of stocks listed grew impressively, there was an equally important surge in daily share volume traded. At the end of 1998, the average daily volume traded on the NASDAQ was higher than the corresponding daily volume at the NYSE. On October 30, 1998, the NASDAQ and the American Stock Exchange merged, creating NASDAQ-AMEX.

3.2.1 A COMPETING MARKET MAKERS SYSTEM

While the NYSE relies on the interaction between a single market maker, an order book and the crowd of floor traders to provide liquidity to trade stocks, the NASDAQ trading system is a competing market makers system. For each stock traded on the NASDAQ, a certain number of market makers[19] **make the market** for the given stock and these market makers have a firm obligation to quote bid-ask prices continuously during the opening hours of the NASDAQ. The competition between the market makers is an essential feature of NASDAQ, and it is a driving force behind the liquidity of the market.

As the NASDAQ is an electronic securities market, the market makers are not physically in the same location (as it is the case for the NYSE). Usually market makers are employees of well known banks and make the market from the trading rooms of their banks. The trading and the quote reporting is done via a communications network that connects all trading participants. Market makers at NASDAQ (and other market participants connected to the NASDAQ communications system) have access to what is called Level 2 or Level 3 screens[20], which give information on all quotes posted by the market makers. However, the exchange only reports the best bid-ask quotes[21] to the outside world. Level 2 screens are now accessible to outside individuals also, but there is a substantial fee involved. The best bid-ask quotes are updated each time a market maker undercuts the best ask, or posts a higher bid. This implies that the best bid quote need not be posted by the same market maker as the best ask quote.

3.2.2 MARKET ORDERS AND LIMIT ORDERS

Market orders and limit orders are handled in the same way at NASDAQ. If a trader (who is not a market maker, for example a trader representing an individual who wishes to buy or sell shares) wants to buy or sell shares, he submits his market or limit order to one of the market makers dealing with the stock. If it is a market order, the market maker executes the order at the best price, which can be against his own inventory or against the quotes of another market maker (i.e. the dealer guarantees the execution at the inside spread). If it is a limit order, the order enters the order book. For large trades and more particularly institutional trades, some evidence points out that order preferencing arrangements exist among traders, i.e. orders are routed to dealers according to established relationships which ensure better transaction prices than those quoted at the inside spread (see Wahal, 1997).

Regarding limit orders, an important change in the way these orders are handled at NASDAQ occurred in 1997.[22] If the limit order submitted by the trader improves the current best bid price or ask price, it sets a new inside spread, and the limit order acts as if it was a quote posted by a market maker (it is thus reported by the exchange as a firm quote to buy or sell). Let us suppose for example that the inside spread for stock A is \$100 bid and \$100$\frac{1}{4}$ ask, and that a given trader X wants to buy shares at a limit price of \$100$\frac{1}{8}$. As his limit price improves upon the existing best bid price, the new quotes for stock A are now \$100$\frac{1}{8}$ bid and \$100$\frac{1}{4}$ ask. Thus, although NASDAQ is a pure market maker system, it also includes features of an order driven system.

3.2.3 OPENING PROCEDURE

There is no formal opening procedure at the NASDAQ. However, from 8 am to 9h30 am, there is a preopening session, where market makers can post non binding bid-ask quotes. As documented by Cao, Ghysels and Hatheway (2000), this gives rise to a price discovery process, where the information events that happened during the night are included in the opening price. Two essential features of this preopening session can be highlighted. First, there seems to be some kind of cooperative game between the market makers, in order to include all information in the opening price, with some market makers acting as leaders (usually well known investment banks). Secondly, the information is included in the price via the mechanism of locked quotes.[23]

Generally speaking and as put forth in the above mentioned paper of Cao, Ghysels and Hatheway (2000) or in Bernhardt, Dvoracek, Hughson and Werner (2000), the multiple market maker structure (as opposed to a centralized trading scheme such as used at the NYSE) gives rise to very different market microstructure effects from those observed at the NYSE. For example, cooperative game behaviors between market makers or intertemporal competition between market makers and traders lead to enduring relationships between market makers and traders.

3.3 THE FOREIGN EXCHANGE MARKET

The foreign exchange market (FOREX) is a continuous, decentralized market operating 24 hours a day. Like the NASDAQ, the FOREX is a pure price driven market; the market participants are market makers (also called dealers) who represent large banks active in currency trading.

3.3.1 A CONTINUOUS MARKET

The continuous, 24 hours a day, trading activity at the FOREX is a unique feature of this market. Actually, the continuous dealing in currencies can be divided into three distinct time zones, corresponding to three geographical markets: Asia, Europe and the US. Shortly after midnight GMT, traders are active in Tokyo, Hong-Kong and Singapore, with a lull around 4 am GMT as this is lunchtime in Asia; around 8 am GMT, currency trading starts in Europe (mainly in London, Frankfurt and Paris) and stops in Asia; the last time zone starts around 3 pm GMT as the markets in New York open. At the same time, trading gradually stops in Europe. This intradaily pattern is well known to market researchers and has been often detailed in the academic literature (see for example Bollerslev and Domowitz, 1993, or Guillaume, 2000).

3.3.2 A PRICE DRIVEN MARKET

As the FOREX market is price driven only, trading takes place between the currency dealers, with each dealer posting bid-ask quotes in a regular way. The dealers post quotes from the trading floors of their banks and the information is immediately transmitted to the other dealers via communications networks such as Reuters and Telerate. When a trade takes place, it involves two dealers who agree on a price; this transaction usually takes place over the phone. Two remarks should be made about the price that is agreed upon:

- the price of the trade can be different from the posted bid-ask quotes, and it is often between those quotes;

- because banks do not wish their trading activity and strategies to be made public, the information regarding the price of the trade, its volume and the dealers involved remain private and is not made public to the other dealers.

Thus the information available to all the market participants consists of the indicative (as they can be bettered) bid-ask quotes posted by the dealers, while the information regarding the trades remain confidential.

3.4 THE PARIS BOURSE

As shown in Pagano (1998), the Paris Bourse has undergone substantial changes in the last decade. Driven by the fear of losing business to London's SEAQ international trading system[24], the Paris Bourse has completely changed its trading system, and this set the trend for other European stock exchanges, such as Brussels, Madrid and Milan. The main innovation regarding the trading system in Paris was the introduction of a continuous (from 10 am to 5 pm) centralized order driven system monitored by computers, the CAC system, where CAC stands for 'Cotation Assistée en Continu'.[25] As briefly outlined in the preceding subsection, trading is continuous for actively traded stocks. For infrequently traded stocks, semi-continuous or fixing mechanisms are used, which ensures that a sufficient liquidity exists. A thorough discussion of the main features of the Paris Bourse is available in Biais, Foucault and Hillion (1997) or Demarchi and Foucault (2000).

3.4.1 AN ORDER DRIVEN MARKET

By definition, an order driven trading system relies exclusively on the buy and sell limit orders to provide liquidity to the market: no market maker is involved. At the Paris Bourse, traders can submit buy and sell limit orders to the computerized system, although the orders can only be entered by the stock exchange member firms, called Sociétés de Bourse. Buy and sell orders that can be matched to existing orders are immediately carried out. If the orders cannot be executed (or can be only partially executed), they (or the remaining parts of the orders) are recorded in the order book, awaiting future execution. With a direct access to the order book, traders can also cancel previously submitted orders.

As in most exchanges, the CAC system enforces time and price priority: if two limit orders feature the same limit price, the order entered in the first place is executed first; the orders yielding the most favorable prices for the trade are executed first (matching of a buy order with the lowest limit sell order, matching of a sell order with the highest limit buy order).

The execution of market orders is somewhat different from the execution of limit orders. The part of the order that can be executed against the best limit orders in the order book is executed immediately. The remaining part is not executed against the second best limit orders, but is transformed into a buy or a sell limit order (there is no 'walking up or down' of the order book). For example, if a market buy order for 1,000 shares is to be executed against the order book as given in Table 1.4, 600 shares will be bought at a price of \$100, and the remaining 400 shares are transformed in a limit buy order at \$100 (the end state of the order book is given Table 1.5). That is the reason why an aggressive trader should use a limit order with a very high (if he wants to buy) or a very low (if he wants to sell) price if he wants to trade all the shares immediately.

Table 1.4. Start state of the order book

Shares	Limit buy ($)	Limit sell ($)	Shares
750	98	100	600
2000	96	102	800
		104	1000

Start state of the order book. Five limit orders are entered into the system, three are limit sell order while two are limit buy orders.

Table 1.5. End state of the order book

Shares	Limit buy ($)	Limit sell ($)	Shares
400	100	102	800
750	98	104	1000
2000	96		

End state of the order book, after a market buy order for 1,000 shares was entered into the system whose state was as given by Table 1.4. 600 shares are immediately bought at a price of $100, while the remaining portion of the order (400 shares) is transformed into a limit buy order at $100.

Although there are no official market makers involved at the Paris Bourse, some stock exchange members provide additional liquidity to the market by entering limit buy and sell orders in the order book. These dealership services were introduced in 1996 to provide additional liquidity for medium and low liquidity stocks (see Demarchi and Foucault, 2000).

The CAC system is characterized by an almost complete information flow[26] to the market participants. Each of them (usually banks which are stock exchange member firms) has access to the complete order book, with the identification of the bank who entered the limit buy or sell orders. Trade reporting is also highly computerized and quickly available to market participants. This almost perfect transparency of the market is one of the main feature of the Paris Bourse. However, as documented in Pagano (1998), this transparency can 'scare' some traders, who would wish more privacy for conducting their trades. For these traders, there still exists the possibility of conducting their trades with the London SEAQ International trading system, which is a market maker system.

3.4.2 OPENING PROCEDURE

The opening procedure, which starts at 9 am and ends at 10 am, at the Paris Bourse is quite similar to the one at the NYSE and relies on a price discovery mechanism close to the Walrasian auction. Shortly before 10 am, the opening price is determined by maximizing the volume of shares that can be traded given the (known at this time) supply and demand curves. Biais, Hillion and Spatt (1999) give a detailed analysis of the price discovery during the preopening period at the Paris Bourse.

4. MARKET MICROSTRUCTURE

Over the past twenty years, there has been a considerable amount of research in market microstructure. This research has focused both on theoretical and on empirical models, on price driven and order driven markets, on liquidity, on the role of information in trading (more particularly the effects of information about trades and quotes on the functioning of the markets), on the importance of information asymmetry between traders and on the interaction between market participants. Underlying the theoretical models are the Walrasian equilibrium and rational expectation (usually featuring noisy rational expectation) models. Even briefly reviewing the main theoretical trends and applications would be beyond the scope of this introductory chapter. O'Hara (1995), Biais, Foucault and Hillion (1997), Goodhart and O'Hara (1997) and more recently Madhavan (2000) provide excellent surveys of the existing theoretical and empirical models developed in this field. Lee (1998) provides a broad review of the informational role of prices in such theoretical models. Last, a growing number of studies make use of 'experiments' to investigate empirical market microstructure models. See Bloomfield and O'Hara (1999) for some recent developments in this field. In this section our more modest aim is to set the stage for some of the applications that will be dealt with in the empirical part of this book, focusing on price driven markets. Thus, we give a very brief summary of some of the models related to the behavior of market makers and how they determine their bid-ask prices.

4.1 BEHAVIOR OF MARKET MAKERS: THEORETICAL MODELS

4.1.1 THE MONOPOLISTIC MARKET MAKER

The first theoretical model explaining the market maker's behavior was proposed by Garman (1976). He considers a single monopolistic market maker who is confronted with a succession of buy and sell orders, which are assumed to be independent stochastic processes. To avoid failure (bankruptcy and failure to provide for liquidity), this market maker sets different buy (bid price) and sell prices (ask price). Garman's model was improved by Amihud and Mendelson (1980). These early models are characterized by the fact that the market maker is assumed to be a risk-neutral monopolist, whose bid-ask prices reflect his market power.

4.1.2 INVENTORY MODELS

Stoll (1978) introduces the notion of a market maker supplier of intermediary services. In his model the market maker is a market participant who buys and sells shares to other market participants. In doing so, he no longer has the optimal amount of wanted securities and thus faces an inventory risk. To safeguard himself against this risk, the market marker buys (at the bid price) and sells (at the ask price) shares at different prices, which gives rise to the existence of the spread, equal to the difference between the ask and bid prices.

A main feature of the so-called inventory models is that the market maker is assumed to be risk averse and that the spread is a cost compensating the market maker for deviating from his optimal inventory. More precisely, it can be shown that the spread is an increasing function of the riskiness of the stock, the coefficient of risk aversion of the market maker, and the volume of shares bought or sold. Thus, large buys and sells give rise to large spreads. However, the spread does not depend on the inventory position of the market maker, but the placement of the bid-ask prices do. When the market maker has a large (low) inventory, he will quote low (high) bid-ask prices to elicit buy (sell) orders but will not change the spread. Because of the link between the bid-ask prices and the inventory of the market maker, the inventory effect is often referred to as a transitory component. Indeed, once the inventory reverts to its original size, bid-ask prices and spread should revert to their previous levels.

Stoll's model was improved by Ho and Stoll (1981) who extend the original model to a multi-period framework. Other possible extensions include the study of inventory models in a multiple market makers framework (see O'Hara, 1995, or Biais, Foucault and Hillion, 1997).

4.1.3 INFORMATION BASED MODELS

The first so-called information based model was introduced in 1985 by Glosten and Milgrom.[27] In these models, traders and market makers (who are assumed to be risk-neutral) do not have the same information regarding the value of the security they are trading. Typically two kinds of traders are trading with the market maker: informed and uninformed traders.

Uninformed traders do not have superior information (with respect to the market makers' information set) regarding the financial asset they are trading and they mainly trade for liquidity reasons. Informed traders, however, have superior information on the asset. Because informed traders know the final value of the asset, they always try to benefit from their private information. They sell if they know bad news, buy if they know good news, and they trade as long as the price quoted by the market maker is different from the price implied by their private information.

The market maker, who is potentially confronted with both types of traders, does not know if he deals with an informed or an uninformed trader. Indeed, the incoming trade can originate from a liquidity trader, in which case the market maker does not lose on the trade, or can be submitted by an informed trader, who trades because the quoted prices do not reflect the private information (either good or bad) yet to be included in the asset. Because the marker maker wishes to protect himself from this possible loss, the information model as introduced by Glosten and Milgrom specifies that the quoted prices are set equal to the market maker's *conditional* expectation of the asset value given the types of trades submitted by the trader. More precisely, the bid price is equal to the conditional expected value of the asset given that the trader wishes to sell the asset to the market maker. As there is always the possibility that this sell order originates from the informed trader, the quoted bid price includes the possibility that bad news has occurred. The opposite is true for the ask price, which is set equal to the conditional expected value of the asset given that the trader wishes to buy the asset from the market maker. Because informed traders only buy when good news is to be released, the ask price must allow for this possibility. In both cases, the market maker assumes that the incoming trade is a signal of possible private information. An important implication of the model is that the bid-ask prices are different, with the ask price greater than the bid price. A positive spread arises, which compensates the market maker for the possible loss due to trading with the informed traders. Thus, the spread is the market maker's compensation for facing adverse selection in the order flow.

As detailed extensively in the original paper of Glosten and Milgrom (1985) or in O'Hara (1995), this kind of model is very close to Bayesian learning models. In a multi-period framework, the quoting strategy outlined above gives rise to a Bayesian updating behavior, with the market makers learning from the sequence of trades. It can be shown that, over time, the quoted prices converge to the expected value of the asset given the informed traders' information set. This implies that bid-ask prices permanently include the information given by the trades, as opposed to the transitory component predicted by inventory models.

Easley and O'Hara (1987) extend this model by allowing for different trade sizes, i.e. traders (informed and uninformed) can choose to submit a small order or a large one. They conclude that there should be order size dependency of the spread, as market makers should beware large size orders which probably originate from informed traders. Another important extension of Glosten and Milgrom's model is provided by Easley and O'Hara (1992), who focus on the role of time in the price adjustment process, i.e. updating of the quotes. Indeed, in the Glosten and Milgrom's model, time does not matter: it is exogenous to the price process. Easley and O'Hara use a similar framework but also argue that the time between trades (also called **duration**) conveys information. In their model, a no-trade outcome (a long duration) means that no new information (either good or bad) has been released. Thus the probability of dealing with an informed trader should be smaller than when a short duration is observed. Consequently, with a low probability of dealing with an informed trader, and because the market maker is assumed to follow a Bayesian updating strategy, the quoted spread decreases. Their model has several important consequences:

- time is no longer exogenous to the price process, which implies that the time between trades should also be a variable to be analyzed. As quoted by O'Hara (1995), "empirical investigations using transaction data[28] will be biased because examining only transaction prices ignores the information content contained in the nontrading intervals".
- the sequence of prices matters and is informative;
- volume brings valuable information to the market maker.[29] More precisely, volume is found to exhibit an informational content that is not contained in the price process as excess volume (with respect to what is usually observed, or normal volume) is indicative of possible arrival of informed traders.

Another consequence of their model is that the release of news (information event) should lead to an increase in the trading intensity and this should imply more frequent revisions of the bid-ask prices posted by the market makers: "quotes converge to their strong form efficient values at exponential rate. Rates of convergence are increasing in the fraction of trades from the informed." (Easley and O'Hara, 1992).

4.2 EMPIRICAL RESEARCH

The amount of research in empirical market microstructure is very large and we do not attempt to give a detailed description of this field here. An introduction to this topic can be found in Campbell, Lo and

MacKinlay (1997) or Biais, Foucault and Hillion (1997), while a recent survey is available in Goodhart and O'Hara (1997). In this section, we briefly present some key empirical studies related to the exchanges described in Section 3.

4.2.1 NYSE

The trading mechanism at the NYSE and its consequences on market characteristics (spread, volatility or traded volume) have been the subject of growing academic research set in the framework of market microstructure. The list of empirical issues often investigated includes the study of the components and intraday variation of the spread, the behavior of NYSE specialists, the impact of information on market characteristics and the econometric modelling of the trade and bid-ask quote processes.

The components of the spread Regarding the study of the spread, two major types of empirical studies exist. The first type focuses on the determination of the components of the spread according to the theoretical inventory or information based models. Generally speaking, it is well accepted that both components play a significant role in explaining the existence of the spread. Empirical studies then try to determine the percentage of the spread that can be attributed to the respective theoretical factors. Early studies of this nature are Roll (1984), Glosten and Harris (1988) or Stoll (1989). Biais, Foucault and Hillion (1997) present a general review of such empirical models.

The intraday behavior of the spread This is the second type of studies focusing on the spread. At the NYSE, both volume and spread are much higher shortly after the opening at 9h30 and before the close at 16h than during the trading day. This is usually referred to as the U shaped curve of the volume or spread. Brock and Kleidon (1992) focus on the quasi-monopolistic behavior of the specialist at these times to explain this U shaped pattern. More precisely, because there is an increased and less elastic demand to trade near the open and close, the monopolistic specialist can charge a higher rent at these times, i.e. increase his quoted spread. The increased demand to trade at the open can be explained by the rebalancing of positions by traders to take into account the overnight information. At the end of the day, a much higher volume is observed as short term traders wish to close their positions prior to the close and because some orders are to be executed at that time precisely (market on close orders or orders submitted by portfolio managers who wish to track the indexes). Brock and Kleidon (1992) do not link the intraday pattern of the spread to inventory or information models but stress the role of institutional features in explaining the variation of the spread at the NYSE. Their study explains why both spread and traded volume are much higher near the open and close of trading than during the day.[30]

Chung, Van Ness and Van Ness (1999) provide a recent detailed study of the intraday pattern in the observed spread. Because the NYSE is a hybrid market, they point out that studies focusing on the exclusive role of the specialist in quoting bid-ask prices are biased. Using a database indicating the origin of the quotes (specialist or limit order), they can investigate the intraday pattern of both types of quotes. They conclude that most quotes originate from limit orders and that the U shaped pattern in observed spreads can be largely explained by the intraday pattern of order placement and execution of limit orders. Specialists quote more actively at the start of the day and for low volume stocks (which is consistent with the role they are supposed to play at the NYSE, i.e. providing liquidity when needed). Furthermore, the spread of the specialist is higher than the spread of limit orders and is also much larger at the start of the day, which is compatible with the adverse selection model of spreads.

The behavior of NYSE specialists In a study on stocks traded on the NYSE, and using databases keeping track of the inventory holdings of the specialists, Madhavan and Sofianos (1998) examine the importance and relative share of dealer trading by NYSE specialists. They conclude that the proportion of the trades involving the specialist is relatively weak and depends very much on the stock. Specialist's participation is found to be more active for low volume stocks, and the timing of their participation is linked to their inventory positions. Thus, while standard inventory models suggest that specialists should adjust their quotes according to their inventory positions, this study argues that specialists adjust the timing of their trades. The behavior of NYSE specialists is also detailed in Chung, Van Ness and Van Ness (1999), see above.

The impact of information on market characteristics (spread, depth) Lee, Mucklow and Ready (1993) study the impact of earnings announcements on spreads and depths. More precisely, they show that liquidity decreases (spreads increase and depths decrease) before, during and shortly after earnings announcements.

Block trades Using the Consolidated Audit Trail Data[31] and TAQ database of the NYSE, Madhavan and Cheng (1997) analyze the trading of block trades in the downstairs and upstairs markets of the NYSE. As suggested by Seppi (1990), they find that upstairs intermediation by block traders helps mitigate the adverse section costs faced by large traders who wish to trade for liquidity reasons. These large traders have a clear incentive of signalling that their trades are not information motivated, which allows them to get a lower marginal price impact for their large trades (with the signal enforced by the reputation of the trader). Traders who cannot signal that their trades are liquidity motivated will mostly trade downstairs, thus facing a larger marginal price impact for their trades. Nevertheless and as previously indicated in Hasbrouck, Sofianos and Sosebee (1993), a large portion (around 80%) of the block trades are executed without any upstairs intermediation, suggesting that downstairs trading provides a significant amount of liquidity for large trades and does not deter traders from routing their orders directly to the floor of the NYSE.

The econometric modelling of the trade and bid-ask quote processes Engle and Russell (1998) introduce a new model of the times between market events (such as trades, quotes, significant changes in price).[32] These so-called duration models are usually set in the framework of market microstructure and information models. Other models for the times between market events are the Log-ACD model of Bauwens and Giot (2000) or the Burr-ACD model of Grammig and Maurer (2000). These models are extensively discussed in Chapters 3 and 4. Focusing on the same topic but in a different framework, Hausman, Lo and MacKinlay (1992) use an ordered Probit model applied to intraday data for stocks traded on the NYSE to examine such issues as the effect of a sequence of price changes, the effect of trade size and the effect of price discreteness.

The dynamics of trade and quote revisions Hasbrouck (1988, 1991) studies the quotes revision process of NYSE specialists in a vector autoregressive (VAR) framework and focuses on the 'information content' conveyed by the trade process. In his model, the information content of a trade is measured as the persistent price impact of the unexpected component of the trade, which is not felt immediately after the trade but with a certain lag. Next to the long term information effect, liquidity and inventory effects affect the short term transitory time paths of prices. See also Escribano and Pascual (2000) for an extension of this model. Information models are also dealt with in Easley, Kiefer and O'Hara (1997), as they extend the paper of Easley and O'Hara (1992) and estimate the model with intraday data for NYSE stocks. More recently, Dufour and Engle (2000) combine Hasbrouck (1991) model with high frequency duration models of the ACD type to investigate the role played by times between trades in the process of price adjustments. They conclude that short trade durations lead to a higher price impact of trades and a faster price adjustment to possible asymmetric information conveyed by the trade.

4.2.2 NASDAQ

The mechanism of competing market makers at NASDAQ has been studied by Chan, Christie and Schultz (1995), who show that it gives rise to a different intraday pattern of the spread than what is usually observed at the NYSE. At the NASDAQ, the inside spread is relatively constant during the day (although a little bit higher at the start of the day), but falls sharply at the end of the trading session. In contrast, the average spread per dealer does not exhibit a specific intraday pattern. Chan, Christie and Schultz (1995) argue that a decreasing inside spread at the end of the day is observed because of the competition between market makers. As the market makers at NASDAQ do not have the obligation of maintaining an orderly market, they can better manage their inventory at the end of the day and post quotes that narrow the inside spread. Their paper also highlights the price discovery process that takes place at the start of trading (there are no formal opening procedures at NASDAQ), as traders quote actively but trade orders with relatively low volume. Focusing on a similar topic, Cao, Ghysels and Hatheway (2000) detail the preopening at NASDAQ (see subsection 3.2 on NASDAQ for a discussion of this paper). Overall, for the NYSE and NASDAQ, most recent studies stress the importance of structural and institutional features of markets in explaining the intraday patterns observed for the spread, volume or quoting activity. See also Chung and Van Ness (2001) for a recent study on the impact of reforms in some trading features at NASDAQ on key market characteristics such as the spread and quoted depth.

In the mid 1990's, market makers at the NASDAQ have been criticized for their abnormally low number of bid-ask quotes on odd-eighth pricing. For example, instead of quoting a \$100 bid and a $\$100\frac{1}{8}$ ask, the quotes were (too often) \$100 bid and $\$100\frac{1}{4}$ ask, yielding a higher spread and thus a higher gain for market makers. This systematic behavior is of course against the trading rules at NASDAQ, as it suggests that dealers tacitly collude to post wide quotes. This behavior was highlighted by academic research (Christie and Schultz, 1994) and also made the headlines of specialized business journals. Recently, a special issue of the *Journal of Financial Economics* was devoted to the analysis of market microstructure of NASDAQ (Schwert, 1997). As detailed in the section on market liquidity, the problem of the persistently high spreads at NASDAQ is also studied in Huang and Stoll (1996), who stress the importance of structural arrangements at this market place.

4.2.3 FOREX

In the early nineties, the Zurich based consultancy Olsen & Associates released a comprehensive database of the indicative bid-ask quotes posted on the FOREX market for several currencies. The availability of this information resulted in a tremendous increase in academic research about intraday patterns and price processes in the FOREX market; today the number of publications is still growing very rapidly, with the NYSE and the FOREX the most closely examined markets as far as academic research is concerned. Among many available papers, one can highlight:

- Bollerslev and Domowitz (1993): a detailed analysis of intraday patterns in the FOREX market, with an application to high-frequency GARCH models;

- Andersen and Bollerslev (1997): an analysis of intraday periodicity in the return volatility in the FOREX and futures market, with an emphasis on the modelling of intraday volatility using GARCH models;

- the academic research conducted by Olsen & Associates, such as Guillaume, Dacorogna, Davé, Muller, Olsen and Pictet (1997), Guillaume, Pictet and Dacorogna (1995) or Guillaume (2000).

4.2.4 PARIS BOURSE

As is the case at the NYSE, trading mechanisms and stock exchange members behaviors are the focus of much academic research, especially of French researchers and academics. Indeed, thanks to the intraday data published by the Paris Bourse, there are growing opportunities to closely study how a computerized order driven market works. The academic research on order driven systems is rather new, as past research usually focused on US markets, which are mainly characterized by market makers system. Let us end this subsection by giving a non exhaustive list of academic research papers on order driven systems:

- Pagano (1998): a review of the trading systems in Europe and an analysis of the competing threat of London SEAQ international trading system regarding continental exchanges (shares of large continental companies can also be bought/sold at London SEAQ International, which features a market making system, and which competes with the continental exchanges);

- Biais, Foucault and Hillion (1995): a detailed analysis of the CAC trading system, with an emphasis on the interaction between the order book and the order flow. They highlight the fact that the flow of order placements is greater at and inside the bid-ask quotes, and show that this flow is increasing when the spread increases (so that liquidity is 'naturally' provided to the market). More precisely, the undercutting behavior of the market participants is an essential feature of the order flow as these participants compete for price and time priority.

- Biais, Hillion and Spatt (1999): an analysis of the opening procedure at the Paris Bourse;

- Gouriéroux, Le Fol and Meyer (1998) and Gouriéroux, Jasiak and Le Fol (1999): an intraday analysis of the trading activity and bid-ask curves at the Paris Bourse using high-frequency data from the order book of several French stocks.

GLOSSARY

Ask price Quoted price for which a market maker is committed to sell an asset. This price is usually valid for a certain volume (depth). In an order book market, the price of the lowest limit sell order is sometimes called the ask price.

Bid price Quoted price for which a market maker is committed to buy an asset. This price is usually valid for a certain volume (depth). In an order book market, the price of the highest limit buy order is sometimes called the bid price.

Block trade Buy or sell order to trade a large amount of shares. At the NYSE, a block order is an order with a volume in excess of 10,000 shares.

Depth Volume for which the bid-ask prices quoted by a market maker are guaranteed.

Downstairs trade Trade that is routed to the floor of the NYSE. See also upstairs trade.

Duration Time between two market events, which can be for example two trades (trade duration) or two quotes (quote duration).

Inside spread Price difference between the best bid-ask prices quoted by market makers (these best quotes can be posted by two different market makers) in a price driven market, or price difference between the price of the lowest limit sell order and the price of the highest limit buy order in an order driven market. See also the definition of the spread.

Internalization Preferencing where brokers fill their customer's orders internally instead of routing them to the marketplace.

Limit order Order to buy or sell an asset up to a given price and within a given time interval. A limit buy order specifies the maximum price at which the asset can be bought, a limit sell order specifies the minimum price at which the asset can be sold.

Making a market In a price driven market, a market maker makes the market for a given asset, meaning that he has an obligation (usually enforced by the exchange) to quote firm bid and ask prices for this asset.

Market maker Designated person (usually employed by the exchange or by banks affiliated with the exchange) who has an obligation to quote firm bid-ask prices for a given asset. These bid-ask prices are valid up to a given number of shares (depth). The market maker buys the asset at the bid price and sells the asset at the ask price.

Market order Order to buy or sell an asset at the best available price. This order is executed 'immediately', i.e. upon receipt of the order by a market maker or by the centralized order book system.

Matching of orders Orders are said to be matched when a buy order (sell order) is crossed with a sell order (buy order), i.e. when a trade occurs between a buyer and a seller.

Order book Complete collection of limit buy and sell orders entered by traders. In an order driven market, the order book is usually managed by a centralized computer. In a price driven market or hybrid system, the order book is maintained by a market maker.

Over-the-counter securities system Trading system where traders deal the securities by phone.

Preferencing In a price driven market, preferencing occurs when traders assign their orders to specific market makers, i.e. their orders are routed to market makers on the basis of prearrangements.

Spread Price difference between the quoted bid-ask prices of a market maker. See also the definition of the inside spread.

Trading post Place on the floor of the New York Stock Exchange where the specialist makes the market for a given stock.

Upstairs trade Trade that is routed to the so-called upstairs market of the NYSE, where block trades are prearranged by a block trader.

Notes

1 Limit buy and sell orders and the computerized trading system at the Paris Bourse and NYSE are detailed later in this chapter.

2 In the pure Walrasian auction, supply is equal to demand at the market clearing price. In most practical applications of this scheme, and because traders submit mostly limit orders, it would be impossible to ensure that all buy orders are matched with all sell orders. That's the reason why the price is usually determined such that the traded volume is maximized.

3 Domowitz (1993) introduces a taxonomy of automated trade execution systems, which allows an easy classification of the existing automatic trading systems.

4 The definition of the technical terms are given in the glossary at the end of this chapter. These terms are set in bold characters the first time they are used.

5 In a market maker system, the buy and sell can take place at different times. For example, the first trader can sell the asset to the market maker at 10 am, and the market maker could sell the asset to the second trader at 11 am.

6 The tick size depends on the stock and is set by rules defined by the exchange where the stock is traded. For example, the tick size of most stocks traded on the NYSE is equal to $\$\frac{1}{16}$. For stocks of which share prices are close to \$1 or \$2, the tick size can be as low as $\$\frac{1}{32}$. Since January 29th, 2001, this rule has been changed as the NYSE now quotes all its stocks in decimal form, with the tick size being equal to 1 cent.

7 Trading mechanisms at the London Stock Exchange have usually been of the price driven types; today, due to increasing competition from the other European Exchanges, the trading system is evolving towards a hybrid system, i.e. a market maker system in combination with an electronic order book.

8 Other rules are possible. For example, at the NYSE, orders entered by traders have time priority over orders entered by specialists in the order book.

9 See for example Pagano (1998) for a survey of European equity markets.

10 Liquidity is an important topic in market microstructure. See for example Pagano (1998), O'Hara (1995) or Biais, Foucault and Hillion (1997) for additional discussion on this topic. Pascual, Escribano and Tapia (1999, 2000) present a recent application to NYSE data and provide numerous references to this subject.

11 Indeed, the viability of a pure order book trading system is not obvious by itself. See Handa, Schwartz and Tiwari (1997) for a discussion regarding the interaction between market orders and limit orders entered in the order book.

12 SEAQ stands for Stock Exchange Automated Quotations and is a computer-based quotation system for the London Stock Exchange where market makers can enter their bid-ask quotes.

13 Lee (1998) provides a general discussion of the role played by exchanges.

14 Gordon (1999) provides a colourful, easy to read, narrative of the emergence of Wall Street.

15 For a complete description of the trading procedures at the NYSE, see Hasbrouck, Sofianos and Sosebee (1993).

16 Super-DOT (Super Designated Order Turnaround) is an electronic trading system meant for small orders. With this system, the brokerage firms can send their customer's orders directly to the trading post of the specialist. Next to Super-DOT, there is also ITS (Intermarket Trading System) which is a telecommunication network binding the NYSE, the NASDAQ and the regional exchanges.

17 For a comprehensive description of orders, see Sharpe, Alexander and Bailey (1999).

18 Market-on-open orders are market orders that are to be executed right at the open of the trading session.

19 For largely traded stocks like Microsoft, Cisco Systems or Dell, this number can easily be over 50!

20 Level 2 screens display continuously the bid-ask quotes of all market makers, while Level 3 screens add the possibility of entering quotes and limit orders in the system.

21 This is called Level 1. The difference between the best bid-ask prices is called the inside spread.

22 See Chung and Van Ness (2001).

23 A locked quote is a quote where the bid price is higher than the ask price.

24 The London Exchange created the SEAQ international quote-driven trading system in 1986 to attract trading volume from continental exchanges, as it allows the trading of non-UK shares listed in Paris, Brussels, Madrid, ...

25 While the acronym CAC is most often used, the trading system was updated in 1996 and is now formally called NSC (Nouveau Système de Cotation).

26 The only exception is what is called hidden orders, i.e. limit orders which are only partially visible to the market participants.

27 Strictly speaking, the first information based model can be traced back to Bagehot (1971), but Glosten and Milgrom (1985) first introduce the key idea that trades reveal informed traders private information, which has become the hallmark of these models.

28 Intraday data are described closely in Chapter 3.

29 Thanks to the information models, volume and the much criticized technical analysis are found to have important implications on the behavior of the market makers. See for example Easley and O'Hara (1992) or Blume, Easley and O'Hara (1994).

30 As Brock and Kleidon (1992) show, information models have trouble explaining why *both* spread and volume are larger at the same period of the day. A high spread at the open can be due to the asymmetric information effect already mentioned, as market makers must take into account the overnight information. But that does not explain why most traders wish to transact at that time too. Liquidity traders in particular should avoid these trading periods because of the large spread.

31 The Consolidated Audit Trail Data is a proprietary database of the NYSE where audit trail records for shares traded on the NYSE are recorded.

32 More precisely, Engle and Russell (1998) introduce the autoregressive conditional duration model (ACD model) to deal with financial durations.

Chapter 2

NYSE TAQ DATABASE AND FINANCIAL DURATIONS

1. INTRODUCTION

In Chapter 1, we reviewed basic concepts in theoretical and applied market microstructure and detailed the trading mechanisms used in several key exchanges. As stated in the introduction, our empirical work focuses on tick-by-tick data for stocks traded on the NYSE. In this chapter, we start by describing the intraday database that is available from this exchange (see Section 2). The Trade And Quote database, also called TAQ database, provides intraday information on the price and quote processes for stocks traded on the NYSE and NASDAQ-AMEX. Although databases featuring financial information have been around for a long time, databases providing intraday information to the general public have only been available since the early nineties. Today, most stock exchanges make available to the general academic community the (more or less) complete record of their intraday activity. The release of this kind of information has given rise to a substantial amount of empirical research conducted on the trading mechanisms, the intraday characteristics of the markets (liquidity, volatility), and the price formation process. While intraday databases provide researchers with a substantial amount of valuable information, we also highlight some of the potential problems that arise when dealing with these databases due to the specific nature of these data.

In Section 3, we explain how we process the basic information contained in the TAQ database in order to build the datasets used for the econometric analyses carried in the subsequent chapters. This processing leads to the computation of trade durations, which are the time intervals between successive trades of a stock, and quote durations, which are the time intervals between successive best quotes for a stock. Other types of durations can be defined as the times between other events defined for a specific purpose. In Section 4, we introduce price and volume durations and motivate their interest.

In the last section, to set the stage for the econometric models and results of the next chapters, we provide a descriptive analysis of the key characteristics of the intraday data for several stocks traded on the NYSE and stress the importance of intraday seasonality and dynamics of the duration data. The main stylized facts can be summarized in a few words. Durations between intraday market events are highly autocorrelated. They are overdispersed in the case of trade, quote and price durations, and underdispersed in the case of volume durations. They feature a strong intraday seasonality which is linked to market and exchange characteristics. While taking into account this intraday seasonality does remove some of the autocorrelation, the so-called time-of-day adjusted durations are still highly autocorrelated, which justifies the use of the dynamic duration models introduced in Chapter 3.

Finally, in an appendix to this chapter, we also give some information regarding two high-frequency databases, released by Olsen & Associates, related to bid-ask quotes posted by market makers in the foreign exchange market.

2. THE TAQ DATABASE

The Trade and Quote database (TAQ database) is released by the New York Stock Exchange and provides intraday information for stocks traded on the NYSE and NASDAQ-AMEX.[1] The information included in this database consists of:

- trade information: all trades, timestamped to the second, for all stocks traded on the New York Stock Exchange, the regional affiliates (such as Boston, Cincinnati, MidWest, ...) and the NASDAQ-AMEX;
- quote information: all best bid-ask quotes posted by specialists (at the NYSE and the AMEX) and by the market makers (at the NASDAQ) for all stocks. These quotes are timestamped to the second.

After this brief introduction, we present the detailed structure of the trade and quote databases.

2.1 THE TRADE DATABASE

The trade database has the following structure:

@SYMBOL	DATE	EX	TIME	PRICE	SIZE	C	CR	TSEQ	G127
IBM	960903	N	93644	11287500	2600		0	2311350	0
IBM	960903	N	93650	11287500	1800		0	2311360	0
IBM	960903	N	93658	11287500	1000		0	2311380	0

Each line of the trade database consists in the recording of a trade actually carried out. The first column is the ticker[2] of the stock, the second is the date at which the trade took place, the third is the exchange (in this example N stands for New York), the fourth is the time in hours/minutes/seconds of the trade, the fifth is the price (multiplied by 100,000) and the sixth is the volume of the trade. The last columns are correction indicators, which give information on the validity of the trade.

In the example given above, the second line indicates that 1,800 shares of IBM were traded on a price of \$112.875 at 9 hours 36 minutes and 50 seconds on the third of September 1996. The trade was made on the NYSE.

2.2 THE QUOTE DATABASE

The quote database has a similar structure:

@SYMBOL	DATE	EX	TIME	BID	SIZ	OFFER	SIZ	MD	QSEQ
IBM	960903	N	93225	11312500	10	11325000	20	12	2311090
IBM	960903	N	93238	11300000	50	11312500	50	12	2311110
IBM	960903	N	93425	11300000	50	11312500	75	12	2311190

Each line of the quote database consists in the recording of the best bid-ask quotes. The first column is the ticker of the stock, the second is the date at which the quotes were posted, the third is the exchange (in this example N stands for New York), the fourth is the time in hours/minutes/seconds of the post, the fifth is the best bid price (multiplied by 100,000), the sixth is the depth (divided by 100) of the bid price, the seventh is the best ask price (multiplied by 100,000) and the eighth is the depth (divided by 100) of the ask price. The last columns are correction indicators, which give information on the validity of the quotes.

For example, the third line indicates that, for IBM, at 9 hours 34 minutes and 25 seconds on the third of September 1996, the best bid price was \$113, with a depth of 5,000 shares, and the best ask price was \$113.125, with a depth of 7,500 shares.

As the TAQ database contains information on all trades and all bid-ask quotes, it is the most accurate source of information available for researchers (who are interested by stocks traded on the NYSE or the NASDAQ).[3] Furthermore, as each transaction and quotes is timestamped to the second, the information set contains the time of the market event (trade, quote) and the time elapsed since the last market event. This is one of the main features of this type of database. As detailed extensively in the next chapters, the inclusion of the time dimension in the information set has given rise to a whole new class of econometric models.

There are however some difficulties associated with the use of the TAQ database. Although they are not serious problems, one must remain careful when working with this type of intraday data and it must be remembered that 'real life' trading on the floor of the NYSE can be very different from what is indicated in the historical data of TAQ. The next subsections indicate the potential pitfalls.

2.3 BEST BID-ASK QUOTES

Although the information regarding the bid-ask quotes leads to a better understanding of the way market makers and specialists revise their prices, it is incomplete in the sense that only the best bid and ask prices are available. This information is usually different from the information that can be gathered by the market participants when trading takes place. Because the trading mechanisms are different for the NYSE and NASDAQ, the information loss is different.

2.3.1 NYSE

As indicated in Chapter 1, the NYSE features a hybrid trading mechanism that combines features from a market maker system (a unique market maker, called the specialist, is assigned to each stock), an order book system and floor trading. Strictly speaking, the specialist is the only market participant that can post quotes. However, the limit orders entered in the order book or supplied by the floor traders can improve on the quotes posted by the specialist, in which case they are equivalent to quotes. Thus, at the NYSE, the best bid-ask quotes reported by the system and recorded in the TAQ database can be

- quotes actually posted by the specialist, which are quotes involving a possible buy or sell by the specialist for his own account;
- quotes from the existing order book, which are either buy or sell limit orders by other market participants;
- quotes originating from limit buy and sell orders submitted by traders in the trading crowd.

As indicated in subsection 4.2.1 of Chapter 1 where intraday studies on the spread were reviewed, Madhavan and Sofianos (1998) show that the participation of the specialist in *trading* at the NYSE is selective: "Over time in an individual stock, specialists participate more actively as sellers (buyers) when holding long (short) inventory positions. This results suggest that dealers control their inventory positions by selectively timing the size and direction of their trades rather than by adjusting their quotes". Furthermore and as indicated by Chung, Van Ness and Van Ness (1999), the participation of the specialist in *quoting* at the NYSE is also selective. Indeed, they show that "a rather large portion of posted bid-ask quotes originates from the limit order book without direct participation by the specialist". Thus, while the specialist monitors the limit order book and the quoting process, all posted quotes do not originate directly from the specialist.

For the traders involved in trading with the specialist, the available quotes are the best bid and ask quotes, which are made public by the specialist. However, the specialist is aware of the state of the order book and of all the limit (buy or sell) orders that were fed into the system. Thus, the specialist has an informational advantage compared to the trading crowd.

By not including the past states of the order book managed by the specialist, the information given in the TAQ database is thus partial.[4] Furthermore, as indicated in Chapter 1, floor traders closely watch the specialist and other floor traders. This implies that their information set includes additional information (which is perhaps hard to quantify) which goes beyond the mere best bid-ask quotes. Last, the reported depth at the bid and ask quotes does not take into account the 'intelligent order book' behavior of the floor traders and tends to understate the available liquidity (see Sofianos and Werner, 2000).

2.3.2 NASDAQ

Since the NASDAQ involves a multiple market maker system (with each market maker managing his own limit order book), the available best bid quote can be posted by market maker A and the available best ask quote can be posted by market maker B (or it can be a limit buy or sell order submitted by a trader). Of course, this situation evolves through time. Thus the best bid-ask quotes are usually not posted by the same market maker. To get a complete picture of the bid-ask quotes updating process by individual market makers at NASDAQ, researchers have to combine the information given by the TAQ database and information on the prices posted by individual market makers, by downloading screens of real-time quotes from information systems as Cao, Ghysels and Hatheway (2000) did, or by using the new tick-by-tick database of NASDAQ.

2.4 DIRECTION OF A TRADE

Regarding the trade database, the information recorded is the time at which the trade took place, the price paid for the trade and the volume of shares that changed hands. More precisely, the direction of the trade is not recorded, i.e. if it is a sell by a trader (and thus a buy by the specialist or matched with a limit buy order) or a buy by a trader (and thus a sell by the specialist or matched with a limit sell order).

The only way to infer the direction of a trade from available intraday historical data is to combine the trade database with the information given by the quote database. It now seems that the algorithm devised by Lee and Ready (1991) gives good results, and it has become the standard algorithm used in empirical market microstructure studies.

The method introduced by Lee and Ready (1991) consists in comparing the price of the trade and the most recent bid-ask prices. If the price of the trade is closer to the bid than to the ask price, then it is assumed that it is a sell initiated trade; when the price of the trade is closer to the ask than to the bid price, then it is a buy initiated trade. For the cases where the price of the trade is equal to the bid-ask midpoint, one has to use the tick rule. The tick rule specifies that, when the price of the trade is equal to the bid-ask midpoint, the direction of the trade is determined by the previously recorded trade. If the price is higher than the price of the previous trade, then it is called an uptick and it is classified as a buy. If the price is lower, then it is called a downtick and it is classified as a sell.

2.5 DOWNSTAIRS OR UPSTAIRS TRADE?

When a large volume of shares is to be traded on the NYSE, the order can be upstairs facilated or routed directly to the floor of the NYSE (see Chapter 1). The two trading mechanisms are different and lead to quantitatively different price impact of trades. However both types of trades are recorded similarly in the TAQ database and it is thus impossible to determine if the trade was upstairs facilitated based on TAQ information alone. An example is given in Madhavan and Cheng (1997).

2.6 RECORDING MISTAKES

As the data is recorded continuously during the day, and is not directly available from a computer system (as would be the case in an electronic order book system), recording mistakes happen from time to time. For example, at the NYSE, an employee of the Exchange, who is called the floor reporter, stands by the specialist and keeps track of the trades not directly reported by the Display Book (Hasbrouck, Sofianos and Sosebee, 1993). Regarding the quotes, it is the duty of the specialist, with the help of his clerk, to report the quotes.

In the TAQ database, each trade and quote is identified by control variables which characterize the validity of the trade and quote (for a list of all control variables used in the TAQ database, see the TAQ database manual). As explained in the next section, the information in the 'raw' TAQ database should first be filtered to remove recording mistakes, prior to using the information.

2.7 BID-ASK BOUNCE

The bid-ask bounce is a familiar problem for researchers working with intraday data. By bid-ask bounce, one means that successions of buy and sell orders take place at different prices, even if the price of the asset is constant. For example, let us assume that a market maker quotes a \$100 bid for 500 shares and a \$100$\frac{1}{8}$ ask for 1000 shares. Assuming that the depths at the bid and at the ask are sufficiently large to accommodate four orders, even if there are no quotes revision a succession of buy/sell/buy/sell orders takes place at the prices \$100$\frac{1}{8}$, \$100, \$100$\frac{1}{8}$ and \$100. Thus, the price of the asset is not unique, but depends on the direction of the trade. As first pointed out by Roll (1984), this gives rise to negative first order autocorrelation when analyzing intraday returns. This must be accounted for when analyzing intraday (trade) data.

3. EXTRACTING INFORMATION FROM THE TAQ DATABASE

As pointed out in the preceding subsections, the information contained in the TAQ database cannot be directly used in an econometric program. On the one hand, recording mistakes must be taken care of, and missing information (such as the direction of the trade) must be inferred from the data. On the other hand, the structure and formatting of the data is usually not directly compatible with the input files accepted by the econometric programs.

In this section, we present the general methodology underlying a typical extraction procedure that can be used with the TAQ database.[5] This extraction procedure proceeds as follows:

- select the ticker of the stock that is under investigation;

- use the extraction program supplied with the TAQ database to retrieve from a given CD-ROM the raw files containing the trade and quote databases (this step has to be repeated for all CD-ROMs available, as the data on one CD-ROM is relative to two trading weeks only);

- using a data processing program, one has to select the trades and quotes that fulfill the regularity conditions ;
- check if there are any errors left (for example, with NASDAQ data, it sometimes happen that the quote reporting is split on two separate lines; these two lines must be combined to get the proper quote);
- finally, select the information needed for both trades and quotes (price, volume, bid and ask prices, quoted depths). Regarding the timestamp of the trade or quote, it is given by a date and a time: for example, a given trade occurred at 961002 (October 2nd, 1996) at 101522 (10 am 15 minutes and 22 seconds). This is highly unpractical for numerical manipulations. To circumvent this difficulty, all timestamps are transformed into the number of seconds after midnight, starting on the first day of the period of time considered. Thus, if the first day is 961001 (October 1st, 1996), the timestamp of the trade considered here will be (961002-961001)*24*3600+10*3600+15*60+22 seconds.

This extraction procedure yields data files for the trade and quote processes that can be directly loaded into standard econometric packages. As the datafiles for the trades and quotes are indexed with respect to time, with market characteristics (price and volume for trades, bid-ask prices and depths for quotes) associated to each timestamp, they can be viewed as realizations of marked point processes. Let us then define a marked point process for the bid-ask quotes Q and a second one for the trades P, where both are indexed by the time in seconds at which the market event (trade, quote) occurred. The two marked point processes thus generated are defined as:

- the trade process (y_j, p_j, v_j), for $j = 1 \dots m$, where m is the total number of trades, y_j is the time (in seconds after midnight of the first day) when the trade was made, p_j designates the price of the trade, and v_j the corresponding volume.
- the quote process (t_i, b_i, a_i), for $i = 1 \dots n$, where n is the total number of quotes, t_i is the time (in seconds after midnight of the first day) at which the quotes were posted, b_i is the bid price posted and a_i is the ask price posted.[6]

By definition, the trade and bid-ask quote datasets contain irregularly time-spaced data as trades and quotes are recorded as soon as they are reported. Thus the durations between two trades $X_t = y_j - y_{j-1}$ and

Table 2.1. Trades and quotes

Time	Index	Type	Bid	Ask	Price	Volume
100405	36245	Q	10	$10\frac{1}{8}$		
100407	36247	T			10	500
100445	36285	T			10	700
100502	36302	T			$10\frac{1}{8}$	450
100506	36306	Q	$10\frac{1}{8}$	$10\frac{1}{4}$		
100507	36307	T			$10\frac{1}{8}$	100
100509	36309	T			$10\frac{1}{8}$	900
100513	36313	Q	$10\frac{1}{4}$	$10\frac{3}{8}$		
100610	36370	T			$10\frac{1}{4}$	2500
100611	36371	T			$10\frac{1}{4}$	250
100812	36492	Q	$10\frac{1}{2}$	$10\frac{5}{8}$		
100822	36502	T			$10\frac{1}{2}$	500
100824	36504	T			$10\frac{1}{2}$	200
100904	36544	T			$10\frac{5}{8}$	400
101547	36947	Q	$10\frac{3}{8}$	$10\frac{5}{8}$		
101548	36948	T			$10\frac{3}{8}$	1500
101550	36950	T			$10\frac{3}{8}$	700
101555	36947	Q	$10\frac{1}{4}$	$10\frac{3}{8}$		

Hypothetical trade and quote dataset. The first column gives the time of the trade or quote (T or Q in the third column), the second column gives the time in number of seconds after midnight, the fourth and fifth columns give the bid-ask prices of the quote (if relevant), the sixth and seventh columns give the price and volume of the trade (if relevant).

between two bid-ask quotes $X_q = t_i - t_{i-1}$ are not constant. Modelling these durations is equivalent to looking at the trading or quoting activity, and is the topic of Chapter 3.

An illustration is given in Tables 2.1, 2.2 and 2.3. Table 2.1 presents a hypothetical dataset for trade and quote data, which could be the result of the extraction procedure given above (the two marked point processes are not listed separately, but are presented in one table). Trade durations are computed as the times between successive trades; they are given in the third column of Table 2.2. Quote durations are computed as the times between successive quotes and are given in the third column of Table 2.3.

Once these datasets are available, the next steps can be:

- sign the trades using the Lee and Ready (1991) algorithm. Merging both databases and using this signing algorithm, the marked point process for the trades is extended to $(y_j, p_j, v_j, s_j, b_j, a_j)$ where s_j indicates if the trade is a buy or a sell, while b_j and a_j indicate the existing bid and ask quotes when the trade was made.

Table 2.2. Trade durations

Time	Index	Trade duration	Price	Volume
100407	36247		10	500
100445	36285	38	10	700
100502	36302	17	$10\frac{1}{8}$	450
100507	36307	5	$10\frac{1}{8}$	100
100509	36309	2	$10\frac{1}{8}$	900
100610	36370	61	$10\frac{1}{4}$	2500
100611	36371	1	$10\frac{1}{4}$	250
100822	36502	131	$10\frac{1}{2}$	500
100824	36504	2	$10\frac{1}{2}$	200
100904	36544	40	$10\frac{5}{8}$	400
101548	36948	404	$10\frac{3}{8}$	1500
101550	36950	2	$10\frac{3}{8}$	700

Trade durations constructed from the dataset given in Table 2.1. The third column gives the trade durations in seconds.

Table 2.3. Quote durations

Time	Index	Quote duration	Bid	Ask
100405	36245		10	$10\frac{1}{8}$
100506	36306	61	$10\frac{1}{8}$	$10\frac{1}{4}$
100513	36313	7	$10\frac{1}{4}$	$10\frac{3}{8}$
100812	36492	179	$10\frac{1}{2}$	$10\frac{5}{8}$
101547	36947	455	$10\frac{3}{8}$	$10\frac{5}{8}$
101555	36955	8	$10\frac{1}{4}$	$10\frac{3}{8}$

Quote durations constructed from the dataset given in Table 2.1. The third column gives the quote durations in seconds.

- filter the data once more to select the observations that occurred during the trading day (i.e. from 9h30 to 16h), thus removing the trades and quotes recorded before the opening of the session and after the end of the session;

- depending on the application that is considered, it is possible to filter the data to retain only a given marked point process. This issue is dealt with in the next section.

4. DURATIONS

It has been shown above that trade durations are defined as the times between consecutive trades while quote durations are defined as the times between consecutive quotes. Other types of durations can however be defined, once the corresponding marks are taken into account. In this new framework, durations are defined conditionally on some specified market event related to the marks. Because the newly defined durations form a subset of the original dataset, they define what is called a thinned point process. Simply put, the new dataset is a transformation of the original one, such that some features of the data are highlighted. Among the possible transformations (see Le Fol and Mercier, 1998, for more information), we look more closely at price and volume durations.

4.1 PRICE DURATIONS

Thinning the marked point process for the quotes with respect to a minimum change in price is a data transformation that is often used in the literature.[7] As first introduced in Engle and Russell (1997), price durations are by definition the times needed to witness a given *cumulative* price change (i.e. total price change since the last point retained) in the price of the asset. To avoid the bid-ask bounce exhibited by the trade process, price durations are usually defined on the mid-point of the bid-ask quote process.

Let us call c_p the predefined threshold, i.e. the minimum cumulative price change that serves to define a price duration. The set of price durations X_p defines a new marked point process Q_p, based on the previously defined Q and P, and is characterized as $(t_{p,i}, b_{p,i}, a_{p,i})$, for $i = 1 \dots n_p$, where n_p is the total number of filtered quotes. By definition, the $t_{p,i}$ are such that the change in the mid-price on the duration $X_{p,i} = t_{p,i} - t_{p,i-1}$ is at least equal to c_p.[8] As indicated in Giot (2000a), price durations defined in this way are convenient to work with for several reasons:

(i) because a price duration is the minimum time needed for the price to change by at least c_p, it can be shown that the resulting point process is strongly related to the underlying instantaneous volatility function for the price of the stock.

Indeed, in the framework of a diffusion model for the stock price, a price duration is the time needed for the price process to 'escape' a $[-c_p, c_p]$ range centered on the current price P_t. This is known as the 'first passage time' problem and we then have that (see Engle and Russell, 1997)

$$E(X_{p,i}|I_{t_{p,i-1}}) = \frac{c_p^2}{P_{t_{p,i-1}}^2} \frac{1}{\sigma^2} \tag{2.1}$$

where σ^2 is the volatility for the diffusion process over the $X_{p,i}$ long period of time (it is assumed constant over that time interval). The conditional expectation of the price durations $E(X_{p,i}|I_{t_{p,i-1}})$ can then be modelled by a high frequency duration model (see Chapter 3).

Thus, the models developed to deal with price durations can easily be used in problems involving the modelling of volatility, such as option pricing for example (Prigent, Renault and Scaillet, 1999). Another application (to a Value-at-Risk problem) is Giot (2000b).

(ii) price durations are relatively 'long' with respect to the (non-filtered) trade or quote durations, which allows the definition of market characteristics for the trading process over the price durations for the quotes. For example, the trading intensity (defined as the number of trades divided by the price duration during which the trades occurred) or average spread per transaction are meaningfully computed as they take into account a relatively large number of trades. When these characteristics are computed over non-filtered quote durations, one or two (on average) trades are available per quote durations, which gives unreliable (and highly variable) results.

(iii) price durations allow the computation of an intuitive measure of market liquidity: VNET (Engle and Lange, 2001). VNET is defined as the amount of one-sided volume that can be traded over the price duration, i.e. the absolute value of the difference between the number of shares bought and sold over the price duration. As reviewed in Chapter 1, a liquid market implies that a large volume can be 'absorbed' by the market without giving rise to a large change in price. This is exactly what underlies the notion of a large VNET: for a given change in price (c_p), a large one-sided volume has been traded. By computing the change in VNET over time (for a given c_p), it is thus possible to retrieve an intuitive measure of the liquidity dynamics.

(iv) when tick-by-tick trade data is analyzed, the bid-ask bounce can be a nuisance and it gives relatively little information.[9] Thinning the bid-ask quotes or trades allows to extract a marked point process where only meaningful price changes are retained. Moreover, as characterized in Engle and Russell (1998) for the NYSE or Biais, Hillion and Spatt (1995) for the Paris Bourse, the bid-ask quote process is often characterized by a short term transitory component which gives little information about the value of the asset. On the contrary, information events lead to movements of the bid-ask quotes in the same direction and thus move significantly the mid-point. Thus, 'significant' market events can be identified and will stand out among the short term trading noise.

An illustration is given in Table 2.4. Thinning the original quote dataset as given in Table 2.1 at the prespecified threshold $c_p = \frac{1}{4}$ leads to the new marked point process as given in Table 2.4. The third column of this table gives the price durations in seconds, while the fourth and fifth columns are the corresponding marks. The last column gives the number of trades made on the price duration.

Table 2.4. Price durations

Time	Index	Price duration	Bid	Ask	Trades
100405	36245		10	$10\frac{1}{8}$	
100513	36313	68	$10\frac{1}{4}$	$10\frac{3}{8}$	5
100812	36492	179	$10\frac{1}{2}$	$10\frac{5}{8}$	2
101555	36955	463	$10\frac{1}{4}$	$10\frac{3}{8}$	5

Price durations for the quotes as given in Table 2.1. c_p is set equal to $\frac{1}{4}$. The third column gives the price durations in seconds, while the last column gives the number of trades made on the corresponding price duration.

4.2 VOLUME DURATIONS

Price durations use information given by the bid-ask quotes to define new durations related to the intraday volatility process. While focusing on the bid-ask quotes Q, another possibility is to use the information given by the traded volume which is contained in the trade process. For example, market participants could be interested by the time between quotes such that a given volume of c_v shares is traded. Thus bid-ask volume durations $X_{v,i}$ are computed by thinning the quote process such that the retained durations are characterized by a total traded volume at least equal to c_v. Strictly speaking, volume durations need not be defined on bid-ask quotes. Indeed, they can be defined on either the quote process (using the above definition) or on the trade process, where they are simply the times between trades such that a volume of c_v shares is traded.[10] Of course, in an active market where trades and quotes occur regularly, there will probably be few differences between volume durations defined on trades or quotes. Volume durations have an immediate appeal for characterizing the liquidity of a stock, as a short $X_{v,i}$ imply that a given volume can be traded quickly.

More precisely, the set of volume durations for bid-ask quotes X_v defines a new marked point process Q_v, based on the previously defined Q and P, which is characterized as $(t_{v,i}, b_{v,i}, a_{v,i})$, for $i = 1 \dots n_v$, where n_v is the total number of filtered quotes. By definition, the $t_{v,i}$ are such that the traded volume on duration $X_{v,i} = t_{v,i} - t_{v,i-1}$ is at least equal to c_v. The change in price (either the bid, the ask or the mid-point) over $X_{v,i}$ can be interpreted as the price response (in the quotes) to a traded volume equal to at least c_v shares. A liquid stock would be characterized by short $X_{v,i}$ with small price changes over these $X_{v,i}$, i.e. it is possible to trade a large amount of shares in a small amount of time without having a large impact on the price.[11]

An illustration is given in Table 2.5. Thinning the original quote dataset as given in Table 2.1 at the prespecified threshold $c_v = 2,000$ leads to the new marked point process as given in Table 2.5. The third column of this table gives the volume durations in seconds, while the fourth and fifth columns are the corresponding marks.

Table 2.5. Volume durations

Time	Index	Volume duration	Bid	Ask
100405	36245		10	$10\frac{1}{8}$
100513	36313	68	$10\frac{1}{4}$	$10\frac{3}{8}$
100812	36492	179	$10\frac{1}{2}$	$10\frac{5}{8}$
101555	36947	455	$10\frac{1}{4}$	$10\frac{3}{8}$

Volume durations for the quotes as given in Table 2.1. c_v is set equal to 2,000. The third column gives the volume durations in seconds.

5. DURATIONS: A DESCRIPTIVE ANALYSIS

The econometric models that are introduced in the next chapters focus on the modelling of durations as defined previously. For several stocks traded on the NYSE, trade, quote, price or volume durations are modelled. However, before tackling this problem, it is useful to conduct a short descriptive analysis of the available data. We focus more particularly on the description of (intraday) characteristics of the trade and quote processes for four stocks traded on the NYSE, Disney (ticker DIS), IBM (IBM), Saks Inc (SKS) and American Water Works (AWK), over a five month period (from January 1997 to May 1997). The first two stocks are well-known, actively traded, and belong to the Dow Jones index.[12] The other two stocks are not so actively traded and were chosen randomly among the list of the stocks belonging to the Standard & Poors MidCap400. For each stock, we document some properties of the trade, quote, price and volume durations and highlight the importance of intraday seasonality, which affects all types of durations and most of the marks (such as the spread and the traded volume).

5.1 TRADES AND QUOTES

The results given in Tables 2.6 and 2.7 indicate that the trading and quoting activity is very active for Disney and IBM. This is not surprising since these stocks are widely held by institutional and small investors. Regarding the trade process, the mean duration is usually smaller than one minute for actively traded stocks, with the standard deviation much larger than the mean. As explained in Chapter 3, this rules out the possibility that the trade process be a Poisson process and calls for more sophisticated econometric models.[13] The quote process features the same characteristics as the trade process, with the standard deviation of the quote durations larger than the mean. Both trade and quote durations feature a very large autocorrelation (the $Q(10)$ for the IBM stock is larger than 19,000!). Thus, trade and quote durations can be characterized as being highly autocorrelated and overdispersed.

While trading and quoting is not so active for American Water Works and Saks Inc (for example, the mean trade duration is higher than three minutes for both stocks), both sets of durations feature the same characteristics as shown for the actively traded stocks, i.e. overdispersion and autocorrelation, albeit the degree of autocorrelation for American Water Works (the least active stock) is less strong than for the other stocks.

For all stocks, the minimum trade duration is equal to 0 second. This is simply due to the fact that orders are recorded as they are reported, with the second being the smallest possible time increase. Thus, two orders executed almost at the same time (within a second) have an identical timestamp.

Table 2.6. Statistics on the trade durations

	AWK	DISNEY	IBM	SKS
Number of trades	6,737	62,177	137,315	12,746
Mean duration	365.2	39.1	17.8	192.4
Standard dev. of durations	440.8	49.9	21.9	335.8
Minimum duration	0	0	0	0
Maximum duration	4,564	1,136	491	5,922
$Q(10)$	209	4,516	19,624	4,365

Data extracted from the January-May 1997 TAQ CD-ROM. All duration statistics are in seconds. $Q(10)$ denotes the Ljung-Box Q-statistic of order 10 on the durations.

Table 2.7. Statistics on the quote durations

	AWK	DISNEY	IBM	SKS
Number of quotes	14,185	90,387	88,083	16,204
Mean duration	171.9	26.8	28.4	148.7
Standard dev. of durations	266.3	31.6	36.0	292.2
Minimum duration	1	1	1	1
Maximum duration	4443	641	1,029	11,949
$Q(10)$	519	7202	6,862	3,309

Data extracted from the January-May 1997 TAQ CD-ROM. All duration statistics are in seconds. $Q(10)$ denotes the Ljung-Box Q-statistic of order 10 on the durations.

5.2 INTRADAY SEASONALITY

An important feature of the trade and quote data is the strong intraday seasonality featured by key characteristics of both processes. Figures 2.1, 2.2 and 2.3 show the intraday seasonality, computed as explained below, featured by the trade durations, average spread for the bid-ask quotes posted by the specialist, and average traded volume.

The intraday seasonality is defined by computing the expectation of the variable (trade duration, spread and traded volume) conditioned on time-of-day, where the expectation is computed by averaging the variable over thirty minute intervals for each day of the week. This is equivalent to assuming that the trading day is divided in thirteen 30 minute bins (from 9h30 to 16h), and that each variable is 'constant' on the 30 minute interval. The last hypothesis is of course not true in practice, as each variable changes throughout the trading day. Assuming that such changes happen gradually, cubic splines are then used on the thirty minute intervals to smooth the time-of-day functions.

Figure 2.1 shows that the trade durations feature a strong intraday effect, with durations being much smaller at the start and at the end of the trading day than around noon. Around noon, trading slows down considerably as traders go for lunch. At the start of the day, trading is very active as the opening of the market prompts traders to take positions such that the information brought about by news events that occurred during the night (macroeconomic news, or news released by companies after the previous market close) is included in the price of the assets. The active trading at the end of the day can be justified by the fact that traders often wish to close their positions before the end of the trading session. Specific types of orders also lead to an increase in the trading activity at those times (see Chapter 1). Although the details are not given here, all types of durations (quote, price and volume) exhibit an

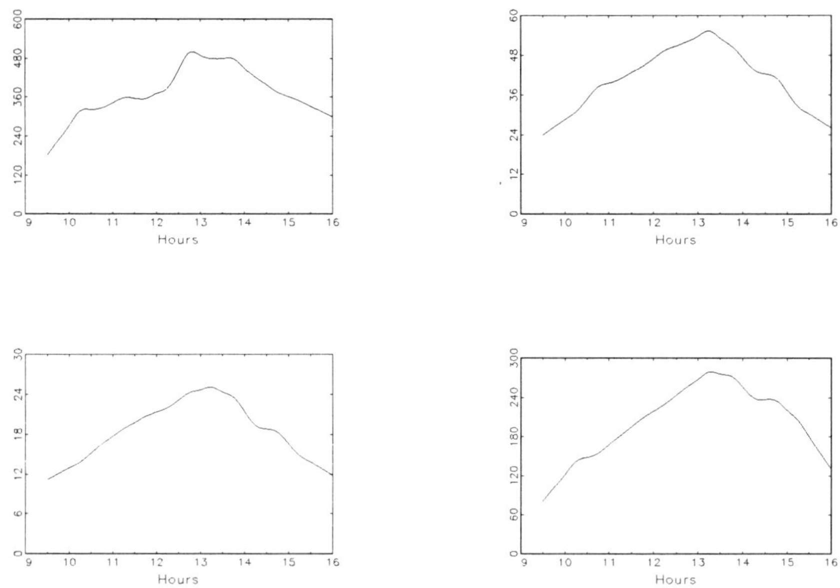

From left to right and up to down: American Water Works, Disney, IBM and Saks Inc.

Figure 2.1. Time-of-day (in seconds) for the trade durations

intraday seasonality akin to the one shown for the trade durations. The pattern displayed by quote durations closely tracks the one displayed by trade durations, as dealers update their quotes more rapidly to accommodate the flow of trades. Regarding price durations, their intraday pattern indicates that durations are much shorter, and thus volatility is much higher, at the open and close of trading than around noon.

Regarding the average spread posted by the specialist, a strong seasonality is also apparent from Figure 2.2, with the spread being higher at the start and at the end of the trading day than around noon (U-shaped pattern, sometimes designated as inverted J-shape). The intraday pattern of the spread has been discussed at length in Chapter 1 and our results are similar to those reported in the empirical market microstructure literature (Brock and Kleidon, 1992, and Chung, Van Ness and Van Ness, 1999).

From Figure 2.3, one sees that traded volume is much higher at the start and end of the day, which is the consequence of the more active trading at these times (short trade durations). Lastly, the average vol-

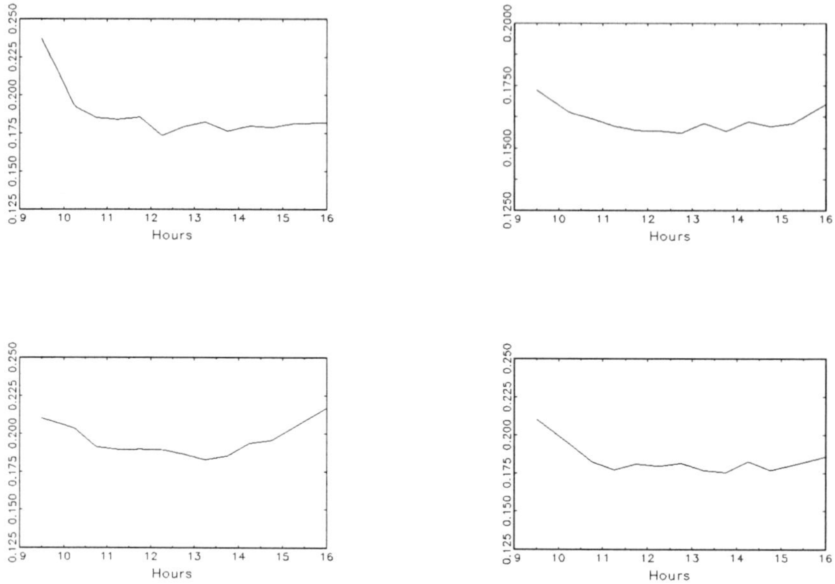

From left to right and up to down: American Water Works, Disney, IBM and Saks Inc.

Figure 2.2. Time-of-day (in \$) for the spread

ume per trade (not shown) seems to be the largest at the start of the day. This is consistent with the fact that traders who want to capitalize on the information releases made public prior to the open place rather large orders, leading to a quick updating of the security prices with respect to the information updates.

5.3 TIME-OF-DAY ADJUSTED DURATIONS

The results given in the previous subsection indicate that most market characteristics related to the trades and quotes exhibit a strong intraday seasonality, which can usually be linked to the behavior of traders or exchange characteristics, such as opening and closing of markets. Regarding durations and to take into account this diurnality, Engle and Russell (1998) suggest computing time-of-day adjusted durations as

$$x_i = X_i/\phi(t_i) \tag{2.2}$$

where X_i is the original duration (computed from the data base), $\phi(t_i)$ is the time-of-day effect at time t_i, and x_i denotes the time-of-day adjusted

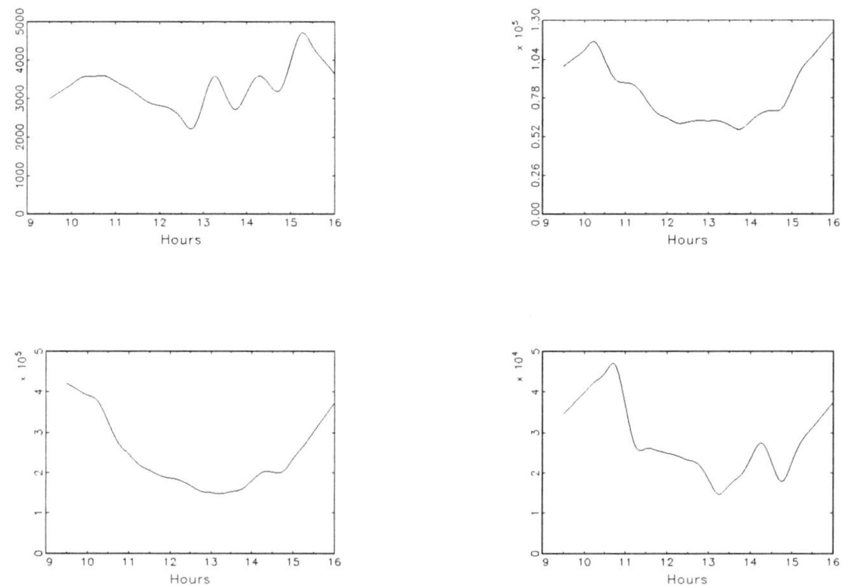

From left to right and up to down: American Water Works, Disney, IBM and Saks Inc.

Figure 2.3. Time-of-day (in shares traded) for the traded volume

duration. The time-of-day effect for each set of durations is defined as the expected duration conditioned on time-of-day. As detailed above, the expectation is computed by averaging the durations over thirty minute intervals, with cubic splines used to smooth the time-of-day function. This procedure can be applied to all types of durations (trade, quote, price and volume) and other market characteristics such as the spread or the traded volume. Basically, this method assumes the existence of a *deterministic* multiplicative intraday seasonality as each new duration x_i is computed as $X_i/\phi(t_i)$, with $\phi(t_i)$ determined by the time t_i at which the duration was recorded.

A possible extension is to introduce a time-of-week effect, which allows for a different time-of-day pattern depending on the day of the week (for example, the deterministic pattern observed on Mondays can be different from the one expected on Tuesdays). This extension is straightforward to implement as all preceding computations can be used provided additional conditioning with respect to the day of the week is provided for. Time-of-day and time-of-week seasonality is used in Bauwens and Giot

Table 2.8. Statistics on the time-of-day adjusted durations

	Trade durations	Price durations	Volume durations
AWK			
Number	6,737	819	285
Dispersion Index	1.17	1.05	0.51
$Q(10)$	129	15	19
First autocorrelation	0.05	0.01	0.12
DISNEY			
Number	62,177	5,985	3,450
Dispersion Index	1.21	1.23	0.64
$Q(10)$	1,900	473	1,079
First autocorrelation	0.08	0.14	0.24
IBM			
Number	137,315	19,680	9,684
Dispersion Index	1.14	1.20	0.7
$Q(10)$	8,704	2,318	7,416
First autocorrelation	0.10	0.16	0.39
SKS			
Number	12,746	1,812	966
Dispersion Index	1.66	1.37	0.98
$Q(10)$	3,636	144	1,151
First autocorrelation	0.20	0.15	0.43

Trade durations are the durations between consecutive trades. Price durations are the durations between bid-ask quotes such that a cumulative change in the mid-price of at least $0.125 is observed. For Disney, IBM and Saks Inc, volume durations are the durations between bid-ask quotes such that a cumulative traded volume of at least 25,000 shares is observed. For AWK, the threshold is reduced to 10,000 shares. The dispersion index is defined as the ratio standard deviation/mean (all means are equal to 1 to the third decimal). $Q(10)$ denotes the Ljung-Box Q-statistic of order 10 on the durations. First autocorrelation is the first-order autocorrelation coefficient. All durations are time-of-day adjusted using formula (2.2) without taking into account a possible time-of-week effect.

(2000) for example. See also Veredas, Rodriguez-Poo and Espasa (2001) for an alternative deseasonalization method based on kernel estimators.

Taking into account the intraday seasonality has an important effect on the statistical properties of the previously defined durations. Because the econometric models are used on the deseasonalized data, it is worthwhile reconsidering the empirical analysis of the durations. To keep the notation short, hereafter time-of-day adjusted durations are called durations.

As shown in Table 2.8, for all stocks the three types of durations feature a large Ljung-Box Q-statistic of order 10, indicating that the durations are strongly autocorrelated, with the strongest autocorrelation observed for the trade durations. Correspondingly, autocorrelation functions (ACF) for the durations usually start at a rather small value (around 0.1-0.15) and slowly decrease to zero. This is illustrated in Figures 2.4 and 2.5, where we plot the ACF of the trade and price durations for the Disney and IBM stocks. Another way of looking at the dynamical structure of these durations is to plot the sequence of the first 5,000 trade and price durations for both stocks (see Figures 2.6 and 2.7), which highlights the clustering.

Taking into account the deterministic intraday seasonality leads to a drop in the autocorrelation exhibited by the durations, but does not remove the dynamic structure as the time-of-day adjusted durations are still highly autocorrelated. For example, taking into account the intraday seasonality of the trade durations for Disney decreases the $Q(10)$-statistic from 4,516 to 1,900, which is still highly significant at any reasonable level. This suggests that the dynamics of durations involve other factors than the intraday seasonality due to market structure such as the open and close of trading (see Chapters 3 and 4).

Table 2.8 also indicates that both trade and price durations are characterized by a dispersion index (the ratio standard deviation to mean) greater than one, i.e. are overdispersed, while volume durations are underdispersed. In Figures 2.8, 2.9 and 2.10, we plot the densities for the three types of durations for the AWK, Disney and IBM stocks. For the IBM stock in Figure 2.10, we give the densities for price durations with $c_p = \$0.25$ and volume durations with $c_v = 50,000$.[14] Price and volume durations were also computed with other thresholds (such as $c_p = \$0.375$ and $c_p = \$0.5$ for price durations, $c_v = 75,000$ and $c_v = 100,000$ for volume durations) for a selection of NYSE stocks and the density plots are quite similar to those given in Figures 2.8, 2.9 and 2.10, which thus do seem to be representative of the general shape of the density functions of trade, price and volume durations. See also Bauwens, Giot, Grammig and Veredas (2000).

Volume durations are characterized by clearly hump-shaped densities, with most of the mass around 0.5-1. This is in contrast with trade and price durations which exhibit essentially decreasing density functions, but with a small hump (at least for the Disney and IBM stocks) at very small durations around 0-0.2 seconds.[15]

APPENDIX 2.A: The Olsen & Associates databases

In the early nineties, the Zurich based Swiss consultancy Olsen & Associates began recording bid-ask quotes related to currency dealing in the FOREX market. The recorded indicative bid and ask quotes are the real time rate quotes displayed on the Reuters screens from October 1992 to September 1993. The resulting dataset, called HFDF93[16], includes

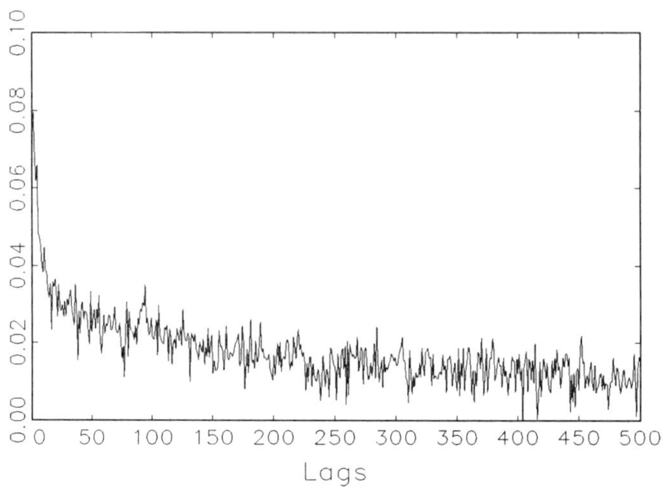

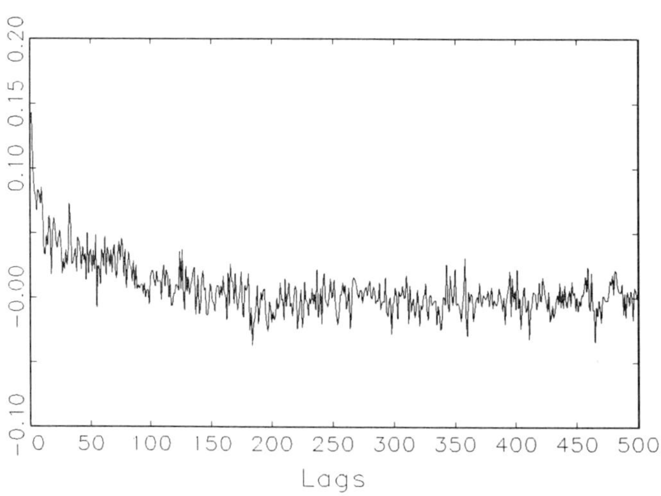

Figure 2.4. Autocorrelation functions for time-of-day adjusted trade (top) and price (bottom) durations (Disney)

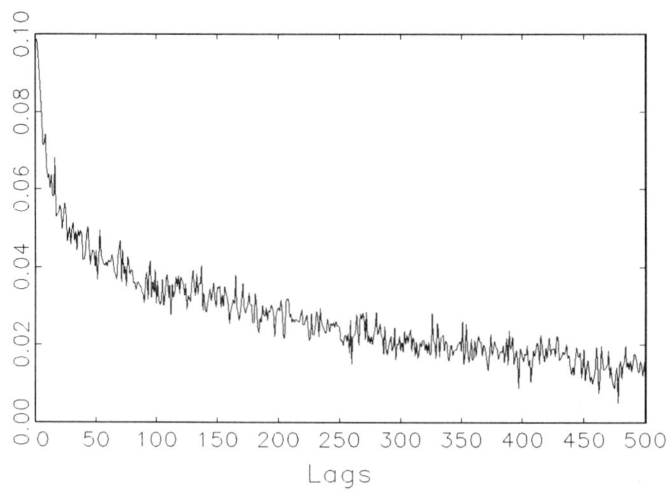

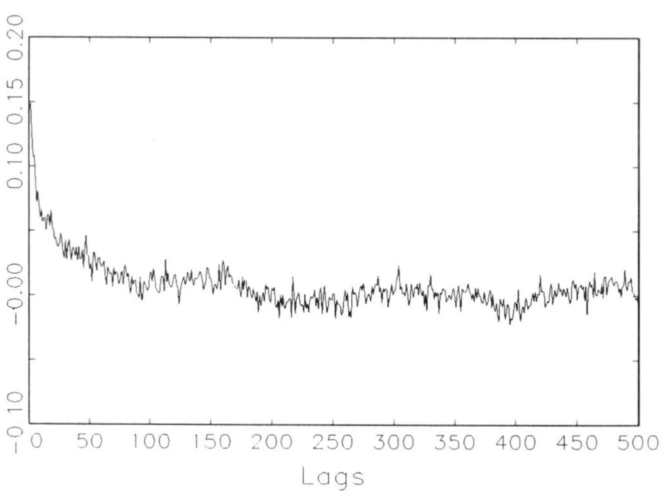

Figure 2.5. Autocorrelation functions for time-of-day adjusted trade (top) and price (bottom) durations (IBM)

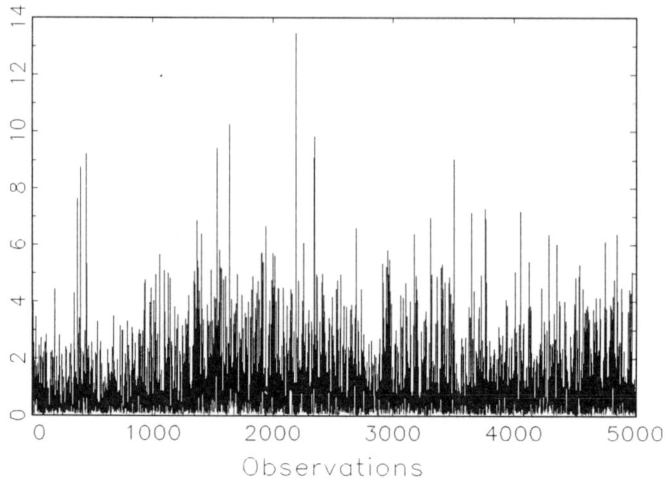

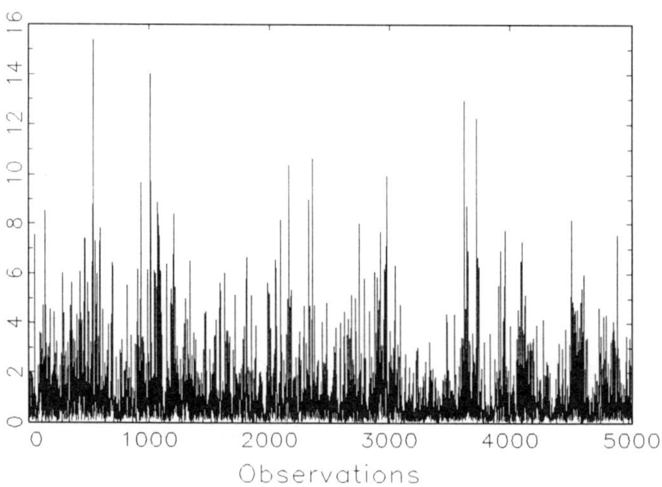

Figure 2.6. Time-of-day adjusted trade (top) and price (bottom) durations (Disney)

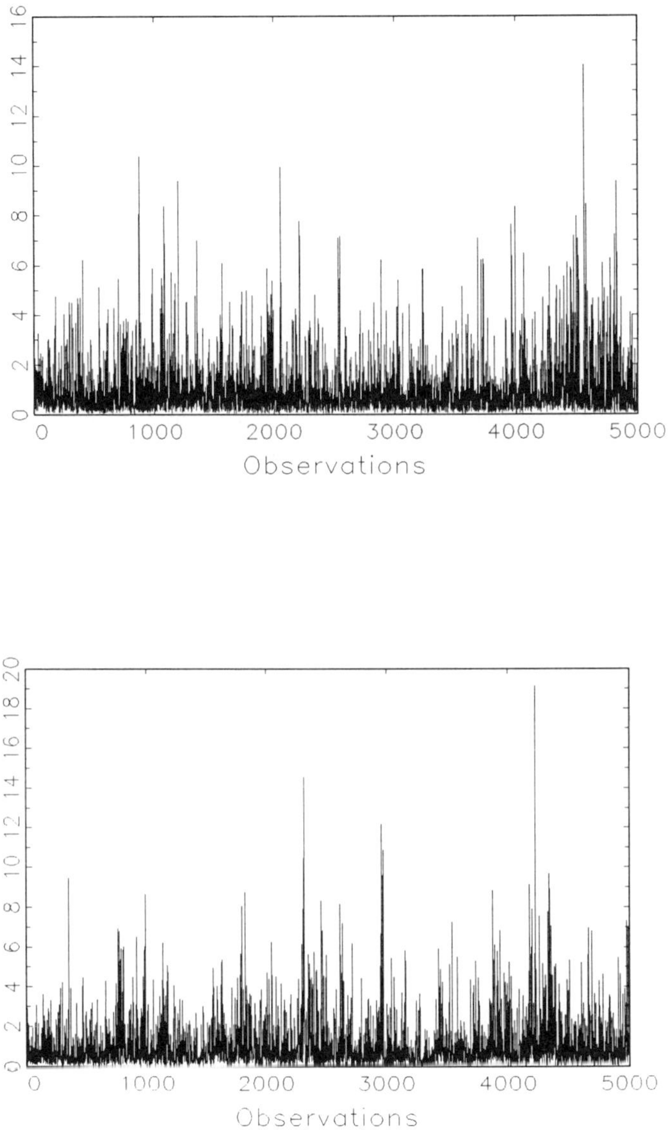

Figure 2.7. Time-of-day adjusted trade (top) and price (bottom) durations (IBM)

tick-by-tick data for USD/DEM, USD/JPY and DEM/JPY rate quotes, three-month maturity interbank deposit rate quotes for USD, JPY and DEM and Money Market Headline News. The database structure is very similar to the structure of the TAQ database: a timestamp (to the second) indicating when the bid-ask quotes were posted, the indicative bid and ask quotes and the name and location of the bank posting the quotes. Thus, with respect to the TAQ database, two important additional piece of information are given:

- the identity of the bank posting the quotes (this is a truly unique feature of this dataset);

- a short text giving the Money Market Headline News.

Unfortunately, because this information is considered private by the banks involved in currency trading, there is no available information on the trades (price agreed upon, volume traded) that were actually carried out.

In 1996, Olsen & Associates released a second database related to intraday trading (called HFDF96). While the first database focused on currency trading and made available tick-by-tick data for the indicative bid-ask quotes, this second database gives intraday *half-hourly* data for FX spot rates, spot metal rates, Eurofutures contracts and indices. Thus, while this second database is larger and gives information on many more assets than the first one, true intraday tick-by-tick data is no longer available.

Notes

1 The information about ordering this database is available at the NYSE Web Site, www.nyse.com. Strictly speaking, the TAQ database is not the first intraday database of the NYSE as a much older database (TORQ database) is routinely used in empirical work (Engle and Russell, 1998). The Trades, Orders Reports, and Quotes (TORQ) dataset was constructed by Hasbrouck and the NYSE in 1991. It provides intraday information on the price and quote processes for a sample of stocks traded on the NYSE over a 3 month period. More recently, the NASDAQ now releases its own database which gives intraday information on the quotes posted by all the market makers active for a given stock traded on NASDAQ (thus not only the best bid-ask quotes but also the other valid quotes).

2 The ticker of the stock is the identification code of the stock used at the exchange. For example, BA is the identification code for BOEING at the NYSE.

3 See also the first footnote of this chapter.

4 It should however be mentioned that some researchers (usually affiliated with the NYSE) were granted access to the historical inventory databases kept by the specialists at the NYSE (e.g. Hasbrouck and Sofianos, 1993).

5 We implemented this procedure using the GAUSS econometric program to get the needed data before estimating the models presented in the next chapters. Our code is available on request.

6 We did not retrieve the quoted depth at the ask and bid prices as we do not include this information in the econometric models of the next chapters, but it is straightforward to do so.

7 See for example Bauwens and Giot (1998, 2000), Engle and Russell (1997, 1998), Giot (2000a) or Gerhard and Hautsch (1999).

8 A formal definition of the rule used to filter the quotes is given in Engle and Russell (1997).

9 However, it is valuable information if the bid-ask spread is to be modelled.

10 Gouriéroux, Jasiak and Le Fol (1999) introduce volume durations for the trade process.

11 See the discussion of liquidity which is provided in subsection 2.4 of Chapter 1. A related measure is VNET which is introduced for price durations.

12 We also looked at other actively traded stocks like Coca-Cola, Boeing, Exxon, ATT, and we found that they generally have the same intraday characteristics as IBM and Disney.

13 In the basic version of the Poisson process, or the corresponding exponential model for the durations, the mean of the durations is by definition equal to their standard deviation.

14 When $c_p = \$0.25$ for the IBM stock, the dispersion index is equal to 1.13 and it is equal to 0.63 for volume durations with $c_v = 50,000$.

15 The hump close to the origin is not an artifact of the kernel density estimation of a density that starts at the origin. We used the gamma kernel proposed by Chen (1998). The bandwidth was set at $(0.9\, s\, n^{-0.2})^2$, where s is the standard deviation of the data and n the number of data.

16 Information about the database and how to order it can be found on the Olsen Web site at www.olsen.ch.

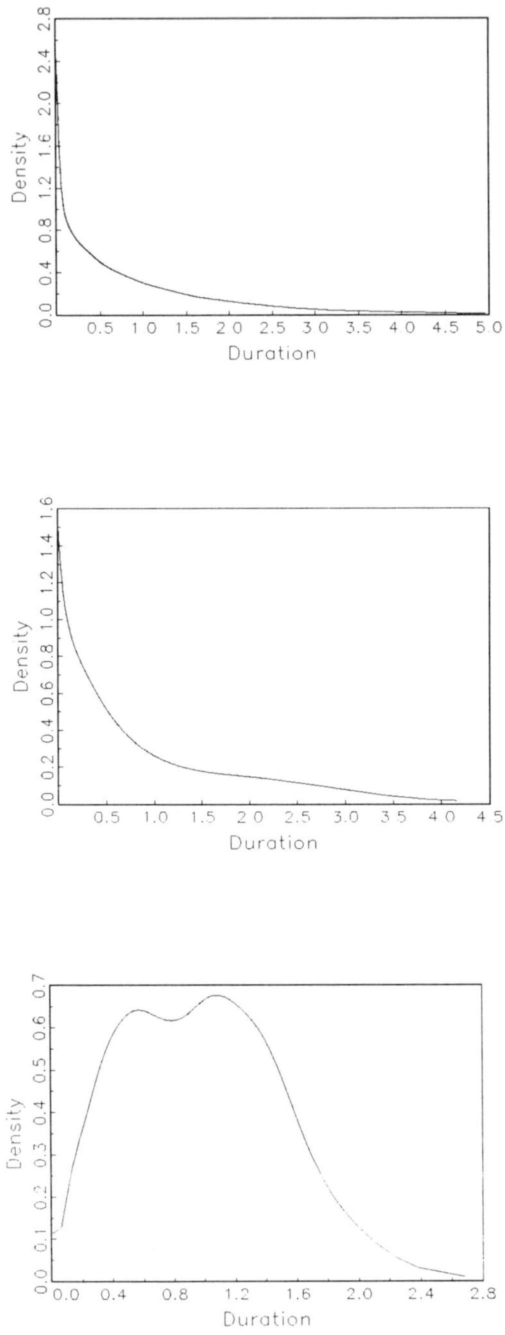

Figure 2.8. Kernel densities for the time-of-day adjusted trade (top), price (middle), and volume (bottom) durations (American Water Works stock)

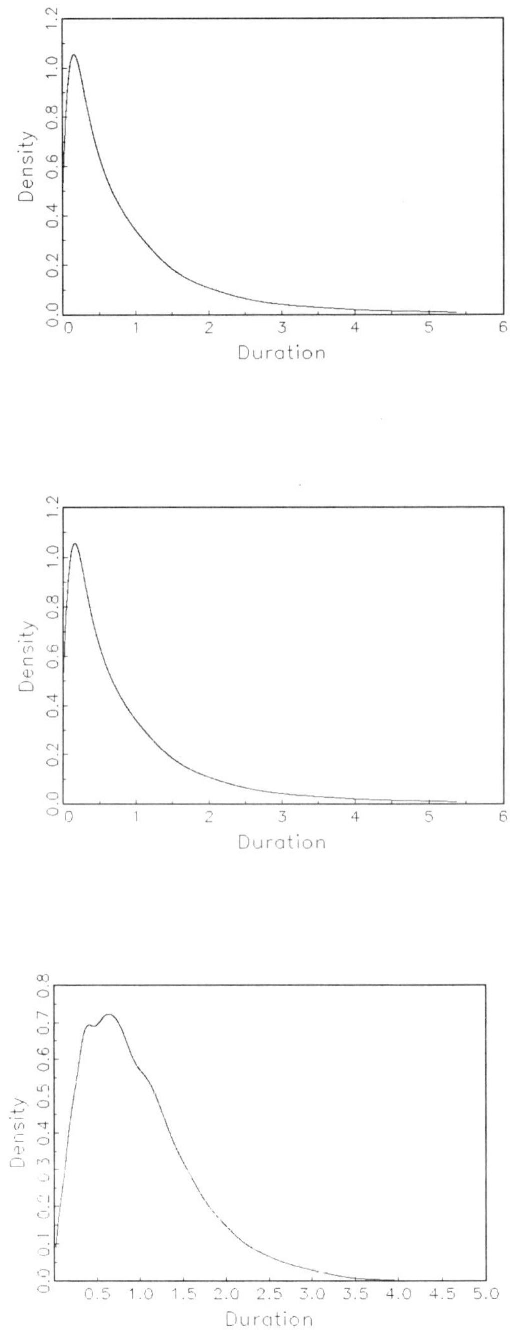

Figure 2.9. Kernel densities for the time-of-day adjusted trade (top), price (middle), and volume (bottom) durations (Disney stock)

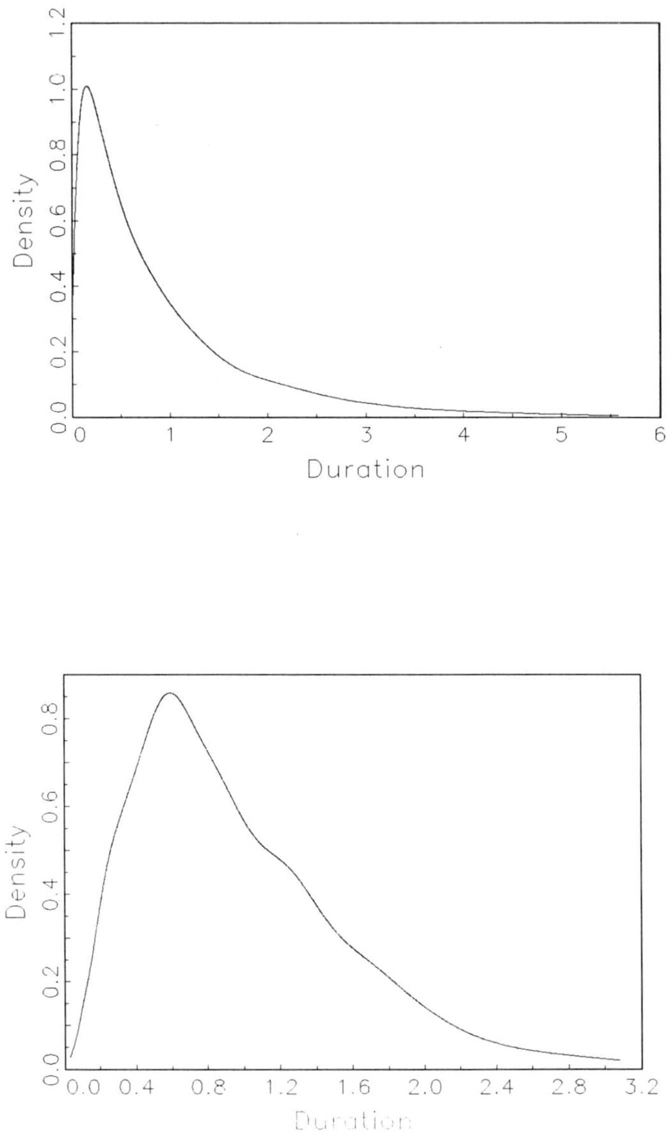

Figure 2.10. Kernel densities for the time-of-day adjusted price durations with $c_p =$ \$0.25 (top) and volume durations with $c_v = 50,000$ (bottom) (IBM stock)

Chapter 3

INTRADAY DURATION MODELS

1. INTRODUCTION

In Chapter 2 we have defined different types of durations that are of interest for the analysis of stock market intraday activity from the viewpoint of characterizing the trading frequency, the volatility, and the liquidity of a market. We also highlighted the main stylized facts of durations: a regular intraday seasonality, and after correcting the data for this pattern, clustering and overdispersion (underdispersion for volume durations). The object of this chapter is to set out econometric models that are compatible with the stylized facts. In Section 2, we introduce some basic statistical concepts relevant to the analysis of durations and make briefly the link with point processes, i.e. collections of points randomly distributed along a time axis. In Section 3, we introduce the class of autoregressive conditional duration models and their logarithmic versions. The models are carefully defined, and their properties are investigated, using a mix of analytical and numerical methods. The estimation of these models by the maximum likelihood method is briefly reviewed, and tools for testing the specification of a model are developed. In Section 4, we provide empirical results that illustrate the estimation and testing procedures. The illustration is done on trade, price, and volume durations of several stocks listed on the NYSE. Applications of the same models to test microstructure effects are pursued in Chapter 4.

2. BASIC STATISTICAL CONCEPTS

Since we are interested in modelling durations between events on the stock markets, it is useful to start with a short reminder of the main concepts of the statistical analysis of durations. More information can be found in survey articles, such as Florens, Fougère and Mouchart (1995), or in specialized books, such as Lancaster (1990). Kamionka (2000) provides a survey of most duration models used for financial intraday data, including joint models for marks and durations.

A duration is a time interval between two events, such as two trades of a stock on a market. Durations are supposed to be measured with sufficient precision to be treated as realisations of (absolutely) continuous random variables. Hence, the usual tools of probability apply: a duration, which is a positive random variable X, has a distribution function $F(x) = \Pr[X \leq x]$, a survivor function $S(x) = 1 - F(x)$, and a density function $f(x) = dF(x)/dx = -dS(x)/dx$. A specific tool relevant to duration analysis is the hazard function $h(x)$. The hazard function is technically computed as

$$h(x) = f(x)/S(x) = -d \ln S(x)/dx. \tag{3.1}$$

In the context of durations between trades, $S(x)$ is the probability that the time elapsed before the next trade is longer than x (say, seconds), and $h(x)$ is the instantaneous rate of occurrence of a trade per second (the unit time period) at x. This interpretation follows from the basic definition of the hazard function:

$$h(x) = \lim_{dx \to 0} \frac{\Pr[x \leq X < x + dx | X \geq x]}{dx} \tag{3.2}$$

In this formula, the numerator is the probability that a trade occurs in an interval dx starting at x, given that no trade has occurred before x. Dividing by dx gives the probability of a trade per second (the rate of occurrence), and taking the limit as dx tends to 0 allows to derive (3.1), since

$$\Pr[x \leq X < x + dx | X \geq x] = \frac{\Pr[x \leq X < x + dx]}{\Pr[X \geq x]} \tag{3.3}$$

and

$$\lim_{dx \to 0} \frac{\Pr[x \leq X < x + dx]}{dx} = f(x). \tag{3.4}$$

Notice that $h(x)$, like a density function, can be larger than 1.

To understand the hazard more intuitively, assume that X is distributed as an exponential variable with parameter $\lambda > 0$ (and thus expectation $1/\lambda$), such that $S(x) = \exp(-\lambda x)$. It follows that $h(x) = \lambda$, and the hazard does not depend on x (a very special case indeed). If λ is equal to 2, this means, loosely speaking, that if you observe the market at any moment, you can expect that two trades will occur in the next second (or equivalently that the expected duration before the next trade is a half second). The fact that $h(x)$ does not depend on x means that when you observe the market, the rate of occurrence of the next trade is the same if the previous trade has occurred one second ago, 10 seconds ago, or 10 hours ago. If for example $h(x) = x$, the rate of occurrence of the next trade is increasing with the time since the last trade: the longer the time since the last trade, the more likely it is to observe a new trade. The reverse would be true if for example $h(x) = 1/\sqrt{x}$. The latter case is called negative duration dependence, and the former positive duration dependence.

Analyzing durations is one possible way to study a point process. A point process is a special kind of stochastic process, one which generates a random collection of points on the time axis; see Cox and Isham (1980), and Veredas (2001). The most well known point process is the Poisson process. Let us assume that in the context of the stock market, a 'point' is a trade (it could be any other event of interest). Denoting by $N(t, t+dt)$ the number of points in the time interval $(t, t+dt]$, and by $\mathcal{H}_t$ the timing of the trades until time t (the history of the process), the Poisson process of rate λ corresponds to the conditions that for all t, as dt $\rightarrow 0$,

$$\Pr[N(t, t+dt] = 1|\mathcal{H}_t] = \lambda dt + o(dt) \quad (3.5)$$

$$\Pr[N(t, t+dt] > 1|\mathcal{H}_t] = o(dt). \quad (3.6)$$

The first condition says that the probability of observing one trade in the next infinitesimal spell of time (dt) is proportional to dt, with λ the constant of proportionality. The second condition says that the probability to observe more than one trade in dt is very small,[1] thus excluding that more than one trade occurs at the same instant. If this condition is fulfilled, the process is called 'orderly'. The two conditions imply that $\Pr[N(t, t+dt] = 0|\mathcal{H}_t] = 1 - \lambda dt + o(dt)$, meaning that 'no trade' occurs with probability $1 - \lambda dt$. Moreover, these probabilities do not depend on $\mathcal{H}_t$, the timing of the trades until time t, and in particular on t itself, the instant at which they are computed. This means that the Poisson process is 'without memory': for example, the fact that many trades have occurred just before t, does not imply that it is more (or less) likely to observe a trade just after t. The Poisson process implies that the durations between the successive trades (points) are distributed independently (a consequence of the 'no memory' feature) and exponentially (with parameter λ, the rate of occurrence, also called the intensity of the process). The converse is also true: IID exponential durations imply that the number of trades in the interval dt follow a Poisson distribution with parameter λdt.

It is not difficult to realize that the occurrence of trades (or quotes) on the stock market does not generally follow a Poisson process. A first obvious reason is the diurnality, or intraday seasonal effect, described in subsection 5.2 of Chapter 2. The markets are more active in some parts of the day than others. This could be modelled by a non-homogeneous (or non-stationary) Poisson process, that is, letting the intensity of the Poisson process be a function of time. However even if that is accounted for, there is usually some dependence left in the durations, which implies that the durations between the trades cannot follow a Poisson process or even a renewal process (that is, a process generating IID durations, although not necessarily with an exponential distribution). This is illustrated in Figures 2.6 and 2.7 (series of durations), where we see duration clustering: long durations tend to occur in clusters, like small durations, which leads to positive autocorrelations, see Figures 2.4 and 2.5.

Dependence between durations can be taken into account by specifying the distribution of the duration conditional on the past history of the process (which is equivalent to the past durations). Thus instead of specifying directly $F(x)$, the unconditional distribution of the duration, we specify $F(x|\mathcal{H}_x)$, where $\mathcal{H}_x$ denotes the sequence of past durations (those preceding x). Equivalently, we can specify the conditional hazard $h(x|\mathcal{H}_x)$, since by equation (3.1) the knowledge of the hazard function implies that of the survivor function.[2] The econometric models presented in the next section are different ways of specifying the conditional distribution of the durations. They aim, in particular, at fitting the stylized facts of stock market durations: clustering (with usually an autocorrelation function that decreases slowly, starting at a low value), and overdispersion (for trade, quotes, and price durations) or underdispersion (for volume durations).[3]

In the appendix of this chapter, we have collected the main distributions that are used in duration modelling, providing their definitions and main properties, in particular information on their hazard function. These distributions include the generalized gamma, which has the gamma, Weibull, and exponential as particular cases, and the Burr, which has also the Weibull and exponential as particular cases.

Instead of characterizing a point process through the duration specification, or through the hazard specification, one can also characterize it through the counting specification, i.e. the joint distribution of the number of points in arbitrary time intervals. Conceptually, the three specifications are equivalent, though it is not always possible to derive analytically one specification from another (contrary to the case of the Poisson process). The analysis of intraday data on the stock market has been done mainly in the framework of duration models, but counting specification models have also been proposed. This is a more recent development that we do not touch upon in this book. A useful textbook for the econometric analysis of count data is Cameron and Trivedi (1998), though it does not deal with applications to the kind of data that we analyze in this book. Papers dealing specifically with stock market intraday data have been written by Shephard (1999) and by Heinen (2000).

3. ECONOMETRIC MODELS

Econometric models for durations are typically conditional models, in the sense that they aim at modelling the duration conditionally on exogenous variables. For example, in analyzing the unemployment duration of individuals, several characteristics of the individuals, such as their level of education, are usually conditioned upon. Likewise, in analyzing stock market durations, we shall condition on some characteristics of the markets. For example, for price durations, possibly relevant variables are suggested by the asymmetric information models mentioned in subsection 1.4. However, even if no such conditioning information is considered, we need to specify a dynamic model that accounts for the dependence in the durations. This can be done by introducing previous durations as explicative variables.

Two types of models are available in the literature to introduce exogenous variables: the proportional hazard (PH) model (also called Cox model), and the accelerated time model. The PH model specifies the hazard function by multiplying a baseline hazard h_0 by a function that depends on the exogenous variables denoted by z:

$$h(x|z,\theta) = h_0(x|\alpha)\, g_1(z,\beta), \tag{3.7}$$

where θ denotes the union of the parameters α and β. One way of introducing dependence is to put lagged durations in z. One drawback of this approach is the need to introduce a lot of lags to account properly for the autocorrelation structure of the durations, which is often found to require a moving average component. Another drawback is that this approach requires numerical integration in the estimation phase. In an interesting contribution, Gerhard and Hautsch (2000) introduce an ARMA structure in a PH model, through the error term that appears after transformation of (3.7). Furthermore, they use a semi-parametric approach in the sense that the baseline hazard is not specified by a parametric assumption.

In accelerated time (AT) models, the effect of the exogenous variables is to modify the time scale, i.e. the duration x is specified as the baseline duration x_0 times a function of the exogenous variables,

$$x = x_0\, g(z,\beta), \tag{3.8}$$

where x_0 follows some distribution with parameter α. This specification allows to interpret $g(z,\beta)$ as $\mathrm{E}(x|z,\theta)$, the conditional expectation of x, if $\mathrm{E}(x_0) = 1$ (which can always be achieved if the expectation of x_0 exists) and if x_0 is independent of $g(z,\beta)$ (in case the latter is stochastic). One advantage of this approach is that it is easy to introduce parismoniously many lagged durations by adopting an ARMA structure for this conditional expectation. Such is the approach followed in the sequel of this book, with the autoregressive conditional duration (ACD) model and its logarithmic versions. From (3.8), the survivor function of x is easily derived from the baseline survivor function S_0: $S(x|z,\theta)) = S_0(x/g(z,\beta))$. Therefore, the hazard function of x corresponding to (3.8) is

$$h(x|z,\theta) = h_0[x/g(z,\beta)|\alpha]/g(z,\beta). \tag{3.9}$$

The difference in the effect of a variable z on the hazard function of a PH model and of an AT one is easily understood when the $g(z,\beta)$ function takes two different values, say 1 when $z = 1$ and 0.5 when $z = 0$. Assuming that $g_1(z,\beta) = 1/g(z,\beta)$ for comparability of the two functions, in the PH model the baseline hazard function is multiplied by 2 when $z = 0$ and unchanged when $z = 1$. In the AT model, the baseline function is unchanged for $z = 1$, and for $z = 0$, it is equal to $2h_0(2x)$, instead of $2h_0(x)$ in the PH model.[4]

From here on, we denote by x_i the duration between two events that happened at times t_{i-1} and t_i, i.e. $x_i = t_i - t_{i-1}$. The data consist of a sequence of n durations, $x_1, x_2, \ldots, x_n$.

3.1 ACD MODELS

The assumption introduced by Engle and Russell (1998) is that the dependence in the durations can be subsumed in their conditional expectations $\mathrm{E}(x_i|\mathcal{H}_i)$, in such a way that $x_i/\mathrm{E}(x_i|\mathcal{H}_i)$ is independent and identically distributed. $\mathcal{H}_i$ denotes the information set available at time t_{i-1} (the beginning of the duration x_i), which includes the past durations. The ACD model specifies the observed duration as the mixing process

$$x_i = \Psi_i \epsilon_i, \tag{3.10}$$

where the ϵ_i are IID positive random variables, with

$$\mathrm{E}(\epsilon_i) = 1 \tag{3.11}$$

$$\mathrm{Var}(\epsilon_i) = \sigma^2, \tag{3.12}$$

so that $\mathrm{E}(x_i|\mathcal{H}_i) = \Psi_i$.

A second equation specifies an autoregressive model for the conditional durations Ψ_i:[5]

$$\Psi_i = \omega + \alpha x_{i-1} + \beta \Psi_{i-1} \tag{3.13}$$

with the following constraints on the coefficients: $\omega > 0$, $\alpha \geq 0$, $\beta \geq 0$ (with $\beta = 0$ if $\alpha = 0$), and $\alpha + \beta < 1$. The last constraint ensures the existence of the unconditional mean of the duration, the others are sufficient to ensure the positivity of the conditional durations.

Several choices are available for the distribution of ϵ_i: exponential, gamma, Weibull, Burr, lognormal, Pareto, generalised gamma..., in principle any distribution with positive support. The choice of a particular distribution should be guided by the desire of having a 'correct' specification, and perhaps by its convenience for estimation (which is discussed in subsection 3.3.3). We assume that these distributions are parameterized in such a way that $\mathrm{E}(\epsilon_i) = 1$: this is not restrictive as long as the first moment exists. Indeed, if $\mathrm{E}(\epsilon_i) = \mu \neq 1$, one can write $x_i = \mu\Psi_i(\epsilon_i/\mu) = \Psi_i^{'}\epsilon_i^{'}$, with $\mathrm{E}(\epsilon_i^{'}) = 1$ and $\mathrm{Var}(\epsilon_i^{'}) = \sigma^2/\mu^2$, whereas the equation for Ψ_i becomes $\Psi_i^{'} = \omega^{'} + \alpha^{'} x_{i-1} + \beta\Psi_{i-1}^{'}$ with $\omega^{'} = \omega\mu$ and $\alpha^{'} = \alpha\mu$.

The autoregressive structure on the conditional expectation of the durations implies that small durations are more likely to be followed by small durations than by large ones (and likewise for long durations). Thus the model accounts for the clustering of the durations.

THEOREM 3.1 *The mean and the variance of the ACD(1,1) process defined by (3.10)-(3.13) are given by*

(i) $\mathrm{E}(x_i) = \mu_x = \omega/(1-\alpha-\beta)$ *if* $0 \leq \alpha + \beta < 1$,

(ii) $\mathrm{Var}(x_i) = \sigma_x^2 = \mu_x^2\,\sigma^2 \dfrac{1-\beta^2-2\alpha\beta}{1-(\alpha+\beta)^2-\alpha^2\sigma^2}$ *if* $(\alpha+\beta)^2 - \alpha^2\sigma^2 < 1$,

and the autocorrelation function (ACF) of x_i *is given by*

$$\rho_1 = \frac{\alpha\,(1-\beta^2-\alpha\,\beta)}{1-\beta^2-2\,\alpha\,\beta} \quad \textit{and } \rho_n = (\alpha+\beta)\rho_{n-1} \ (n \geq 2).$$

Note: If $\mathrm{E}(\epsilon_i) = \mu$, *one has to substitute* $\mu\omega$ *for* ω, $\mu\alpha$ *for* α, *and* σ^2/μ^2 *for* σ^2 *in the formulas above.*

Proof: From (3.10), for all $k > 0$,

$$\mathrm{E}(x_i^k) = \mathrm{E}(\Psi_i^k\,\epsilon_i^k) = \mathrm{E}(\Psi_i^k)\,\mathrm{E}(\epsilon_i^k), \tag{3.14}$$

by virtue of the independence of the ϵ_i process.

For $k = 1$, this gives $\mu_x = \mathrm{E}(\Psi_i)$. By writing equation (3.13) as

$$\Psi_i = \omega + \alpha\epsilon_{i-1}\Psi_{i-1} + \beta\Psi_{i-1} \tag{3.15}$$

and taking the expectation on both sides, we get

$$\mathrm{E}(\Psi_i) = \omega + \alpha\mathrm{E}(\epsilon_{i-1})\mathrm{E}(\Psi_{i-1}) + \beta\mathrm{E}(\Psi_{i-1}),$$

whence (i) follows by using (3.11).

For $k = 2$, equation (3.14) yields $\mathrm{E}(x_i^2) = (1+\sigma^2)\mathrm{E}(\Psi_i^2)$. By squaring equation (3.15) and taking the expectation, one gets

$$\mathrm{E}(\Psi_i^2) = \omega^2 + (\alpha^2 + \alpha^2\sigma^2 + \beta^2 + 2\alpha\beta)\mathrm{E}(\Psi_{i-1}^2) + 2\omega(\alpha + \beta)\mu_x.$$

Then (ii) follows by substitution in $\sigma_x^2 = (1 + \sigma^2)\mathrm{E}(\Psi_i^2) - \mu_x^2$ and some manipulations.

To obtain the ACF, one adds x_i to both sides of (3.13), moves Ψ_i to the right-hand side, and gets

$$x_i = \omega + (\alpha + \beta)x_{i-1} + u_i - \beta u_{i-1}, \tag{3.16}$$

where $u_i = x_i - \Psi_i$ is a martingale difference that is an innovation[6] for x_i. This equation shows that an ACD(1,1) process is equivalent to an ARMA(1,1) for x_i, with autoregressive coefficient $\alpha + \beta$, and moving average coefficient $-\beta$. The ACF follows by the standard formulas for the ARMA(1,1) model. ◇

Figure 3.1 shows the ACF for four sets of parameters. A slowly decaying ACF requires β to be close to 1, but the decrease is necessarily at a geometric rate $(\alpha+\beta)$. A variety of shapes can be produced by the model. Notice the strong effect of increasing α on the starting point of the ACF: compare the top panels and see also Table 3.1. The parameter α has two conflicting impacts: if it increases, the degree of dispersion increases, but the first autocorrelation also increases. If one wants to keep the first autocorrelation at a low value, one has to keep α even lower (see the formula of ρ_1). To have a small ρ_1 and a large degree of overdispersion, one must increase σ.

From the expression of σ_x^2, we see that σ_x/μ_x is greater than σ whenever α is greater than 0: increasing α makes the x_i more dispersed than the ϵ_i. If the latter is overdispersed ($\sigma > 1$), the duration is even more overdispersed. It could even be overdispersed when σ is smaller than 1, if α is large enough to compensate for that. It is also possible to have underdispersion of the duration, if there is enough underdispersion of the error (σ sufficiently smaller than 1), despite the fact that a positive α then reduces the degree of underdispersion.

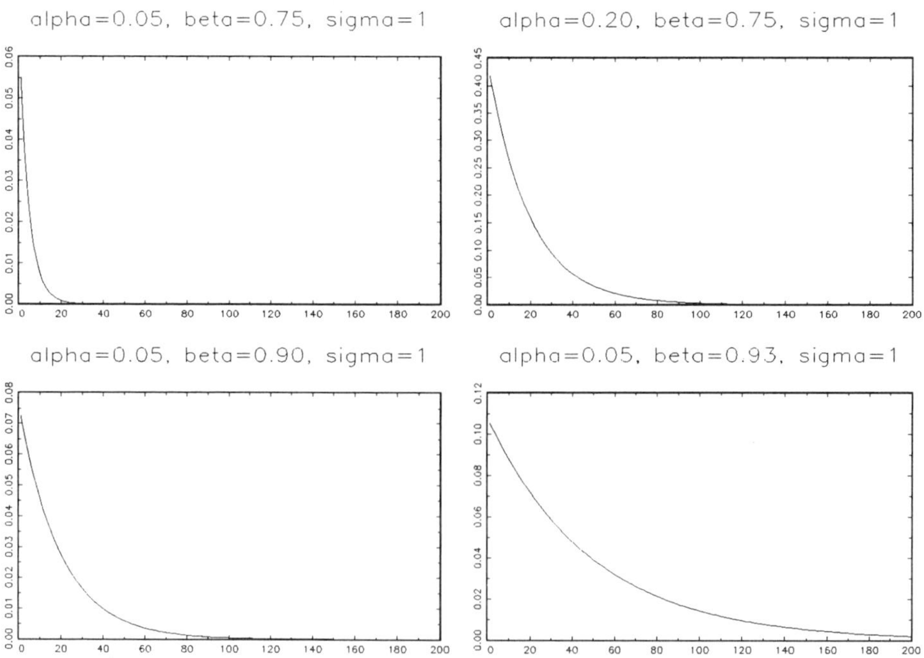

Figure 3.1. ACF of ACD Models

To illustrate numerically the relation between the degree of dispersion and the parameters, we report in Table 3.1 the dispersion index, defined as the ratio standard deviation/mean, for several sets of parameters. To keep things as simple as possible, we have fixed $\mu_x = 1$ by setting $\omega = 1-\alpha-\beta$, but it should be noticed that the ratio does not depend on ω. A large degree of overdispersion requires a relatively large value of α when $\sigma = 1$. Of course, it is easy to increase the degree of overdispersion of x_i by using an overdispersed baseline distribution: for example, with $\beta = 0.9$, the same dispersion ratio is obtained with $\alpha = 0.05$, $\sigma = 1.14$, and with $\alpha = 0.08$, $\sigma = 1$. If the baseline distribution is underdispersed ($\sigma < 1$), a positive value of α also increases the ratio σ_x/μ_x with respect to the baseline distribution. For the dispersion index of x_i, an increase of α has the same effect as an increase of σ in the case of baseline overdispersion, but a counteracting effect in the case of baseline underdispersion (it reduces underdispersion).

Table 3.1. Features of ACD models

β	α	σ	σ_x/μ_x	ρ_1
0.75	0.05	1	1.007	0.055
0.75	0.10	1	1.037	0.126
0.75	0.20	1	1.546	0.418
0.75	0.05	1.5	1.517	0.055
0.75	0.05	0.5	0.502	0.055
0.75	0.10	1.5	1.593	0.126
0.75	0.20	1.5	6.423	0.418
0.90	0.05	1	1.026	0.073
0.90	0.08	1	1.177	0.205
0.90	0.05	1.14	1.174	0.073
0.90	0.05	0.5	0.508	0.073
0.90	0.08	0.5	0.550	0.205
0.93	0.05	1	1.065	0.105
0.93	0.05	1.5	1.670	0.105
0.93	0.05	0.5	0.520	0.105

The dispersion index σ_x/μ_x, and the first-order autocorrelation ρ_1, as defined in Theorem 3.1, are computed for the parameters given in the first columns.

Table 3.2. Definition of simulated ACD processes

DGP	α	β	ω	γ	λ	Cond. Disp.	Unc. Disp.	Representative of
ACD1	0.00	0.00	1.00	1.00	0.00	1.00	1.00	Poisson process
ACD2	0.07	0.90	0.03	1.05	0.20	1.21	1.65	trade durations
ACD3	0.10	0.80	0.10	1.20	0.30	1.19	1.35	price durations
ACD4	0.10	0.80	0.10	1.70	0.08	0.64	0.66	volume durations

Cond. Disp. is the dispersion index of the distribution of ϵ_i. Unc. Disp. is the dispersion index of the unconditional distribution. γ and λ are the parameters of the Burr distribution.

Although the moments of the ACD model can be computed analytically, its unconditional distribution cannot. Simulation of large samples can be used to get an idea of the shapes of the density (by a kernel method), for several distributions of ϵ_i and parameter values. The parameters of the simulated data generating processes are provided in Table 3.2.

In Figures 3.2 and 3.3, we display the (unconditional) densities obtained from 15,000 simulated observations, and compare them with a standard exponential distribution. All the distributions have their mean equal to 1. The Poisson process (ACD1) generates IID exponential durations (EXPO in the figures) and it serves as a benchmark. The

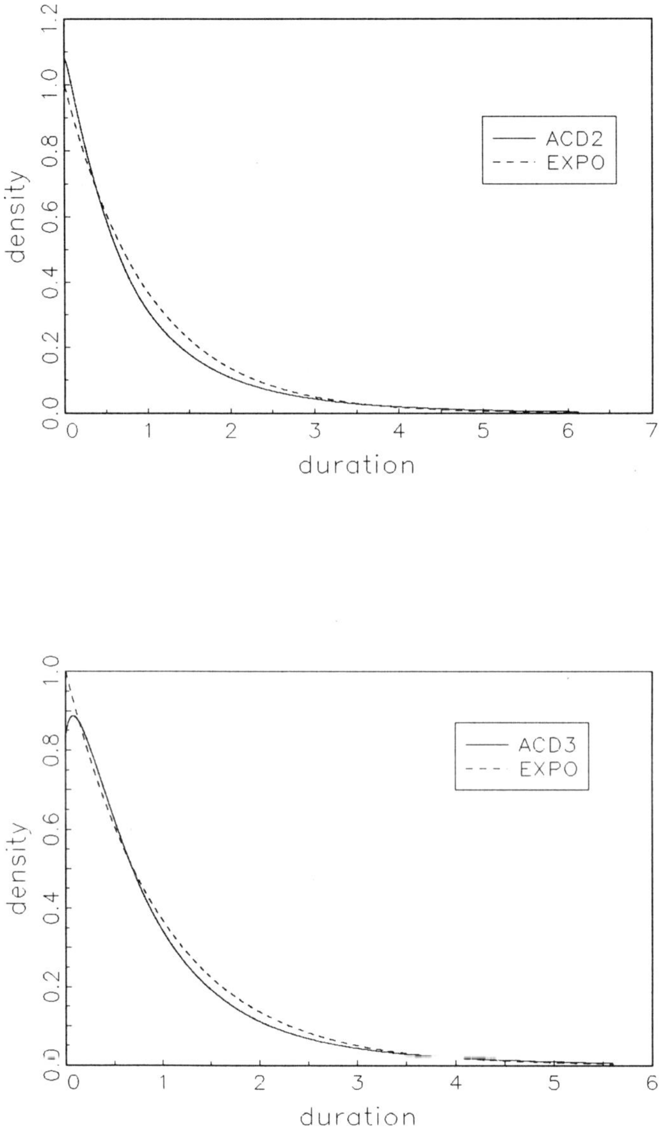

See Table 3.2 for definition of processes. EXPO refers to the exponential density.

Figure 3.2. Kernel Densities of Simulated ACD2 and ACD3 Processes

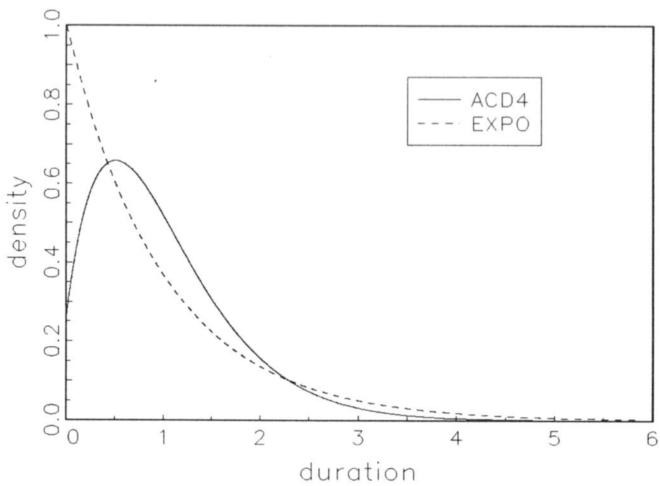

See Table 3.2 for definition of the process. EXPO refers to the exponential density.

Figure 3.3. Kernel Density of Simulated ACD4 Process

decreasing density in panel ACD2 is typical for trade durations and is overdispersed.[7] The ACD density has more mass for small durations (between 0 and 0.4, approximately) and for large durations (over 3.5) than the exponential density. The density in panel ACD3 is typical for price durations, with a mode close to the origin, and is also overdispersed. Notice that the ACD density, due to its mode close to the origin, has less mass than the exponential density (until 0.2), then it has successively more mass (until 0.6), less mass (until 3.5), and again more mass. This type of shape is also found for trade durations in several cases. The density in panel ACD4, with a clear hump, is typical for volume durations, which are usually underdispersed. Underdispersion is clearly visible, with the ACD density having less mass at the two tails than the exponential density. Qualitatively, the shape of the baseline distribution (which is the distribution of the duration conditional to the past history) is transmitted to the unconditional distribution.

3.2 LOGARITHMIC ACD MODELS

When additional explanatory variables are added linearly to the right-hand side of equation (3.13) and have negative coefficients, Ψ_i may become negative, which is not admissible. Imposing the non-negativity restrictions on these coefficients is tantamount to delete the corresponding variables, which is self-destructive. This motivated Bauwens and Giot (2000) to introduce logarithmic versions of the ACD models. In Log-ACD models equation (3.10) is written as

$$x_i = \exp(\psi_i)\,\epsilon_i, \tag{3.17}$$

such that ψ_i is the logarithm of the conditional duration[8]

$$\Psi_i = \exp(\psi_i). \tag{3.18}$$

The main difference with respect to the ACD model is that the autoregressive equation bears on the logarithm of the conditional duration rather than on the conditional duration itself. Two possible specifications of this equation are:

$$\begin{aligned} \text{Log-ACD}_1: \quad \psi_i &= \omega + \alpha \ln \epsilon_{i-1} + \beta\psi_{i-1} \\ &= \omega + \alpha \ln x_{i-1} + (\beta - \alpha)\psi_{i-1}, \end{aligned} \tag{3.19}$$

and

$$\begin{aligned} \text{Log-ACD}_2: \quad \psi_i &= \omega + \alpha\epsilon_{i-1} + \beta\psi_{i-1} \\ &= \omega + \alpha(x_{i-1}/\exp\psi_{i-1}) + \beta\psi_{i-1}. \end{aligned} \tag{3.20}$$

Notice that no sign restrictions are needed on the parameters to ensure the positivity of the conditional duration. The hypotheses about ϵ_i (for $i = 1, \ldots, n$) are the same as in ACD models, as well as the possible probability distributions. Analytic expressions for the moments and the ACF of Log-ACD models are provided by Bauwens and Giot (2001). These expressions are not as explicit as for the ACD model since they involve converging infinite products which, however, can be easily programmed on a computer. A summary of these results is provided in the next theorem. For ease of reference, we write the autoregressive equation of the conditional duration as

$$\psi_i = \omega + \alpha g(\epsilon_{i-1}) + \beta\psi_{i-1}, \tag{3.21}$$

so that $g(\epsilon_{i-1})$ can be either $\ln \epsilon_{i-1}$ or ϵ_{i-1}.

THEOREM 3.2 *The Log-ACD(1,1) process defined by (3.17) and (3.21) is covariance-stationary if* $|\beta| < 1$, $\mathrm{E}\{\epsilon_i \exp[\alpha g(\epsilon_i)]\}$ *and* $\mathrm{E}\exp[2\alpha g(\epsilon_i)] < \infty$. *Its mean and variance are given by*

(i) $\mathrm{E}(x_i) = \mu_x = \mathrm{E}(\epsilon_i)\exp\left(\frac{\omega}{1-\beta}\right)\prod_{j=1}^{\infty} \mathrm{E}\exp[\alpha\beta^{j-1}g(\epsilon_i)]$

(ii) $\mathrm{Var}(x_i) = \sigma_x^2 = \mathrm{E}(\epsilon_i^2)\exp\left(\frac{2\omega}{1-\beta}\right)\prod_{j=1}^{\infty}\mathrm{E}\exp[2\alpha\beta^{j-1}g(\epsilon_i)] - \mu_x^2,$

and its autocorrelation function is given by

$$\rho_n = \frac{\mathrm{E}(\epsilon_i)\mathrm{E}[\epsilon_i e^{\alpha\beta^{n-1}g(\epsilon_i)}]\prod_{j=1}^{n-1}\mathrm{E}[e^{\alpha\beta^{j-1}g(\epsilon_i)}]\prod_{j=1}^{\infty}\mathrm{E}[e^{\alpha(1+\beta^n)\beta^{j-1}g(\epsilon_i)}]}{\mathrm{E}(\epsilon_i^2)\prod_{j=1}^{\infty}\mathrm{E}e^{[2\alpha\beta^{j-1}g(\epsilon_i)]} - [\mathrm{E}(\epsilon_i)]^2\prod_{j=1}^{\infty}[\mathrm{E}e^{\alpha\beta^{j-1}g(\epsilon_i)}]^2}$$
$$-\frac{\mu_x^2}{\sigma_x^2},\ for\, n \geq 1. \tag{3.22}$$

Proof: Starting from (3.18) and (3.21), we have

$$\Psi_i = \exp(\omega)\exp[\alpha g(\epsilon_{i-1})]\,\Psi_{i-1}^{\beta}. \tag{3.23}$$

By recursive substitutions on lagged Ψ_i, one obtains

$$\Psi_i = \exp\left(\omega\sum_{j=0}^{n-1}\beta^j\right)\exp\left[\alpha\sum_{j=1}^{n}\beta^{j-1}g(\epsilon_{i-j})\right]\Psi_{i-n}^{\beta^n} \tag{3.24}$$

$$\rightarrow \exp\left(\frac{\omega}{1-\beta}\right)\exp\left[\alpha\sum_{j=1}^{\infty}\beta^{j-1}g(\epsilon_{i-j})\right] \tag{3.25}$$

as $n \rightarrow \infty$. Raising both sides to the power $m(= 1$ or $2)$, multiplying by ϵ_i^m, and taking the unconditional expectation gives

$$\mathrm{E}(x_i^m) = \mathrm{E}(\epsilon_i^m)\exp\left(\frac{m\omega}{1-\beta}\right)\prod_{j=1}^{\infty}E\{\exp[m\alpha\beta^{j-1}g(\epsilon_i)]\} \tag{3.26}$$

using the hypothesis that $\{\epsilon_i\}$ is IID, and the existence of $\mathrm{E}\exp[m\alpha g(\epsilon_i)]$ which implies that of $\mathrm{E}\exp[m\alpha\beta^{j-1}g(\epsilon_i)]$ (since $|\beta| < 1$).

To get the ACF, one needs $\mathrm{E}(x_i x_{i-n})$ since $\rho_n = [\mathrm{E}(x_i x_{i-n}) - \mu_x^2]/\sigma_x^2$. By multiplying both sides of (3.24) by Ψ_{i-n}, we get an expression for $\Psi_i\Psi_{i-n}$, we multiply it with $\epsilon_i\epsilon_{i-n}$, and we take the expectation. This yields

$$\begin{aligned}\mathrm{E}(x_i x_{i-n}) = {} & \mathrm{E}(\epsilon_i)\exp\left(\omega\tfrac{1-\beta^n}{1-\beta}\right)\textstyle\prod_{j=1}^{n-1}\mathrm{E}\{\exp[\alpha\beta^{j-1}g(\epsilon_i)]\} \\ & \mathrm{E}\{\epsilon_{i-n}\exp[\alpha\beta^{n-1}g(\epsilon_{i-n})]\}\,\mathrm{E}[\Psi_{i-n}^{1+\beta^n}],\end{aligned} \tag{3.27}$$

which exists using the assumption that $\mathrm{E}\{\epsilon_i \exp[\alpha g(\epsilon_i)]\}$ exists. Using (3.25) (with $i-n$ instead of i) raised to the power $1+\beta^n$, we get $\mathrm{E}[\Psi_{i-n}^{1+\beta^n}] = \exp[\omega(1+\beta^n)/(1-\beta)]\prod_{j=1}^{\infty}\mathrm{E}[e^{\alpha\beta^{j-1}g(\epsilon_i)}]$. Substituting this in the right-hand side of (3.27), we get the numerator of the first term of (3.22) multiplied by $\exp[2\omega/(1-\beta)]$ which can be simplified since it appears also in σ_x^2. ◇

Notice from the proof that the condition $|\beta| < 1$ is necessary for the existence of unconditional moments of x_i.

If we assume that α and β are both positive, computing the moments given in the previous theorem requires to know $\mathrm{E}(\epsilon^p)$ for $p > 0$ in the Log-ACD$_1$ case, and $\mathrm{E}[\exp(p\epsilon)]$ in the Log-ACD$_2$ case. The (non-integer) moments $\mathrm{E}(\epsilon^p)$ are available for the generalized gamma and Burr distributions, and all their particular cases. The moment generating function which provides $\mathrm{E}[\exp(p\epsilon)]$ is only available for the gamma distribution (including the exponential), not for all the other distributions encompassed by the generalized gamma and the Burr classes (such as the Weibull). For the latter cases, one can compute $\mathrm{E}[\exp(p\epsilon)]$ by numerical integration using a deterministic rule (such as Simpson's rule). As an alternative, one can proceed also by simulation of a very large sample of the process to estimate the moments; the unconditional density can then also be estimated by a non-parametric technique.

The infinite products that appear in the moments can be truncated after a sufficiently large number of terms since β^j tends to 0 under the stationarity condition. For example, if we use an exponential distribution, $\mathrm{E}(\epsilon^{\alpha\beta^j}) = \Gamma(1+\alpha\beta^j)$ and $\mathrm{E}[\exp(\epsilon\alpha\beta^j)] = 1/(1-\alpha\beta^j)$, so that both expectations tend to 1 when j tends to infinity.

Log-ACD models can fit the stylized facts of durations as well as ACD models. The extent of clustering increases with the parameter β, which in this respect is equivalent to $\alpha+\beta$ in the ACD model. The degree of dispersion depends on the baseline distribution and on the parameters β and α. The latter also influences the starting value of the ACF: the larger α, the larger ρ_1 (other things being equal). We illustrate these results in Table 3.3 which is directly comparable to Table 3.1 (β in the second table is equal to $\alpha+\beta$ in the corresponding row of the first one). A slight difference arises between the ACD and the Log-ACD models in the behaviour of the ACF: for the ACD the ACF decreases at the geometric rate $\alpha+\beta$ from ρ_2, whereas for the Log-ACD, the geometric decrease at the rate β is only asymptotic in n (the lag order); for small n, the ratio ρ_n/ρ_{n-1} is slightly smaller than β.

The results in Table 3.3 also show that the two versions of the Log-ACD model do not provide very different results for a given value of the

Table 3.3. Features of Log-ACD models

β	α	σ	σ_x/μ_x	ρ_1
0.80	0.05	1	1.011 - 1.007	0.058 - 0.058
0.85	0.10	1	1.054 - 1.042	0.137 - 0.139
0.95	0.20	1	1.588 - 1.587	0.420 - 0.448
0.80	0.05	1.5	1.524 - 1.539*	0.049 - 0.087*
0.80	0.05	0.5	0.503 - 0.502*	0.063 - 0.048*
0.85	0.10	1.5	1.621 - 1.836*	0.117 - 0.241*
0.95	0.20	1.5	3.004 - 17.87*	0.340 - 0.445*
0.95	0.05	1	1.040 - 1.028	0.084 - 0.076
0.98	0.08	1	1.249 - 1.182	0.241 - 0.213
0.95	0.05	1.14	1.192 - 1.182*	0.081 - 0.083*
0.95	0.05	0.5	0.512 - 0.506*	0.088 - 0.062*
0.98	0.08	0.5	0.570 - 0.540*	0.253 - 0.173*
0.98	0.05	1	1.099 - 1.068	0.130 - 0.109
0.98	0.05	1.5	1.731 - 1.844*	0.113 - 0.168*
0.98	0.05	0.5	0.528 - 0.516*	0.133 - 0.088*

In the last two columns, the first result is for a Log-ACD$_1$ model, defined by (3.17) and (3.19), while the second result is for a Log-ACD$_2$, defined by (3.17) and (3.20). The parameters are given in the first columns. When $\sigma = 1$, the baseline distribution is exponential, while it is Weibull with parameter γ selected to yield the given value of σ in the other cases ($\gamma = 2.101, 0.8795, 0.6848$ correspond to $\sigma = 0.5, 1.14, 1.50$, respectively). The dispersion index σ_x/μ_x and the first-order autocorrelation ρ_1 are computed according to the formulas given in Theorem 3.2, except the values marked with a *, which have been computed by averaging the results of 500 simulated samples of size 20,000 each.

parameters. The dispersion index is larger with the first version than with the second (except when $\sigma = 1.5$), but the difference is important only when β is close to 1 (0.98 in the table). The first-order autocorrelation is slightly larger with the Log-ACD$_1$ in the same circumstances, and for small n, the ACF of the Log-ACD$_2$ decreases less quickly than the ACF of the Log-ACD$_1$.

Figure 3.4 shows a few autocorrelation functions computed with (3.22). A variety of shapes can be generated, and the comments made about the ACF of the ACD model apply also for the Log-ACD models. Figure 3.5 shows an exponential density and the kernel densities estimated from 15,000 observations simulated from Log-ACD$_1$ and Log-ACD$_2$ processes with parameters $\alpha = 0.07, \beta = 0.92$ and $\omega = 0.041$ (Log-ACD$_1$) and -0.0713 (Log-ACD$_2$), chosen so that the mean of the durations is equal to 1. The distribution of ϵ_i is a Burr with parameters $\gamma = 1.10$ and $\lambda = 0.3$. Its dispersion index is equal to 1.35, while the dispersion index of the simulated durations is 1.37 for the two Log-ACD processes. The kernel densities of the two Log-ACD processes are almost indistinguish-

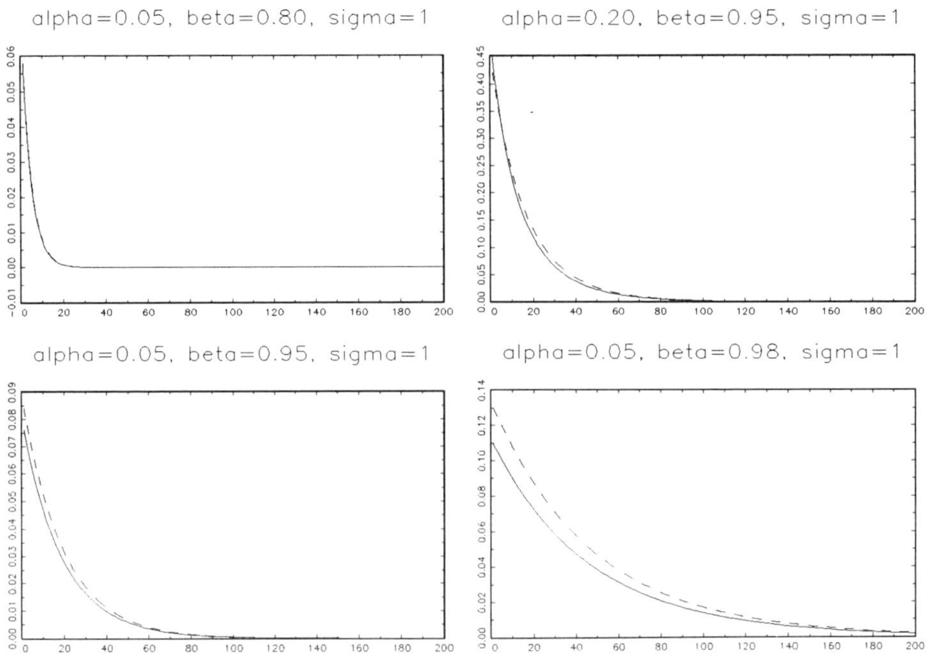

Figure 3.4. ACF of Log-ACD$_1$ (dashed lines) and Log-ACD$_2$ (solid lines) models

able, and the overdispersion is quite visible. Actually, Log-ACD models can generate the same variety of unconditional densities as ACD models.

3.3 ESTIMATION

Given a parametric assumption about the distribution of ϵ_i, it is straightforward to write the likelihood function. If $f_\epsilon(\epsilon_i;\theta_2)$ stands for the density function of ϵ_i, which can depend on some parameters θ_2, the density function of x_i given $\mathcal{H}_i$ is

$$f_x(x_i|\mathcal{H}_i;\theta) = f_\epsilon(\frac{x_i}{\Psi_i};\theta_2)\,\Psi_i^{-1}, \tag{3.28}$$

so that the log-likelihood function for the parameter $\theta = (\theta_1, \theta_2)$ where θ_1 corresponds to the parameters of the autoregressive equation (typically ω, α, and β) is

$$l(\theta) = \sum_{i=1}^{n} \ln f_x(x_i|\mathcal{H}_i;\theta) = \sum_{i=1}^{n}\left[\ln f_\epsilon(\frac{x_i}{\Psi_i};\theta_2) - \ln \Psi_i\right]. \tag{3.29}$$

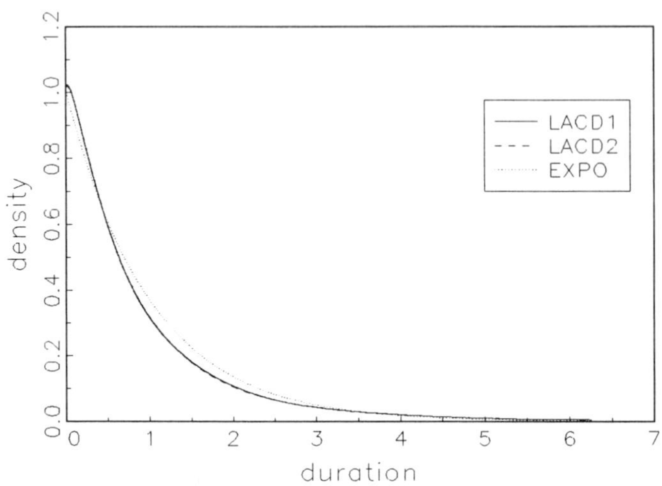

See text for definition of the simulated processes. EXPO refers to the exponential density.

Figure 3.5. Kernel Densities of Simulated Log-ACD Processes

In this expression, Ψ_i can be any of the specifications introduced above, see equations (3.13), (3.19), and (3.20), the last two with $\Psi_i = \exp(\psi_i)$.

The log-likelihood function can be maximized by a standard numerical algorithm, which at convergence delivers the maximum likelihood estimate (MLE) $\hat{\theta}$. In this book, we proceed under the presumption that the usual asymptotic properties of $\hat{\theta}$ hold, namely that in large samples

$$\hat{\theta} \sim N(\theta^0, V(\theta^0)) \tag{3.30}$$

where θ^0 is the so-called true value. The variance-covariance matrix $V(\theta^0)$ can be estimated consistently by A^{-1} or B^{-1} evaluated at the MLE, where

$$A = -\sum_{i=1}^{n} \frac{\partial^2 \ln f_x(x_i|\mathcal{H}_i;\theta)}{\partial\theta\partial\theta'} \tag{3.31}$$

and

$$B = \sum_{i=1}^{n} \Big[\frac{\partial \ln f_x(x_i|\mathcal{H}_i;\theta)}{\partial\theta}\Big]\Big[\frac{\partial \ln f_x(x_i|\mathcal{H}_i;\theta)}{\partial\theta}\Big]'. \tag{3.32}$$

The usefulness of (3.30) is that one can conduct hypothesis tests on θ by usual standard normal and chi-square tests.

When using a precise hypothesis about the distribution of ϵ_i, one runs the risk of making a mistake, in which case the MLE is not even consistent. A simple alternative is to rely on the quasi-maximum likelihood estimate (QMLE) $\tilde{\theta}_1$. The appropriate quasi-log-likelihood function is obtained by proceeding as if the distribution of ϵ_i were exponential. It is given by

$$ql(\theta_1) = -\sum_{i=1}^{n}[\frac{x_i}{\Psi_i} + \ln \Psi_i], \tag{3.33}$$

and the score by

$$\frac{\partial ql}{\partial \theta_1} = \sum_{i=1}^{n}(\frac{x_i}{\Psi_i} - 1)\frac{1}{\Psi_i}\frac{\partial \Psi_i}{\partial \theta_1}. \tag{3.34}$$

The score is readily seen to be a martingale difference with respect to the information set $\mathcal{H}_i$, so that the QMLE is consistent and asymptotically normal if $\mathrm{E}(x_i|\mathcal{H}_i) = \Psi_i$, that is, if the conditional expectation of x_i is correctly specified, even though the distribution of ϵ_i is not exponential.[9] Thus we can rely on a result similar to (3.30),

$$\tilde{\theta}_1 \sim N(\theta_1^0, V_q(\theta_1^0)) \tag{3.35}$$

where θ_1^0 is the pseudo-true value of θ_1 and $V_q(\theta_1^0)$ can be estimated consistently by $A^{-1}BA^{-1}$ (the so-called sandwich estimator). In this case, A and B are defined as in (3.31) and (3.32) with f_x the exponential density. Remark that the QML approach is robust to misspecifiction of the baseline distribution, but it does not provide an estimate of its parameters (θ_2).

3.4 DIAGNOSTICS

The (Log-)ACD models that have been presented are based on several hypotheses: a precise form of the conditional expectation of the duration, IID error terms, and possibly a precise distribution of the error. Since these assumptions are crucial to validate inferences that are made with the model, it is recommended to test them. Such tests are called diagnostic checks.

The independence assumption of the errors is usually not testable as such, because it involves too many dimensions. One important dimension that can be tested easily is the absence of autocorrelation of the errors, and of functions of the errors (like their squares). A check of this assumption can be made through the residuals, defined as

$$e_i = \frac{x_i}{\widehat{\Psi}_i}, \tag{3.36}$$

where $\widehat{\Psi}_i$ is the expected duration evaluated at the (Q)MLE, see equations (3.13) for the ACD model, and (3.19), (3.20) with $\Psi_i = \exp(\psi_i)$ for the Log-ACD models. If the residuals look like white noise, the postulated model successfully captures the autocorrelation of the durations. This can be tested with Ljung-Box Q-statistics and can be visualized by plotting the ACF of the residuals. The Q-statistic of order s is defined as

$$Q(s) = n(n+2) \sum_{k=1}^{s} \frac{r_k^2}{n-k}, \tag{3.37}$$

where n is the sample size and r_k is the autocorrelation coefficient of order k, i.e.

$$r_k = \frac{\sum_{i=k+1}^{n} (e_i - \bar{e})(e_{i-k} - \bar{e})}{\sum_{i=1}^{n} (e_i - \bar{e})^2}, \tag{3.38}$$

with $\bar{e}$ the mean of the residuals. The statistic $Q(s)$ is distributed as $\chi^2(s)$ if n is large (which is the case in the data sets that we use in this book). For example, if we obtain a $Q(10) > 18.3$ (the 95% quantile of the $\chi^2(10)$ distribution), we can consider that the residuals are significantly autocorrelated up to the order 10, at the 5% level. Similarly, Q-statistics can be computed using the squared residuals, to test for autocorrelation in the squares of the errors.

In the framework of ML estimation (excluding QML), it is crucial to check the distributional assumption. Before choosing a distribution for ϵ_i, we advise to estimate the density of the durations x_i by a non-parametric method. As mentioned at the end of subsection 3.3.1, the shape of the density of ϵ_i (which is the density of x_i conditional on the past), should be compatible with the shape of the unconditional density of x_i. It is highly implausible, for example, to have a conditional density that is monotone decreasing, like a $W(\gamma, 1)$ with $\gamma \leq 1$, and to have an unconditional density which is hump-shaped. Once the model has been estimated, the assumed distribution should be confronted with the data. Several procedures for doing this are available: some are applicable with any distribution, some are specific to some distributions. For example, Engle and Russell (1998) use a test of the hypothesis that the Weibull distribution is valid.[10]

The first general method consists of checking if the distribution of the residuals e_i is compatible with the assumed distribution of ϵ_i at the MLE estimate. One can use a chi-square test of goodness-of-fit; for a description, see e.g. Mood, Graybill, and Boes (1987, pp 442-448).

The second general method is based on the analysis of density forecasts. A density forecast, in our context, is a density that is assumed for the next duration: if we are at the end of the duration x_{i-1}, i.e. at time t_{i-1}, we wonder what is the density of the next duration x_i, given the past history of the durations (and possibly, other past information). Thus, it is a 1-step-ahead prediction, not of the next expected duration, but of the complete distribution of the next duration. For example, if we assume a (Log-)ACD model with a $Burr(\gamma, \sigma^2, 1)$ distribution for ϵ_i, the density forecast of x_i implied by the model is the $Burr(\gamma, \sigma^2, \Psi_i)$ distribution.

Since the evaluation of density forecasts provides not only a test of distributional assumption, but also an indirect test of the IID assumption on the ϵ_i, we develop this approach in the next subsection.

Density forecast evaluation

Methods for evaluating density forecasts have been advanced by Diebold, Gunther and Tay (1998) (referred to as DGT hereafter). DGT's approach makes it possible to evaluate a model forecasting performance regardless of the users' loss functions.[11] The basic ideas behind DGT's method are easily understood.

Let us denote by $\{f_i(x_i \mid \mathcal{H}_i)\}_{i=1}^m$ a sequence of one step ahead density forecasts produced by one of the (Log-)ACD models and $\{p_i(x_i \mid \mathcal{H}_i)\}_{i=1}^m$ the sequence of densities defining the data generating process of the duration series x_i.[12] DGT show that the correct density is weakly superior to all other forecasts, i.e. will be preferred, in terms of expected loss, by all forecast users regardless of their loss functions. This suggests that forecasts should be evaluated by assessing whether the forecasting densities are correct, i.e. whether

$$\{f_i(x_i \mid \mathcal{H}_i)\}_{i=1}^m = \{p_i(x_i \mid \mathcal{H}_i)\}_{i=1}^m . \tag{3.39}$$

At first sight, testing whether (3.39) is true appears difficult because $p_i(x_i \mid \mathcal{H}_i)$ is not known. The distributional properties of the probability integral transform

$$z_i = \int_{-\infty}^{x_i} f_i(u)du \tag{3.40}$$

provide the solution to this problem. Rosenblatt (1952) derived that the distribution of the probability integral transform under the null hypothesis (3.39) is uniform. DGT extend this result and show that under the null hypothesis, the distribution of the sequence of probability transforms $\{z_i\}$ of $\{x_i\}$ with respect to $\{f_i(x_i \mid \mathcal{H}_i)\}$ is IID uniform. Hence, the empirical sequence of probabilty integral transforms produced by the forecasts of some model can be used for testing. DGT propose graphical tools that can be complemented by goodness-of-fit (GOF) and independence tests for IID uniformity. By plotting a histogram based on an empirical z-sequence, departures from uniformity can easily be detected.

A visual inspection often provides obvious hints to the reasons for model failure. For instance, an inverted U-shape of the z-histogram would indicate that the issued forecast densities are too narrow and that the tails of the true density are not accounted for. On the other hand, a U-shape of the histogram would suggest that the model issues forecasts that either underestimate or overestimate too frequently. Confidence intervals for the z-histogram bins as well as a chi-square goodness-of-fit test can easily be computed by exploiting familiar statistical properties of the histogram under the null hypothesis of uniformity. As a complement to a check of uniformity, autocorrelograms of $(z_i - \bar{z}), (z_i - \bar{z})^2 \ldots$ and corresponding Ljung-Box Q-statistics can be used to uncover potential deficiencies of the independence assumption of the errors.

We can use density forecasts either for 'in-sample' evaluation of a model, or for 'out-of-sample' evaluation. In the former case, once the model is estimated, one computes and evaluates (with graphical and complementary tools) the z_i series for the sample used for estimation (using the MLE to compute the forecast densities). In the latter case, one uses a first part of the sample of durations for estimation, and then computes and evaluates the z_i series for the remaining part of the sample (using the model with the MLE frozen at the end of the estimation period). The out-of-sample evaluation is clearly more demanding than the in-sample one, but more useful to reveal a possible predictive failure of the model.

Although the basic ideas behind DHT's approach are straightforward, the implications for testing and comparing non-nested models are far reaching. Indeed, one can apply the tools to compare competing models: see Bauwens, Giot, Grammig, and Veredas (2000). Note that the method does not require that the data generating process remains the same over time. Instead, the true data generating process $\{p_i(x_i \mid \mathcal{H}_i)\}$ may exhibit all kinds of structural change, as indicated by its time subscript. The important point is that a model density forecasts $\{f_i(x_i \mid \mathcal{H}_i)\}$ are able to account for these features.

To illustrate the use of density forecasts to evaluate duration models, we have simulated several data generating processes (DGP) and for each of them we estimated a range of models. If the DGP is encompassed by an estimated model, the probability integral transforms computed with the density forecasts implied by the estimated model should have the required properties (uniformity and independence). On the contrary, if the estimated model is incorrectly specified, some features of the forecast densities should reveal this, as explained above.

We have used the data simulated from the four DGP of the ACD class defined in Table 3.2, whose densities are shown in Figures 3.2 and 3.3.

Table 3.4. Density forecast evaluation results for simulated ACD processes

DGP	Model	In-sample		Out-of-sample	
		GOF	AC(z)	GOF	AC(z)
	GGACD	38	2	17	2
	BACD	41	2	13	2
	WACD	41	2	15	2
	EACD	15	2	15	2
	POISSON	20	2	18	2
	GGLACD$_1$	30	2	13	2
ACD1	BLACD$_1$	68	2	16	2
	WLACD$_1$	68	2	16	2
	ELACD$_1$	60	2	28	2
	GGLACD$_2$	46	2	18	2
	BLACD$_2$	52	2	33	2
	WLACD$_2$	52	2	31	2
	ELACD$_2$	50	2	43	2
	GGACD*	17	2	7.5	2
	BACD	9	2	26	2
	WACD	0.4	2	0.0	2
	EACD	0.1	2	0.0	2
	POISSON	0.0	19	0.0	19
ACD2	GGLACD$_1^*$	45	2	0.5	3
	BLACD$_1^*$	60	2	8.2	3
	WLACD$_1^*$	0.2	3	0.0	3
	GGLACD$_2^*$	53	2	0.8	2
	BLACD$_2^*$	20	2	28	2
	WLACD$_2^*$	0.4	2	0.0	2
	GGACD*	26	2	8.7	2
	BACD	16	2	37	2
	WACD	16	2	9.5	2
	EACD	0.0	2	0.0	2
	POISSON	0.0	16	0.0	16
ACD4	GGLACD$_1^*$	68	2	6.9	2
	BLACD$_1^*$	68	2	15	2
	WLACD$_1^*$	70	2	13	2
	GGLACD$_2^*$	19	2	13	2
	BLACD$_2^*$	19	2	45	2
	WLACD$_2^*$	22	2	14	2

A sample of 15,000 observations was generated from each DGP. In-sample: the last 5,000 observations were used both for estimation and forecasting. Out-of-sample: the first 10,000 observations were used for estimation, the rest for forecasting. See Table 3.2 for the definition of the DGP. The models acronyms GGACD, BACD, WACD, EACD stand for generalized gamma, Burr, Weibull, and exponential-ACD, respectively. For the Log-ACD$_1$ (Log-ACD$_2$) models, the suffix ACD is changed into LACD$_1$ (LACD$_2$). A * superscript on a model name means that the model is not encompassed by the DGP. Under GOF we report the p-value (in percent) of the chi-square goodness-of-fit statistic (with 19 degrees of freedom) for a uniform distribution of the probability integral transforms (z), and under AC(z)the number of autocorrelations (out of the first 50) that are outside of the 95 % confidence interval.

The first one (ACD1) is a Poisson process, such that durations are IID with a standard exponential distribution. It is encompassed by all the estimated models. The other DGP are Burr-ACD ones which are not encompassed by any model except the Burr-ACD itself.

The results, reported in Table 3.4 are computed 'in-sample' and 'out-of-sample'. For each DGP, 15,000 observations were generated. The first 10,000 were used for estimation and the last 5,000 for out-of-sample forecasting. For in-sample forecasting, the last 5,000 observations were used for estimation and once again for 'forecasting'. In this way, exactly the same 5,000 observations were used for evaluation, making the results more comparable than if different samples had been used.

For each experiment (estimation of a model with data generated by a DGP), we report the p-value (in percent) of the chi-square goodness-of-fit (GOF) statistic, with 19 degrees of freedom, for an uniform distribution of the probability integral transforms (z), and the number of autocorrelations (out of the first 50) of the same z-series, which are outside of the 95 % confidence interval. For example, if the DGP is the Poisson process (ACD1), and the estimated model is a Burr Log-ACD of type 1 ($BLACD_1$), the uniform distribution is accepted both 'in-sample' and 'out-of-sample' at the usual levels of significance (p-values are 68 % and 16 %, respectively), and in both cases, there are two autocorrelations outside of the 95 % confidence interval. Graphs of histograms of the z and of their autocorrelogram are shown in Figure 3.6.

As expected, all models are able to forecast correctly when they are encompassed by the DGP (results for the ACD3 DGP are not reported because they are very similar to those obtained for the DGP ACD2).[13] Other less obvious but more interesting findings are the following:

1) When the estimated model is a Log-ACD one and the distribution of ϵ_i is not too restrictive with respect to that of the DGP (as are the exponential and Weibull when the DGP uses a Burr distribution), the results are as good as when the estimated model is an ACD one.

2) Even if the estimated model uses a generalized gamma distribution, the p-values for the GOF statistic are above 5 percent (with two exceptions), implying that to a large extent it is not crucial to use a Burr distribution instead of a generalized gamma for estimation despite the fact the DGP uses the Burr. In the ACD2 and ACD3 cases, the rejection of uniformity (p-values of the GOF statistic below 5 percent) occurs when exponential or Weibull models are estimated. This is due to the fact that these distributions are too restrictive to fit the shape of the Burr distribution specified for these two DGP. For the ACD4, the Weibull models are not rejected, because they can fit

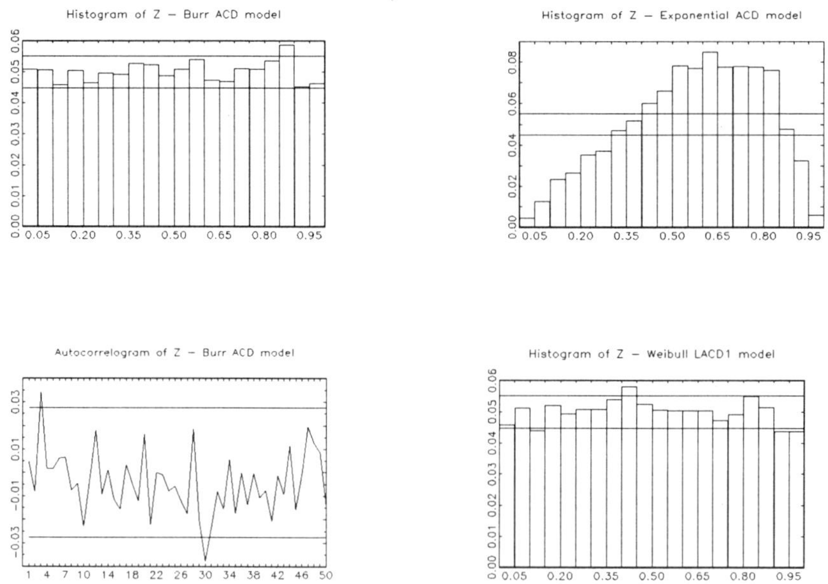

Figure 3.6. Histograms and Autocorrelogram (out-of-sample) of Estimated Models, Simulated Data from ACD4 DGP

the shape of the Burr distribution of the DGP (hump shaped), but the exponential models are rejected, because the exponential distribution cannot be hump-shaped. Figure 3.6 contains three histograms: two of them show cases when uniformity is not rejected, and one when it is clearly rejected. To understand the latter case, refer to Figure 3.7, which shows the standard exponential density together with the Burr density with parameters $\gamma = 1.70$ and $\lambda = 0.10$ (these being the estimates for the Burr-ACD model): assuming that the durations used for computing the z_i have been generated by the estimated Burr-ACD model, there are not enough small and large durations compared to what would be the case if the DGP were the exponential ACD, see the thin tails of the Burr density. Consequently there are too few z_i close to 0 and to 1, and too many in the middle range, as is the case on the top right panel of Figure 3.6.

3) Even the estimated model is based on a too restrictive distribution with respect to that of the DGP, the number of significant autocorrelations—'significant' meaning outside of the 95 % confi-

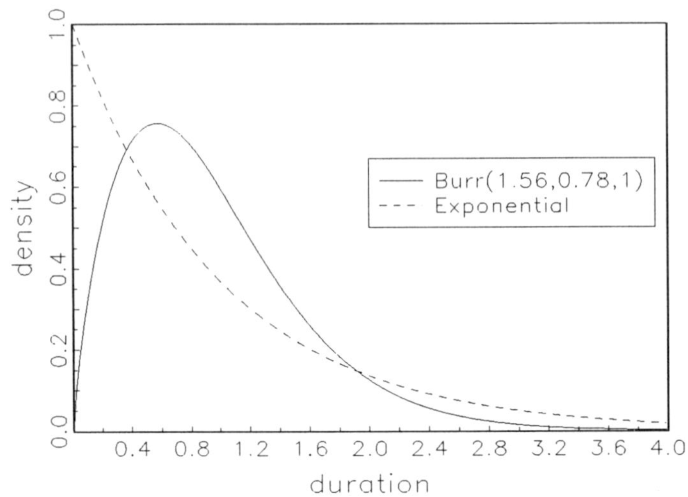

Figure 3.7. **Comparison of Exponential and Burr Densities**

dence interval—is low (2 out of 50). One panel of Figure 3.6 illustrates the autocorrelations and the confidence interval for the Burr-ACD model, but the corresponding graphs for the other estimated models, except the Poisson model, are almost identical. An inspection of the autocorrelations reveal that they are marginally significant, so that actually no Ljung-Box Q-statistic of order up to 50 is significant at the 5 percent level. The only case when there are many significant autocorrelations and the first 50 Q-statistics are all significant at least at the 5 percent level, is when there is no dynamics in the estimated model, i.e. in the case of the Poisson model.

4) In-sample evaluation usually gives the same conclusions in terms of the hypothesis of uniformity of the z as out-of-sample evaluation (although the p-values are usually higher in the former case). We conclude that in-sample evaluation can be used as an evaluation device. This is useful if the available sample is not large enough to break it into an estimation sample and a forecast sample.

To conclude, ACD and Log-ACD models are able to capture well the dependence in the data, but some care has to be taken in the choice of the distribution of ϵ_i. In that respect, we advise to use the Burr or the generalized gamma distributions as a starting hypothesis, and to

Table 3.5. Estimation results for Exxon trade durations

	EACD		BACD		GGACD	
ω	0.030	(0.0099)	0.055	(0.011)	0.12	(0.018)
α	0.044	(0.077)	0.061	(0.0065)	0.084	(0.070)
β	0.93	(0.017)	0.89	(0.016)	0.80	(0.024)
γ	1		1.09	(0.0094)	0.45	(0.013)
λ or ν	1		0.27	(0.015)	3.79	(0.20)
GOF all-out	0 - 0		0 - 0		0 - 0	
AC(z) all-out	9 - 4		9 - 4		14 - 10	
	ELACD$_1$		BLACD$_1$		GGLACD$_1$	
ω	0.034	(0.0029)	0.044	(0.0035)	0.040	(0.0034)
α	0.056	(0.0047)	0.071	(0.0053)	0.065	(0.0052)
β	0.88	(0.015)	0.84	(0.017)	0.85	(0.017)
γ	1		1.10	(0.0094)	0.37	(0.015)
λ or ν	1		0.29	(0.015)	5.54	(0.44)
GOF all-out	0 - 0		0 - 0		0 - 0	
AC(z) all-out	11 - 6		9 - 8		8 - 7	
	ELACD$_2$		BLACD$_2$		GGLACD$_2$	
ω	-0.045	(0.0068)	-0.057	(0.0050)	-0.052	(0.0049)
α	0.045	(0.0066)	0.057	(0.0050)	0.053	(0.0049)
β	0.96	(0.011)	0.94	(0.010)	0.94	(0.010)
γ	1		1.09	(0.0094)	0.38	(0.016)
λ or ν	1		0.27	(0.015)	5.27	(0.41)
GOF all-out	0 - 0		0 - 0		0 - 0	
AC(z) all-out	8 - 4		9 - 4		9 - 4	

Sample size = 28,371. Data from TAQ database, September-November 1996.
E for exponential, B for Burr, GG for generalized gamma; λ for B, ν for GG, $\nu = 1$ for E.
ACD for ACD models. LACD$_1$ for Log-ACD of type 1. LACD$_2$ for Log-ACD of type 2.
ML estimates and asymptotic standard errors in parentheses, from complete sample.
GOF: p-value (in percent) of chi-square goodness-of-fit test.
AC(z): number of autocorrelations (in the first 50) out of the 95 percent confidence interval.
all = in-sample evaluation on complete sample (all data).
out = out-of-sample evaluation on last third of data (estimation on first 2/3).

test if it can be restricted to a simpler distribution. Nevertheless, the dependence in the duration process is well captured whatever the choice of the distribution.

4. ILLUSTRATION ON NYSE DATA

We have estimated the ACD and Log-ACD models combined with different distributions of ϵ_i, for different stocks and types of durations. We report the QML estimates (using the exponential density) and the ML estimates using either the Burr or the generalized gamma density. They are the most flexible densities that we consider for durations (they

Table 3.6. Estimation results for Coca-Cola price durations

	EACD		BACD		GGACD	
ω	0.16	(0.038)	0.16	(0.045)	0.19	(0.048)
α	0.11	(0.023)	0.11	(0.024)	0.11	(0.023)
β	0.73	(0.047)	0.73	(0.056)	0.69	(0.056)
γ	1		1.15	(0.043)	0.54	(0.041)
λ or ν	1		0.33	(0.068)	2.85	(0.39)
GOF all-out	0 - 1.8		1.3 - 6.1		48 - 46	
AC(z) all-out	4 - 0		4 - 0		3 - 0	
	ELACD$_1$		BLACD$_1$		GGLACD$_1$	
ω	0.054	(0.011)	0.064	(0.015)	0.060	(0.014)
α	0.10	(0.015)	0.10	(0.018)	0.10	(0.018)
β	0.71	(0.049)	0.71	(0.053)	0.71	(0.056)
γ	1		1.17	(0.045)	0.36	(0.063)
λ or ν	1		0.36	(0.071)	6.01	(1.99)
GOF all-out	0 - 0.4		1 - 9.2		55 - 51	
AC(z) all-out	3 - 0		4 - 0		3 - 0	
	ELACD$_2$		BLACD$_2$		GGLACD$_2$	
ω	-0.090	(0.018)	-0.087	(0.019)	-0.086	(0.019)
α	0.088	(0.017)	0.088	(0.018)	0.085	(0.018)
β	0.84	(0.035)	0.84	(0.044)	0.84	(0.047)
γ	1		1.15	(0.043)	0.38	(0.063)
λ or ν	1		0.33	(0.068)	5.34	(1.67)
GOF all-out	0 - 12		0.1 - 15		15 - 71	
AC(z) all-out	6 - 0		4 - 0		4 - 0	

Sample size = 1,609. Data from TAQ database, September-November 1996.
E for exponential, B for Burr, GG for generalized gamma; λ for B, ν for GG, $\nu = 1$ for E.
ACD for ACD models. LACD$_1$ for Log-ACD of type 1. LACD$_2$ for Log-ACD of type 2.
ML estimates and asymptotic standard errors in parentheses, from complete sample.
GOF: p-value (in percent) of chi-square goodness-of-fit test.
AC(z): number of autocorrelations (in the first 50) out of the 95 percent confidence interval.
all = in-sample evaluation on complete sample (all data).
out = out-of-sample evaluation on last third of data (estimation on first 2/3).

depend on two parameters to be estimated, for one in the Weibull and none in the exponential). Both are of interest since they are non nested. We use the TAQ data for the period September-November 1996, and the durations have been adjusted for the intraday seasonality as explained in Chapter 2 (see subsection 5.3). Table 3.5 gives the results for the trade durations of the Exxon stock. Table 3.6 contains the same sort of results for the price durations (with a threshold of \$1/8 on the mid-quote) of the Coca-Cola stock, and Table 3.7 for the volume durations (with threshold of 25,000 shares) of the Boeing stock. The first block of each table gives the results for the ACD specifications, the second

Table 3.7. Estimation results for Boeing volume durations

	EACD		BACD		GGACD	
ω	0.032	(0.012)	0.031	(0.010)	0.032	(0.011)
α	0.13	(0.020)	0.13	(0.017)	0.12	(0.017)
β	0.83	(0.028)	0.85	(0.023)	0.85	(0.023)
γ	1		1.65	(0.052)	1.47	(0.11)
λ or ν	1		0.066	(0.042)	1.13	(0.14)
GOF all-out	0 - 0		94 - 10		82 - 8	
AC(z) all-out	2 - 2		1 - 3		1 - 3	
	ELACD$_1$		BLACD$_1$		GGLACD$_1$	
ω	0.024	(0.0060)	0.023	(0.0040)	0.023	(0.0040)
α	0.097	(0.020)	0.094	(0.013)	0.093	(0.013)
β	0.86	(0.034)	0.86	(0.023)	0.86	(0.023)
γ	1		1.65	(0.053)	1.36	(0.12)
λ or ν	1		0.086	(0.045)	1.28	(0.18)
GOF all-out	0 - 0		86 - 19		90 - 15	
AC(z) all-out	2 - 3		3 - 3		3 - 3	
	ELACD$_2$		BLACD$_2$		GGLACD$_2$	
ω	-0.14	(0.020)	-0.14	(0.017)	-0.14	(0.017)
α	0.14	(0.020)	0.14	(0.017)	0.14	(0.017)
β	0.95	(0.016)	0.95	(0.014)	0.95	(0.014)
γ	1		1.64	(0.051)	1.41	(0.12)
λ or ν	1		0.066	(0.042)	1.20	(0.16)
GOF all-out	0 - 0		97 - 12		96 - 4.1	
AC(z) all-out	1 - 2		1 - 2		2 - 2	

Sample size = 1,576. Data from TAQ database, September-November 1996.
E for exponential, B for Burr, GG for generalized gamma; λ for B, ν for GG, $\nu = 1$ for E.
ACD for ACD models. LACD$_1$ for Log-ACD of type 1. LACD$_2$ for Log-ACD of type 2.
ML estimates and asymptotic standard errors in parentheses, from complete sample.
GOF: p-value (in percent) of chi-square goodness-of-fit test.
AC(z): number of autocorrelations (in the first 50) out of the 95 percent confidence interval.
all = in-sample evaluation on complete sample (all data).
out = out-of-sample evaluation on last third of data (estimation on first 2/3).

block for the Log-ACD of type 1, and the last for the Log-ACD of type 2. In the second block of columns (those starting with E, like EACD) the likelihood function is built using the exponential distribution, and the standard errors are computed using the QML sandwich estimator (see subsection 3.3). In the third block (names starting with B) and in the last block (names starting with GG), the likelihood is built using the Burr distribution, and the generalized gamma distributions, respectively. In these cases, the standard errors are computed from the inverse of the Hessian matrix. Each set of results also contains the diagnostics based on the probability integral transforms, both 'in-sample' and 'out-

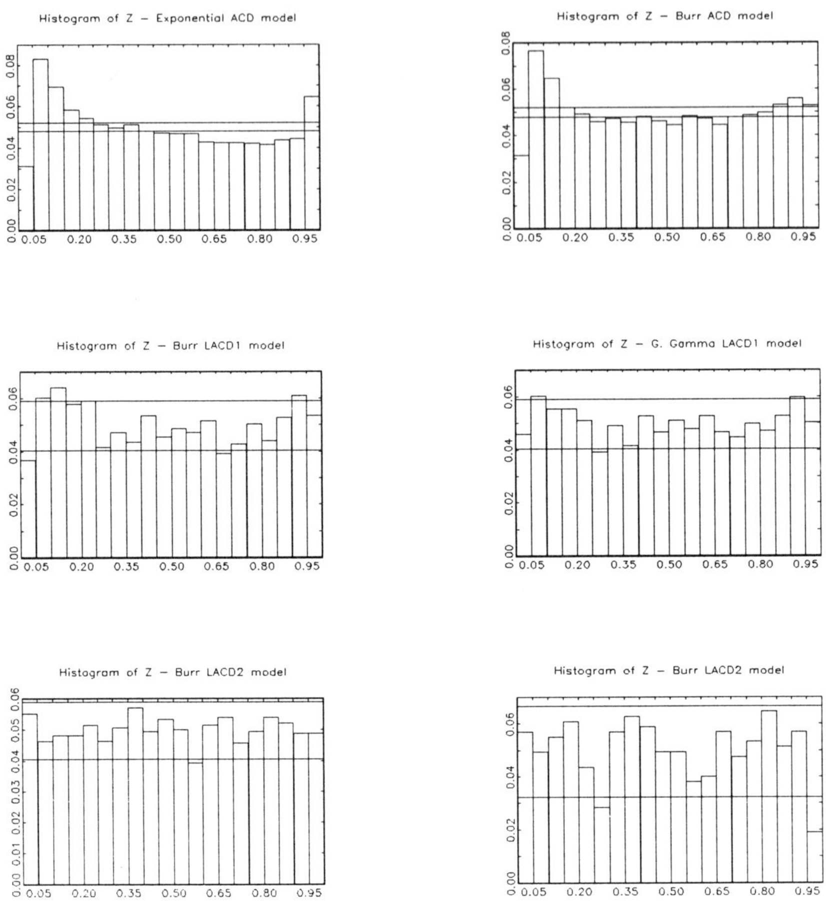

Top panels: Exxon trade durations (complete sample). Middle: Coke price durations (complete sample). Bottom panels: Boeing volume durations (left panel: complete sample; right panel: out-of-sample).

Figure 3.8. Histograms of Probability Integral Transforms

of-sample'. The 'in-sample' diagnostics (and the reported estimates of the parameters) are based on all the observations of the available sample (not the last third like in Table 3.4). The 'out-of-sample' results are based on estimates (not reported) for the first two-thirds of the observations, and probability integral transforms of the last part of the sample (exactly like in Table 3.4).

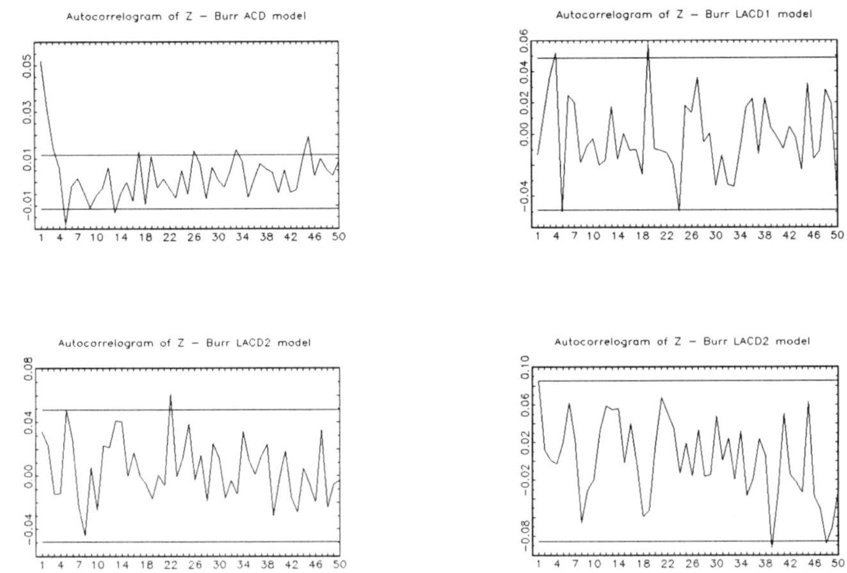

Top left panel: Exxon trade durations (complete sample). Top right panel: Coke price durations (complete sample). Bottom panels: Boeing volume durations (left panel: complete sample; right panel: out-of-sample).

Figure 3.9. ACF of Probability Integral Transforms

The following conclusions can be drawn from the reported results and from similar results for other stocks or periods of estimation.

1) The autoregressive coefficients of the ACD and Log-ACD equations vary between 0.75 and 1, according to the stock and the type of durations. This is in agreement with the stylized fact of duration clustering, that implies a slowly decreasing auotocorrelation function. The estimates are usually closer to 1 for trade durations than for price and volume durations, since the former are more persistent than the latter. Notice that the higher value of the β estimates for the Log-ACD$_2$ models does not indicate a difference in this respect with the other models, since β in the Log-ACD$_2$ is comparable to $\alpha + \beta$ in the other models, see equations (3.19) and (3.20).

2) For a given dataset and type of model, the estimates of the parameters ω, α, and β of the equation of the conditional duration do not change much with the choice of the distribution of ϵ_i. This corresponds to

asymptotic independence between the estimators of the parameters of the conditional duration equation and of the assumed distribution of the error term.

3) For a given dataset, the estimates of the parameters of the Burr distribution are almost the same across the three different types of models (ACD, Log-ACD$_1$, and Log-ACD$_2$), whereas the estimates of the parameters of the generalized gamma distribution are more variable. The estimates of the parameters of the distributions imply conditional overdispersion for trade and price durations, and underdispersion for volume durations, as can be checked using Tables 3.A.1 and 3.A.2 with the parameter estimates.

4) For trade durations, the assumption of a Burr or generalized gamma distribution is rejected according to the goodness-of-fit tests based on the probability integral transforms obtained from the density forecasts. For volume durations, the two sorts of distribution are not rejected, and for price durations there are some cases of rejection. A few histograms, which should correspond to uniform distributions if the specifications are correct, are shown in Figure 3.8, illustrating cases of rejection or acceptance of uniformity. Notice that the widths of the confidence intervals (all of level 90 %) vary according to the sample sizes: for example the intervals for trade durations are very thin because the sample size is large (of the order of 30,000). The histograms for the trade durations show clearly the lack of uniformity due to an inadequate distribution, even if the Burr distribution performs a little better than the exponential one (see the right part of the histograms). The histograms for the price durations (middle panels) show that there is hardly a difference between the Burr and the generalized gamma distributions in this case. The histograms for the volume durations illustrate a case where there is a better fit of a Burr distribution in the evaluation based on the complete sample than in the evaluation based on the forecast sample. Finally, the exponential distribution assumption is strongly rejected for all types of data and models. This can also be inferred by testing the restrictions $\gamma = \lambda = 1$ or $\gamma = \nu = 1$ from the Burr or generalized gamma estimation results, respectively.

5) In almost all cases, the probability integral transforms are not significantly autocorrelated, indicating that the dynamic specification of the models are good enough. Q-statistics (nor reported) of order 1 to 50 for the probability integral transforms are not significant at 5%, except for the trade durations (Exxon stock), when the evaluation

is done on the complete estimation sample. Figure 3.9 illustrate the first fifty autocorrelations and the associated 95 % confidence bands of four cases, including a deficient case (see the top left panel). Direct tests of autocorrelation could be done using the Q-statistics of the residuals, as explained in subsection 3.4, see (3.36).

APPENDIX 3.A: Probability distributions

For ease of reference in this appendix, we define the gamma function by the usual integral identity

$$\Gamma(\nu) = \int_0^\infty x^{\nu-1} \exp(-x)dx \quad \text{for } \nu > 0. \tag{3.A.1}$$

Integration by parts produces the gamma recursion

$$\Gamma(\nu) = (\nu - 1)\Gamma(\nu - 1) \quad \text{for } \nu > 1. \tag{3.A.2}$$

The digamma function $\psi(\nu)$ is defined by

$$\psi(\nu) = \frac{\partial \ln \Gamma(\nu)}{\partial \nu} \tag{3.A.3}$$

and the trigamma function, noted $\psi'(\nu)$, is the first derivative of the digamma function.

Gamma distribution

The gamma density function for the random variable $\epsilon > 0$, with parameters $\nu > 0$ and $c > 0$, is given by

$$f_G(\epsilon) = C_G^{-1}(\nu, c)\epsilon^{\nu-1} \exp(-\epsilon/c), \tag{3.A.4}$$

i.e. $\epsilon \sim G(\nu, c)$, where

$$C_G(\nu, c) = \Gamma(\nu)c^\nu. \tag{3.A.5}$$

Clearly, if $\epsilon \sim G(\nu, c)$, then $\epsilon/c \sim G(\nu, 1)$. Many useful properties of the gamma distribution follow from such a standardization, combined with the definition of the gamma function in equation (3.A.1). In particular, the uncentered moments of order p of ϵ are given by

$$\mu_p = \frac{C_G(\nu + p, c)}{C_G(\nu, c)} = c^p \frac{\Gamma(\nu + p)}{\Gamma(\nu)} \quad \text{for } \nu + p > 0 \tag{3.A.6}$$

(where p can be negative provided that $\nu + p > 0$). Its variance is equal to νc^2, so that the variation coefficient,[14] defined as $\mu_2\mu_1^{-2} - 1$, is

$$CV_G = \frac{1}{\nu}. \tag{3.A.7}$$

Overdispersion corresponds to $\nu < 1$, underdispersion to $\nu > 1$, and equidispersion to $\nu = 1$. The gamma survivor and hazard functions are not known analytically (except if $\nu = 1$) since they include the incomplete gamma function. However, it can be shown that the hazard is monotone decreasing (starting at ∞) if $\nu < 1$, flat if $\nu = 1$, and monotone increasing (starting at 0) and concave if $\nu > 1$. Notice the correspondence between the presence of overdispersion and the decreasing hazard (or underdispersion and increasing hazard).

The moment generating function is

$$\mathrm{E}(e^{p\epsilon}) = \left(\frac{c^{-1}}{c^{-1} - p}\right)^{\nu} \quad \text{for } p < c^{-1}. \tag{3.A.8}$$

Remark: the parameter c is a scale parameter that is set equal to 1 when the gamma distribution is used in (Log-)ACD models, where this parameter is replaced by Ψ_i. The same remark applies to the other distributions of this appendix where this parameter appears.

Weibull distribution

The Weibull density function for the random variable $\epsilon > 0$, with parameters $\gamma > 0$ and $c > 0$ is given by

$$f_W(\epsilon) = \frac{\gamma}{c}\left(\frac{\epsilon}{c}\right)^{\gamma-1} \exp\left[-\left(\frac{\epsilon}{c}\right)^{\gamma}\right], \tag{3.A.9}$$

i.e. $\epsilon \sim W(\gamma, c)$. Its uncentered moments of order p are given by

$$\mu_p = c^p\,\Gamma(1 + p\gamma^{-1}). \tag{3.A.10}$$

The variation coefficient is equal to

$$CV_W = \frac{\Gamma(1 + 2\gamma^{-1})}{[\Gamma(1 + \gamma^{-1})]^2} - 1. \tag{3.A.11}$$

Overdispersion corresponds to $\gamma < 1$ and underdispersion to $\gamma > 1$ (see in Table 3.A.1 the row for $\nu = 1$). The survivor function is

$$S_W(\epsilon) = \exp\left[-\left(\frac{\epsilon}{c}\right)^{\gamma}\right] \tag{3.A.12}$$

and the hazard function is

$$h_W(\epsilon) = \frac{\gamma}{c}\left(\frac{\epsilon}{c}\right)^{\gamma-1}. \tag{3.A.13}$$

The hazard is monotone decreasing (starting at ∞) if $\gamma < 1$, flat if $\gamma = 1$ (which corresponds to the exponential case), and monotone increasing (starting at 0) if $\gamma > 1$ (concave if $1 < \gamma < 2$, linear if $\gamma = 2$, convex if $\gamma > 2$). Remark the correspondence between the overdispersion and the decreasing hazard. These properties are similar to those of the gamma distribution. There is a difference, however, in that as $\epsilon \to \infty$, $h_G(\epsilon)$ tends to the exponential case (a constant hazard), which is not the case for $h_W(\epsilon)$ (one says that the gamma hazard is asymptotically exponential because the hazard of the exponential distribution is flat, see below).

Exponential distribution

If $\epsilon \sim G(1, c)$ or if $\epsilon \sim W(1, c)$, the density of ϵ is called the exponential density with parameter equal to c:

$$f_E(\epsilon) = (1/c)\ \exp(-\epsilon/c), \tag{3.A.14}$$

i.e. $\epsilon \sim Expo(c)$. Its uncentered moments of order p are given by

$$\mu_p = c^p\,\Gamma(1 + p), \tag{3.A.15}$$

so that

$$CV_E = 1 \tag{3.A.16}$$

(the distribution is equidispersed). Its survivor function is

$$S_E(\epsilon) = \exp(-\epsilon/c), \tag{3.A.17}$$

and its hazard function is

$$h_E(\epsilon) = 1/c, \tag{3.A.18}$$

which is flat.

Generalized gamma distribution

The generalized gamma density function for the random variable $\epsilon > 0$, with parameters $\nu > 0$, $\gamma > 0$ and $c > 0$, is given by

$$f_{GG}(\epsilon) = \frac{\gamma}{c^{\nu\gamma}\Gamma(\nu)}\epsilon^{\nu\gamma-1}\exp\left[-\left(\frac{\epsilon}{c}\right)^{\gamma}\right], \tag{3.A.19}$$

i.e. $\epsilon \sim GG(\nu, \gamma, c)$. If $\gamma = 1$, the $GG(\nu, \gamma, c)$ distribution becomes the $G(\nu, c)$ distribution. If $\nu = 1$, the $GG(\nu, \gamma, c)$ becomes the $W(\gamma, 1)$. The uncentered moments of order p of ϵ are given by

$$\mu_p = c^p\frac{\Gamma(\nu + p\gamma^{-1})}{\Gamma(\nu)}. \tag{3.A.20}$$

Table 3.A.1. Dispersion index of gen. gamma, gamma, and Weibull distributions

		γ								
		0.30	0.40	0.50	0.70	1.00	1.20	1.50	2.00	3.00
	0.50	*8.50*	*4.71*	*3.27*	*2.08*	*1.41*	$\underline{1.19}$	$\underline{0.97}$	0.76	0.53
	0.70	*6.85*	*3.88*	*2.72*	*1.76*	*1.20*	$\underline{1.00}$	0.81	0.63	0.44
	1.00	*5.41*	*3.14*	*2.24*	*1.46*	1.00	0.84	0.68	0.52	0.36
	1.20	*4.78*	*2.82*	*2.02*	*1.33*	0.91	0.76	0.62	0.47	0.33
	1.50	*4.10*	*2.47*	*1.79*	**1.19**	0.82	0.68	0.55	0.42	0.29
ν	2.00	*3.37*	*2.08*	*1.53*	**1.03**	0.71	0.59	0.48	0.36	0.25
	3.00	*2.55*	**1.64**	**1.22**	**0.83**	0.58	0.48	0.39	0.29	0.20
	4.00	**2.11**	**1.39**	**1.05**	**0.72**	0.50	0.42	0.34	0.25	0.17
	5.00	**1.82**	**1.22**	**0.93**	**0.64**	0.45	0.37	0.30	0.23	0.15
	6.00	**1.62**	**1.10**	**0.85**	**0.59**	0.41	0.34	0.27	0.21	0.14
	8.00	**1.35**	**0.94**	**0.73**	**0.51**	0.35	0.29	0.24	0.18	0.12

Entries are the square roots of the variation coefficient (i.e. the dispersion index). The row with $\nu = 1$ corresponds to Weibull distributions, the column with $\gamma = 1$ corresponds to gamma distributions. A boldface entry corresponds to an inverted U-shaped hazard ($\gamma\nu > 1$ and $\gamma < 1$). An underlined entry corresponds to a U-shaped hazard ($\gamma\nu < 1$ and $\gamma > 1$). An italicized entry corresponds to a decreasing hazard. Other entries correspond to an increasing hazard (except at $\gamma = \nu = 1$, when the hazard is flat).

The variation coefficient is

$$CV_{GG} = \frac{\Gamma(\nu + 2\gamma^{-1})\Gamma(\nu)}{[\Gamma(\nu + \gamma^{-1})]^2} - 1. \tag{3.A.21}$$

All types of dispersion are thus feasible, see Table 3.A.1. If γ or ν increase, the coefficient of variation decreases. Like in the case of the gamma distribution, the survivor function requires the incomplete gamma function, so that is not available analytically (and the hazard also). The hazard function can take many shapes. If $\gamma\nu > 1$ and $\gamma < 1$, the hazard is hump-shaped (i.e. inverted U-shaped), starting at 0 and tending to 0 as ϵ tends to infinity. If $\gamma\nu < 1$ and $\gamma > 1$, the hazard is U-shaped, starting at ∞, and tending to ∞ as ϵ tends to ∞. Otherwise, if $\gamma < 1$, the hazard is monotone decreasing (from ∞ to 0), whereas if $\gamma > 1$, it is monotone increasing from 0 to ∞ (similar to the hazard of the Weibull distribution, see below). More specific shapes are obtained in the particular cases: if $\gamma = 1$, the gamma hazards result, and if $\nu = 1$, the Weibull hazards result. Notice that there is no one-to-one correspondence between the shape of the hazard and the type of dispersion, like in the case of the gamma and Weibull distributions. With the generalized gamma, the hazard can be non monotone while there is overdispersion (or underdipersion).

Table 3.A.2. Dispersion index of Burr and Weibull distributions

		γ						
		0.50	0.70	1.00	1.20	1.50	2.00	3.00
	0.00	*2.24*	*1.46*	1.00	0.84	0.68	0.52	0.36
	0.05	*2.56*	*1.59*	*1.05*	**0.87**	**0.70**	**0.54**	**0.37**
	0.10	*3.05*	*1.75*	*1.12*	**0.92**	**0.73**	**0.56**	**0.38**
	0.30		*4.06*	*1.58*	**1.19**	**0.89**	**0.65**	**0.43**
λ	0.50				**2.07**	**1.22**	**0.79**	**0.49**
	0.70					**2.80**	**1.06**	**0.58**
	0.90						**1.95**	**0.71**
	1.00							**0.81**
	1.40							**2.11**

Entries are the square roots of the variation coefficient (i.e. the dispersion index). The row with $\lambda = 0$ corresponds to Weibull distributions. Missing entries correspond to a non existing variance, which occurs if $\gamma \leq 2\lambda$. A boldface entry corresponds to an inverted U-shaped hazard. An italicized entry corresponds to a decreasing hazard. Other entries correspond to an increasing hazard (except at $\gamma = 1$, $\lambda = 0$, when the hazard is flat).

The mean and variance of $\ln \epsilon$ are

$$\mathrm{E}(\ln \epsilon) = \log c + \frac{\psi(\nu)}{\gamma} \tag{3.A.22}$$

and

$$\mathrm{Var}(\ln \epsilon) = \frac{\psi'(\nu)}{\gamma^2}, \tag{3.A.23}$$

where $\psi(\nu)$ is defined by (3.A.3).

In the top panel of Figure 3.A.1, we show a standard exponential density and two generalized gamma densities. Their parameters ν and γ have been chosen as representative of the estimation results presented in Section 4, and the parameter c such that the mean is equal to 1. This is easily achieved by fixing the parameter c equal to $\Gamma(\nu)/\Gamma(\nu + \gamma^{-1})$, see formula (3.A.20).

Burr distribution

We define the Burr density function for the random variable $\epsilon > 0$, with parameters $\gamma > 0$, $\lambda > 0$, and $c > 0$ as[15]

$$f_B(\epsilon) = \frac{\gamma}{c}\left(\frac{\epsilon}{c}\right)^{\gamma-1}\left[1 + \lambda\left(\frac{\epsilon}{c}\right)^{\gamma}\right]^{-(1+\lambda^{-1})}, \tag{3.A.24}$$

i.e. $\epsilon \sim Burr(\gamma, \lambda, c)$. Its uncentered moments of order p are given by

$$\mu_p = c^p \frac{\Gamma(1 + p\gamma^{-1})\Gamma(\lambda^{-1} - p\gamma^{-1})}{\lambda^{1+p\gamma^{-1}}\Gamma(1 + \lambda^{-1})}, \text{ for } \gamma/\lambda > p, \tag{3.A.25}$$

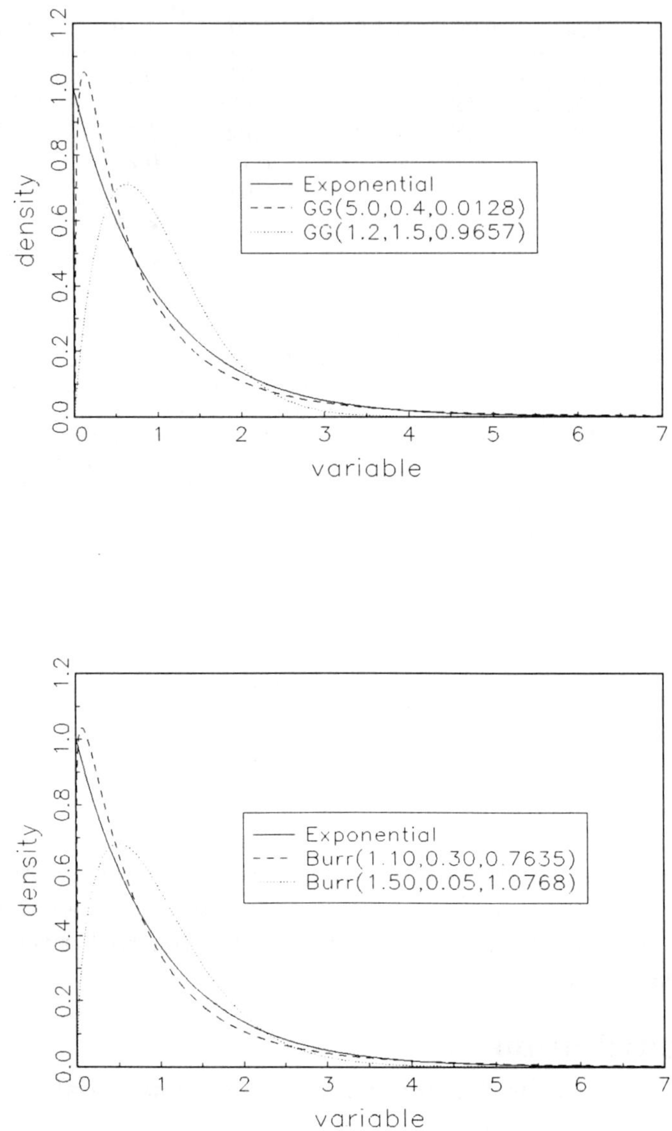

All distributions have been parametrized to have their expectation equal to 1.

Figure 3.A.1. **Generalized Gamma and Burr Densities**

so that if c is chosen as

$$c = \frac{\lambda^{1+\gamma^{-1}}\Gamma(1+\lambda^{-1})}{\Gamma(1+\gamma^{-1})\Gamma(\lambda^{-1}-\gamma^{-1})} \tag{3.A.26}$$

then $\mu_1 = 1$ (if $\gamma > \lambda$). The variation coefficient is equal to

$$CV_B = \lambda\Gamma(1+\lambda^{-1})\frac{\Gamma(1+2\gamma^{-1})\Gamma(\lambda^{-1}-2\gamma^{-1})}{[\Gamma(1+\gamma^{-1})\Gamma(\lambda^{-1}-\gamma^{-1})]^2}. \tag{3.A.27}$$

When $\gamma \leq 1$, there is overdispersion, which increases with λ. When $\gamma > 1$ and λ is small, there is underdispersion, while if λ is large enough, there is overdispersion. See Table 3.A.2 (where the effect of increasing λ is similar to the effect of decreasing ν in Table 3.A.1). The Burr survivor function is

$$S_B(\epsilon) = (1+\lambda c^{-\gamma}\epsilon^{\gamma})^{-1/\lambda}, \tag{3.A.28}$$

and its hazard function is

$$h_B(\epsilon) = \frac{\gamma}{c}\left(\frac{\epsilon}{c}\right)^{\gamma-1}(1+\lambda c^{-\gamma}\epsilon^{\gamma})^{-1}. \tag{3.A.29}$$

When $\gamma > 1$, the Burr hazard is not monotone: starting at 0, it increases, and finally decreases (it has an inverted U-shape). When $\gamma = 1$, the hazard is monotone decreasing starting at a finite value, but it becomes flatter and flatter when λ tends to 0. When $\gamma < 1$, the hazard is monotone decreasing starting at ∞. With the Burr distribution (like with the generalized gamma), the hazard can be non monotone while there is overdispersion, which is not possible with the gamma and Weibull distributions.

The $Burr(\gamma, 1, c)$ distribution is called the log-logistic distribution, that is, the logarithm of a log-logistic random variable follows a logistic distribution (like the logarithm of a lognormal variable is normal).

For λ tending to 0, the $Burr(\gamma, \lambda, c)$ density tends to the $W(\gamma, c)$ density.

The mean and variance of $\ln\epsilon$ are

$$\mathrm{E}(\ln\epsilon) = \log c + \frac{1}{\gamma}[\psi(1) - \psi(\lambda^{-1}) - \ln\lambda] \tag{3.A.30}$$

and

$$\mathrm{Var}(\ln\epsilon) = \frac{1}{\gamma^2}[\psi'(1) + \psi'(\lambda^{-1})], \tag{3.A.31}$$

where $\psi(.)$ is defined by (3.A.3).

In the bottom panel of Figure 3.A.1, we show a standard exponential density and two Burr densities. Their parameters γ and λ have been chosen as representative of the estimation results presented in Section 4, and the parameter c such that the mean is equal to 1, see formula (3.A.26). They are quite comparable to the corresponding generalized gamma densities on the top panel of the same figure.

Lognormal distribution

The lognormal density function for the random variable $\epsilon > 0$, with parameters μ and $\tau^2 > 0$, is given by

$$f_{LN}(\epsilon) = \frac{1}{\epsilon\sqrt{2\pi\tau^2}} \exp\left[-\frac{1}{2\tau^2}(\ln\epsilon - \mu)^2\right] = \frac{1}{\epsilon\tau}\varphi\left(\frac{\ln\epsilon - \mu}{\tau}\right) \quad (3.A.32)$$

i.e. $\epsilon \sim LN(\mu, \tau^2)$, where $\varphi(.)$ denotes the standard normal density. If $\epsilon \sim LN(\mu, \tau^2)$, then $\ln\epsilon \sim N(\mu, \tau^2)$ (where N denotes the normal distribution). Its uncentered moments of order p are given by

$$\mu_p = \exp\left(p\mu + \frac{1}{2}p^2\tau^2\right). \quad (3.A.33)$$

Its variance is

$$\mathrm{Var}(\epsilon) = e^{2\mu}e^{\tau^2}(e^{\tau^2} - 1), \quad (3.A.34)$$

so that the variation coefficient is

$$CV_{LN} = e^{\tau^2} - 1, \quad (3.A.35)$$

which can be smaller or larger than 1. The distribution can be over-, under- or equidispersed. The lognormal survivor function is

$$S_{LN}(\epsilon) = 1 - \Phi\left(\frac{\ln\epsilon - \mu}{\tau}\right), \quad (3.A.36)$$

where $\Phi(.)$ denotes the distribution function of a standard normal variable. The hazard function is the ratio of (3.A.32) and (3.A.36). It starts at 0, increases, and finally decreases (tending to 0). Like for the Burr distribution, there is no equivalence between the shape of the hazard and the presence or absence of overdispersion. However, the lognormal distribution cannot produce a decreasing hazard.

Pareto distribution

The Pareto density function for the random variable $\epsilon > k > 0$, with parameters $\rho > 0$ and $k > 0$, is given by

$$f_P(\epsilon) = \frac{\rho k^\rho}{\epsilon^{\rho+1}}, \quad (3.A.37)$$

i.e. $\epsilon \sim P(\rho, k)$. Its uncentered moments of order p are given by

$$\mu_p = \frac{\rho k^p}{\rho - p} \text{ if } \rho > p. \tag{3.A.38}$$

Its variation coefficient is equal to

$$CV_P = \frac{1}{\rho(\rho - 2)} \text{ if } \rho > 2. \tag{3.A.39}$$

It decreases from ∞ as ρ increases from 2, being equal to 1 if $\rho = 1 + \sqrt{2} \approx 2.41$. The survivor function is

$$S_P(\epsilon) = (k/\epsilon)^{\rho}. \tag{3.A.40}$$

The hazard function,

$$h_P(\epsilon) = \rho/\epsilon, \tag{3.A.41}$$

is monotone decreasing from ρ/k to 0. Notice that this is compatible with overdispersion, underdispersion, or equidispersion.

In the context of estimation, the parameter k should be set at a small value compatible with the data.

Notes

1 Technically the probability being $o(dt)$ means that the probability divided by dt tends to 0 when dt tends to 0.

2 Specifically, $S(x) = \exp(-\int_0^x h(u)du)$.

3 Overdispersion means that the standard deviation is greater than the mean, and underdispersion the contrary.

4 See Cox and Oakes (1984, p 72) for a graphical illustration when $h_0(x)$ is a step function.

5 This model is the ACD(1,1). More lags of x_i and Ψ_i can be added. As we use only one lag, we use the short notation ACD.

6 $\mathrm{E}(u_i x_{i-p}) = 0, \ \forall p \geq 1$.

7 In the figures, we report the densities for a limited range of durations, in order to enhance the visibility. It should be noticed that the simulated data contain a few extreme values (as big as 30) in the case of the ACD2 and ACD3 processes.

8 The conditional duration is the conditional expectation of the duration.

9 Sufficient conditions for the asymptotic normality of the QMLE in the ACD(1,1) model are presented in Engle and Russell (1998). They are taken from results obtained for the GARCH(1,1) model by Lee and Hansen (1994) and by Lumsdaine (1996).

10 This test is discussed in Kalbfleish and Prentice (1980).

11 The loss function specifies the loss incurred by the user who chooses an action from a choice set, given the available data. In the context of density forecasting, a user should choose the action that minimizes his expected loss, where the expectation is computed with respect to the correct density of the data.

12 For notational convenience, we shall sometimes use an abbreviated notation and suppress the information set $\mathcal{H}_i$ and, in one-period contexts, the subscript i. However, the dependence on $\mathcal{H}_i$ and the dependence of the forecasts on the index i should always be kept in mind.

13 Obviously, this should be interpreted as a mere indication in favour of the evaluation method. A more solid 'proof' of its validity would require to repeat each experiment a large number of times and to check in what proportion the evaluation fails. That proportion should not exceed the nominal level chosen, for example for the uniformity test.

14 The variation coefficient is the square of the dispersion index.

15 See Lancaster (1990, p 68) for a derivation of the Burr distribution as a gamma mixture of Weibull distributions.

Chapter 4

EMPIRICAL RESULTS AND EXTENSIONS

1. INTRODUCTION

In this chapter we consider two extensions of the models presented in Chapter 3. Firstly, we use the intraday duration models to test some market microstructure effects. The models presented in Chapter 3 introduce a new way of modelling the times between market events and are directly related to quantitative tools developed in labour econometrics. While the models can be used to characterize the point processes defined by trade, quote, price or volume durations, they can also be used to test market microstructure effects such as presented in Chapter 1. This has been one of the main motivations for the use of such intraday duration models, and most recent papers focusing on the econometric modelling of the durations usually include a market microstructure section (Engle and Russell, 1997, 1998; Engle and Lunde, 1998; Bauwens and Giot, 1998, 2000; Grammig and Wellner, 1999). In Section 2 of this chapter, we review some possible applications of the Log-ACD model to the testing of market microstructure issues which deal with the (bid-ask quotes) updating behavior of a market maker with respect to the information flow.

In Section 3, we introduce the asymmetric Log-ACD model, which extends the Log-ACD models of Chapter 3 by letting the duration process depend on the state of the price process. If the price has increased, the parameters of the model can differ from what they are if the price has decreased. Simultaneously, we model the direction of the price change from the beginning to the end of a duration. As in Chapter 3, the models are applied to intraday data for stocks traded on the NYSE.

Most of the material presented in this chapter is based on earlier work first presented in Bauwens and Giot (2000), for the application to market microstructure issues, and Bauwens and Giot (1998), for the asymmetric Log-ACD model. However, we extend the results presented in these two papers by applying the models to new data sets.

2. MARKET MICROSTRUCTURE EFFECTS

2.1 ADDING VARIABLES IN THE ACD MODEL

As introduced in Engle and Russell (1998) and Bauwens and Giot (2000), the ACD and Log-ACD models provide a convenient framework for testing market microstructure issues related to the updating behavior of a market maker. Indeed, the equation for the conditional expectation of the duration can be modified to include additional terms related to the state of current or past market characteristics. More specifically, equation (3.13) can be modified into

$$\Psi_i = \omega + \alpha x_{i-1} + \beta \Psi_{i-1} + \eta Z_{i-1} \tag{4.1}$$

where Z_{i-1} is the added explicative variable. The reason for including the lagged variable, instead of Z_i itself, is that the variables we want to include depend on the duration with respect to which they are defined, as will be obvious from their definition given in subsection 2.2.1 below. Hence the variable cannot be considered exogenous with respect to the duration model. When η is positive, this indicates a positive relation between the expected duration and the included market microstructure variable: an increase (decrease) in Z_{i-1} leads to a larger (lower) expected duration. This extension of the ACD model is similar to the extension of ARMA models to ARMAX models in the time series literature. Moreover, because the quasi-maximum likelihood estimator (see Section 3 of Chapter 3) is also valid in this framework, the η parameters in (4.1) can be estimated using the exponential ACD model. This simple estimation procedure is particularly attractive in the context of intraday data, since the tick-by-tick databases usually contain a very large number of observations and QML estimation is justified by its asymptotic properties.[1]

Although the ACD model with additional explicative variables has been applied to high frequency tick-by-tick data (for example IBM stock trades on the NYSE by Engle and Russell, 1998), the positivity constraints on the coefficients of the model may be quite restrictive: the right-hand side of (4.1) must remain strictly positive whatever the included variables. The additional variables could be added in a nonlinear way, such that the expected duration should be hopefully positive.

However, this raises the issue of which functional form to use. The logarithmic ACD model allows to enter the variables linearly even if they have negative coefficients.

In this framework, the Log-ACD model is much preferable, as no positivity constraints need to be imposed on the parameters of the model. For example, the Log-ACD of type 2 with the additional variable Z_{i-1} is defined by

$$x_i = \exp(\psi_i)\,\epsilon_i, \tag{4.2}$$

and

$$\psi_i = \omega + \alpha(x_{i-1}/\exp\psi_{i-1}) + \beta\psi_{i-1} + \eta Z_{i-1} \tag{4.3}$$

where η can be positive or negative.

2.2 EMPIRICAL APPLICATION

In this section (based on Bauwens and Giot, 2000), we apply the Log-ACD model to durations defined by bid-ask quotes updates by the specialist at the NYSE. We use price durations defined on the bid-ask quotes process as these allow a more convenient and meaningful definition of market characteristics (see Chapter 2, subsection 4.1). Before estimating the econometric models, we deseasonalize the data as explained in Chapter 2 (see subsection 5.2). Thus, all durations should be viewed as time-of-day adjusted durations.

2.2.1 MARKET MICROSTRUCTURE VARIABLES

Based on the theoretical models describing the bid-ask quotes updating behavior of a single market maker, we consider the following proposals for the choice of Z_{i-1}:

- The spread: Easley and O'Hara (1992) extend the information model introduced by Glosten and Milgrom (1985) by focusing on the role of time in price adjustment. Easley and O'Hara argue that the duration between two trades conveys information. In their model, a no-trade outcome (a long duration) means that no new information has been released. Thus the probability of dealing with an informed trader is small, relative to the case where the duration would be small. Consequently, with a low probability of dealing with an informed trader, the market maker decreases his bid-ask spread. This should lead to a negative coefficient for the lagged spread when introduced in the specification of the expected conditional duration. Because the spread features a pronounced intraday seasonality due to market and exchange characteristics (see Chapter 1), we deseasonalize it using the same techniques as those used for the durations as the unanticipated or 'surprise' component of the spread (with respect to the time-of-day component) is probably more meaningful for the econometric analysis. Furthermore, this is consistent with the fact that we work with time-of-day adjusted durations, i.e. durations of which the 'expected' component has also been removed.

- The trading intensity: Bauwens and Giot (2000) introduce the lagged trading intensity as an explicative variable for the expected conditional duration. Over each bid-ask quote duration, the trading intensity is defined as the number of trades divided by the bid-ask quote duration. Thus, the trading intensity is a hybrid variable, which is based on information given by the trade and quote processes. The model of Easley and O'Hara (1992) implies that an increase in the trading intensity (due for example to a release of news) should lead to more frequent revisions of the quotes and thus to a shortening of the durations between the posting of bid-ask quotes by the market maker. This should also lead to a negative coefficient for the trading intensity when introduced in the specification of the expected conditional duration. In the empirical application, we use the deseasonalized trading intensity for the same reasons as above for the spread.

- The volume: Introducing a link between the price process and the volume is one of the main feature of technical analysis, an empirical tool much favored by market practitioners. This issue is also closely studied by Easley and O'Hara (1992), and by Blume, Easley, and O'Hara (1994). In the Easley and O'Hara (1992) paper, the argument presented above regarding the influence of the spread and trading intensity is extended to the volume. More precisely, it is the unexpected volume that matters most.[2] To capture the influence of volume on the bid-ask quotes process, we use the average volume per trade. As it is the unexpected component of the variable that matters, the variable included in the model is the time-of-day adjusted average volume per trade (i.e. deseasonalized average volume per trade). If unexpected volume is related to informed trading, this should shorten the next expected duration: a negative coefficient is expected for this variable when included in the specification of the model.

2.2.2 QML ESTIMATION RESULTS

QML estimation results for the Log-ACD model

$$\psi_i = \omega + \alpha(x_{i-1}/\exp\psi_{i-1}) + \beta\psi_{i-1} + \eta_1 ti_{i-1} + \eta_2 avol_{i-1} + \eta_3 sp_{i-1} \quad (4.4)$$

with the market microstructure variables *ti* (trading intensity), *avol* (average volume per trade) and *sp* (spread) are given in Tables 4.1 and 4.2. Table 4.1 gives the results when only one variable is included in the model—i.e. equation (4.3) is estimated—while Table 4.2 presents the outcomes of the estimation procedures when all variables are included—i.e. equation (4.4) is estimated.

The model is estimated on the January-May 1997 period for several active stocks and with two different thresholds c_p. The estimation is performed with GAUSS using the BHHH algorithm and the variance-covariance matrices are estimated according to the usual sandwich estimator (see subsection 3.3 of Chapter 3).

In most cases, the coefficients of the market microstructure variables have the expected negative sign, although the evidence is weak in a few instances (for example for some data configurations when all three variables are included at the same time). When the model is estimated with one variable included at a time, then the η coefficients are all negative, and usually strongly significant. The inclusion of one or several additional market microstructure variables in the model does not appear to have a strong influence on the dynamics of the model as β remains strongly significant and rather close to one in all cases.

Bauwens and Giot (2000) report the same kind of results for another time period (September to November 1996). They also estimate the model on sub-samples of the original dataset and find that the estimated coefficients are quite stable. The evidence presented here (although featuring sometimes mixed results when all variables are included at the same time) is supportive of the role played by the market microstructure variables as explained in the previous subsection. Related results are also available in Engle and Russell (1998) and Engle (2000).

3. A JOINT MODEL OF DURATIONS AND PRICE CHANGE INDICATORS

The econometric duration models presented in Chapter 3 and in the previous section share a common feature: conditionally on the past durations (for the models of Chapter 3) and also on some explicative variables (for those of Section 2), they are univariate models of durations between market events. A possible extension is to model jointly the durations and some market characteristics (i.e. the marks attached to the point process that lies behind the durations), such as features of the price process, or the traded volume. This issue was first addressed by Engle in 1996[3], who proposed an ACD-GARCH model, which consists of a marginal ACD model for the duration, and a GARCH model for the volatility of the returns, conditionally on the duration. The ACD-GARCH model is

Table 4.1. Separate influence of market microstructure variables

	EXXON	IBM	EXXON	IBM
	$c_p = \$\frac{1}{4}$		$c_p = \$\frac{1}{8}$	
		Trading intensity		
β	0.991 (0.004)	0.938 (0.013)	0.994 (0.002)	0.956 (0.009)
η_1	-0.005 (0.007)	-0.036 (0.010)	-0.006 (0.002)	-0.022 (0.005)
		Average volume per trade		
β	0.983 (0.004)	0.940 (0.013)	0.994 (0.002)	0.962 (0.007)
η_2	-0.029 (0.006)	-0.031 (0.007)	-0.007 (0.002)	-0.015 (0.003)
		Spread		
β	0.953 (0.010)	0.952 (0.012)	0.983 (0.004)	0.968 (0.006)
η_3	-0.081 (0.018)	-0.007 (0.024)	-0.021 (0.005)	-0.003 (0.007)

QML estimation results for the Log-ACD model as defined by (4.3). η_1 is the coefficient of the lagged trading intensity, η_2 is the coefficient of the lagged average volume per trade and η_3 is the coefficient of the lagged spread. All microstructure variables are computed over price durations with $c_p = \$\frac{1}{4}$ or $c_p = \$\frac{1}{8}$. The estimation period is January-May 1997.

Table 4.2. Joint influence of market microstructure variables

	BOEING	DISNEY	EXXON	IBM
		$c_p = \$\frac{1}{4}$		
β	0.885 (0.020)	0.921 (0.037)	0.947 (0.011)	0.927 (0.016)
η_1	-0.022 (0.018)	-0.004 (0.021)	-0.023 (0.011)	-0.034 (0.010)
η_2	0.015 (0.013)	0.018 (0.018)	-0.021 (0.007)	-0.030 (0.007)
η_3	-0.234 (0.041)	-0.044 (0.066)	-0.072 (0.018)	0.016 (0.025)
		$c_p = \$\frac{1}{8}$		
β	0.918 (0.013)	0.932 (0.024)	0.983 (0.004)	0.949 (0.011)
η_1	-0.033 (0.007)	-0.023 (0.009)	-0.006 (0.003)	-0.022 (0.006)
η_2	0.006 (0.004)	0.005 (0.005)	-0.003 (0.002)	-0.016 (0.003)
η_3	-0.129 (0.021)	-0.006 (0.027)	-0.019 (0.005)	0.016 (0.009)

QML estimation results for the Log-ACD model as defined by (4.4). η_1 is the coefficient of the lagged trading intensity, η_2 is the coefficient of the lagged average volume per trade and η_3 is the coefficient of the lagged spread. All microstructure variables are computed over price durations with $c_p = \$\frac{1}{4}$ or $c_p = \$\frac{1}{8}$. The estimation period is January-May 1997.

also studied by Ghysels and Jasiak (1998), and Grammig and Wellner (1999).

As mentioned in the introduction of this book, other recent papers present joint models for the price and duration processes. Darolles,

Gouriéroux and Lefol (2000) model the transaction price dynamics by taking into account both the irregular spacing of the data and the discreteness of the price. Russell and Engle (1998), with the autoregressive conditional multinomial model, combine an ACD model on the durations and a generalized linear model on conditional transition probabilities of the price process. Hafner (1999) specifies an ACD model for the duration, and a non-parametric model for the return conditionally on current duration, lagged returns and lagged volume.

In this section, we present a joint model of the duration process and of the price process, more specifically of the direction, upward or downward, of the price change that occurs over a price duration. The model consists of a marginal Log-ACD model for the price duration and a conditional model for the direction of the current price change. The two components of the model are conditional on the direction of the previous price change, and (as usual) on the past of the duration process. The joint model is a two-state transition model (in a competing risk framework) combined with a Log-ACD model, the two states being the upward and downward price movements. The model can also be interpreted as an asymmetric Log-ACD model, in the sense that the duration dynamics depends on the direction of the previous price change.

3.1 THE MODEL

We begin by presenting a simple two-state competing risk model that highlights the features we want to include in the model, in order to get the asymmetric ACD model which is then presented in the second part of this section.

3.1.1 A TWO-STATE TRANSITION MODEL

A multi-state transition model has been applied to data from the Paris Bourse by Bisière and Kamionka (2000), who model the possible transitions between the different types of orders that can be submitted by traders: each type of order (for example a large buy, a small buy, a small sell, ...) corresponds to a given state and the succession of these states is represented as a transition model based on competing risks.

We consider the marked point process consisting of the pairs (x_i, y_i), where x_i is the duration between two bid-ask quotes posted by a market maker and y_i is a variable indicating the direction of change of the mid-price defined as the average of the bid and ask prices, i.e

- $y_i = 1$ if the mid-price increased over duration x_i;

- $y_i = -1$ if the mid-price decreased over duration x_i.

At the end of duration x_i, there are only two possible end states:[4] $y_i = 1$ or $y_i = -1$. For simplicity, let us assume that the hazard function is constant, which is equivalent to an exponential distribution for x_i. The idea of the transition model is to let the hazard vary with the end state. In this case there are two hazard functions since y_i is binary. Moreover, in each case the hazard can be a function of the previous state y_{i-1} (in the next subsection, we let the hazard depend on the previous durations). If we define λ_i^+ (respectively λ_i^-) as the hazard of duration x_i when the end state is $y_i = 1$ (respectively -1), then

$$\begin{aligned} \lambda_i^+ &= \beta_1 I_{i-1}^+ + \beta_2 I_{i-1}^- \\ \text{and} & \\ \lambda_i^- &= \beta_3 I_{i-1}^+ + \beta_4 I_{i-1}^-, \end{aligned} \tag{4.5}$$

where I_{i-1}^+ is an indicator variable equal to 1 if $y_{i-1} = 1$ and 0 otherwise, and I_{i-1}^- is the complementary indicator variable (equal to 1 if $y_{i-1} = -1$ and 0 otherwise).

At the end of duration x_i, either state $y_i = 1$ or state $y_i = -1$ is observed. In the framework of a competing risk model, the duration corresponding to the state that is not realized is truncated, since the observed duration is the minimum of two possible durations: the one which would realize if $y_i = 1$, and the one which would realize if $y_i = -1$. The realized state contributes to the likelihood function via its density function, while the truncated state contributes to the likelihood function via its survivor function. Assuming independence (conditionally on the past state) between the durations ending at states $y_i = 1$ and $y_i = -1$, the joint 'density' of duration x_i and state y_i, given the previous state, is equal to

$$f(x_i, y_i | y_{i-1}) = (\lambda_i^+)^{I_i^+} e^{-\lambda_i^+ x_i} (\lambda_i^-)^{I_i^-} e^{-\lambda_i^- x_i}. \tag{4.6}$$

For example, if state $y_i = 1$ is observed ($I_i^+ = 1$ and $I_i^- = 0$), x_i contributes to the likelihood function via its density function $\lambda_i^+ e^{-\lambda_i^+ x_i}$ and via the survivor function $e^{-\lambda_i^- x_i}$. A possible refinement of the model would consist of introducing interdependence between the two 'competing' durations, as suggested in the recent literature in labor econometrics.[5]

Based on the density function given in equation (4.6), the transition probabilities for given past and end states can be obtained by integrating this expression with respect to the duration x_i. The results are derived in the appendix of this chapter and summarized in Table 4.3. In the appendix, it is also proved that the transition probabilities of moving from state y_{i-1} to state y_i are independent of x_i, which is a particular

Table 4.3. Transition probabilities for two-state transition model

	$y_i = +1$	$y_i = -1$
$y_{i-1} = +1$	$\pi_{1,1} = \frac{\beta_1}{\beta_1+\beta_3}$	$\pi_{1,-1} = \frac{\beta_3}{\beta_1+\beta_3}$
$y_{i-1} = -1$	$\pi_{-1,1} = \frac{\beta_2}{\beta_2+\beta_4}$	$\pi_{-1,-1} = \frac{\beta_4}{\beta_2+\beta_4}$

π_{y_{i-1},y_i} is the transition probability of moving from state y_{i-1} to state y_i.

feature due to the fact that the hazard functions (4.5) do not depend on x_i.

Although this model is too simple to capture the dynamics of the duration and price processes inherent in intraday quote data, it puts forward a simple way of combining a duration model and a transition model for the direction of the price process.

3.1.2 THE ASYMMETRIC LOG-ACD MODEL

Instead of assuming a constant static hazard ('static' with respect to previous durations) for the two-state transition process, we can use a non-constant hazard of the Weibull-Log-ACD type, i.e. we let the hazard depend not only on the previous state, but also on the previous durations. Combining a two-state competing risk model with a Log-ACD model yields an asymmetric Log-ACD model, which is defined as follows.

- If the end state of duration x_i is $y_i = 1$ and, assuming a Weibull distribution, the hazard for x_i, conditional on the information set $\mathcal{F}_{i-1}$ (that includes the past states and durations), is given by

$$h(x_i|y_i = 1, \mathcal{F}_{i-1}) = \frac{\gamma^+}{\Psi_i^+}\left(\frac{x_i}{\Psi_i^+}\right)^{\gamma^+-1}, \tag{4.7}$$

  with $\Psi_i^+ = e^{\psi_i^+}$, and the autoregressive process on ψ_i^+ is defined as

$$\psi_i^+ = (\omega_1 + \alpha_1\epsilon_{i-1}^+)I_{i-1}^+ + (\omega_2 + \alpha_2\epsilon_{i-1}^+)I_{i-1}^- + \beta^+\psi_{i-1}^+, \tag{4.8}$$

  with $x_i = e^{\psi_i^+}\epsilon_i^+$. When $\gamma^+ = 1$, the hazard simplifies to $h(x_i|y_i = 1, \mathcal{F}_{i-1}) = 1/\Psi_i^+$, and thus Ψ_i^+ is similar to the inverse of λ_i^+ of the previous subsection (the difference being that Ψ_i^+ depends on the previous duration and its own lag).

- If the end state of duration x_i is $y_i = -1$, the hazard for x_i is given by

$$h(x_i|y_i = -1, \mathcal{F}_{i-1}) = \frac{\gamma^-}{\Psi_i^-}\left(\frac{x_i}{\Psi_i^-}\right)^{\gamma^--1} \tag{4.9}$$

with $\Psi_i^- = e^{\psi_i^-}$, and the autoregressive process on ψ_i^- is defined as

$$\psi_i^- = (\omega_3 + \alpha_3 \epsilon_{i-1}^-) I_{i-1}^+ + (\omega_4 + \alpha_4 \epsilon_{i-1}^-) I_{i-1}^- + \beta^- \psi_{i-1}^-, \tag{4.10}$$

with $x_i = e^{\psi_i^-} \epsilon_i^-$.

This model exhibits the main features of the Log-ACD model (i.e. a dynamic structure on the conditional expectation of the duration) while including conditioning information on the underlying bid-ask mid-price change. The autoregressive structure of the conditional expectation of the duration process can differ according to the direction (upward or downward) of the mid-price. In this framework, the density function of x_i and y_i, given the past information (that now includes past states and durations) is given by

$$\begin{aligned} f(x_i, y_i|\mathcal{F}_{i-1}) &= \left[\frac{\gamma^+}{\Psi_i^+}\left(\frac{x_i}{\Psi_i^+}\right)^{\gamma^+-1}\right]^{I_i^+} e^{-\left(\frac{x_i}{\Psi_i^+}\right)^{\gamma^+}} \\ &\quad \times \left[\frac{\gamma^-}{\Psi_i^-}\left(\frac{x_i}{\Psi_i^-}\right)^{\gamma^--1}\right]^{I_i^-} e^{-\left(\frac{x_i}{\Psi_i^-}\right)^{\gamma^-}} . \end{aligned} \tag{4.11}$$

We can estimate the parameters by maximizing the likelihood which is the product of the densities (4.11) over all observations, or, equivalently, we can estimate the parameters relative to the price increase and decrease separately (by splitting the log-likelihood function into two parts which depend on different parameters).

In the model, we could assume an identical (Weibull) distribution for ϵ^+ and ϵ^-, i.e. that $\gamma^+ = \gamma^-$ (a testable hypothesis). In the appendix of this chapter, it is shown that this hypothesis implies that the transition probabilities, conditionally on the past durations, do not depend on the current duration x_i, but that otherwise this conditional independence does not hold.[6] Because Ψ_i^+ and Ψ_i^- depend on the past through the autoregressive process of the conditional durations, the transition probabilities change through time: at the start of each duration x_i, the transition probabilities can be updated on the basis of the information set available at the start of this duration. This is an important feature of the asymmetric ACD model, as it provides evolving forecasts regarding the next price movement.

3.2 EMPIRICAL APPLICATION

Using data over a three month period in 1996 for Disney and IBM, and a five month period in 1997 for Boeing and Exxon, we estimated the asymmetric Log-ACD model defined in the previous section. We deal with price durations based on the quote process (see subsection 4.1 of Chapter 2), which gives two possible end states y_i, and we consider several possible thresholds c_p ranging from \$0.125 to \$0.5. As usual, the price durations are deseasonalized as explained in subsection 5.3 of Chapter 2. The model is estimated by maximizing the likelihood as given by expression (4.11) using the BHHH algorithm of GAUSS. Using the data for the four stocks and three different thresholds c_p, this gives a total of 11 estimation outcomes for the coefficients of the model.[7] As the numerical results are very similar across stocks and thresholds c_p, we give only four sets of results in Table 4.4. The upper block of Tables 4.4 is for the part of the model when the end state is a price increase - see equations (4.8) - and the lower block is for the part when the end state is a price decrease - see (4.10). The main features of the 11 sets of results are:

1) Strong autoregressive effects (β coefficients) in all cases, indicating a strong persistence in the dynamics of the duration process. This result is similar to those reported in Section 4 of Chapter 3 for the symmetric Log-ACD model.

2) The estimates of the γ parameters are close to 1 for the Disney, IBM, and Boeing stocks, and lower than 1 (around 0.86) for the Exxon stock.[8] Exponential distributions for the innovations are thus acceptable for the Disney and IBM stocks and (almost) acceptable for the Boeing stock. The results given in Table 4.4 indicate a high degree of similarity in the estimated values of γ^+ and γ^-. The hypothesis that $\gamma^+ = \gamma^-$ is not rejected at conventional levels of significance for the Disney, IBM and Exxon stocks, but is rejected for the Boeing stock.[9]

3) When the end state is a price increase ($y_i = 1$), α_1 is significantly smaller than α_2 at the five percent level for all stocks except Disney:[10] the expected conditional duration of witnessing a transition from state +1 to state +1 is smaller than the expected duration of witnessing a transition from state -1 to state +1. When the end state is a price decrease ($y_i = -1$), α_3 is larger than α_4, although the difference is significant at the five percent level only for the Disney and Exxon stocks:[11] the expected duration of witnessing a transition from state -1 to state -1 is smaller than the expected duration of witnessing a transition from state +1 to state -1.

Because the model exhibits a dynamic structure, the information given by the estimated coefficients is not straightforward to capture. In the next subsection we thus consider an empirical application of the

Table 4.4. ML Results for asymmetric Log-ACD model

	DISNEY	IBM	BOEING	EXXON
		End state: price increase		
ω_1	-0.076 (0.019)	-0.089 (0.012)	-0.045 (0.034)	-0.023 (0.005)
ω_2	-0.008 (0.023)	-0.055 (0.011)	-0.152 (0.036)	-0.032 (0.007)
α_1	0.113 (0.031)	0.107 (0.019)	0.187 (0.060)	0.049 (0.008)
α_2	0.125 (0.035)	0.204 (0.026)	0.532 (0.069)	0.075 (0.013)
β^+	0.969 (0.012)	0.985 (0.004)	0.878 (0.031)	0.995 (0.002)
γ^+	0.956 (0.021)	1.001 (0.013)	0.976 (0.020)	0.865 (0.008)
		End state: price decrease		
ω_3	-0.112 (0.019)	-0.072 (0.011)	-0.071 (0.023)	-0.035 (0.006)
ω_4	0.013 (0.019)	-0.077 (0.012)	-0.090 (0.024)	-0.015 (0.005)
α_3	0.187 (0.037)	0.189 (0.025)	0.284 (0.053)	0.070 (0.010)
α_4	0.079 (0.028)	0.143 (0.022)	0.199 (0.037)	0.042 (0.007)
β^-	0.987 (0.006)	0.989 (0.003)	0.930 (0.019)	0.996 (0.001)
γ^-	1.012 (0.023)	1.001 (0.013)	1.088 (0.021)	0.864 (0.008)

For a definition of the model, see equation (4.8) for the price increase and equation (4.10) for the price decrease. BHHH asymptotic standard errors are given in parentheses. For the Boeing (price durations with $c_p = \$\frac{1}{4}$) and Exxon stocks, the data refers to the Jan-May 1997 period while the time period is Sep-Nov 1996 for the Disney and IBM data (price durations with $c_p = \$\frac{1}{8}$).

model based on these estimated results, which helps us shed some light on the way the model works.

3.3 FORECASTING AND TRADING RULES

As detailed in subsection 3.1.2, an interesting property of the asymmetric Log-ACD model is to provide two hazards (one for the exit at a price increase, the other for the exit at a price decrease) that change over time as they depend on the previous state and durations. This feature implies a time-varying transition probability matrix for the mid-price. In this section, we use this feature to assess the forecasting performance of the model on the available intraday data. We also combine the 'predictions' of the model regarding the next price movement with a possible trading strategy in order to present a possible empirical use of the model.

3.3.1 FORECASTING INTRADAY PRICE CHANGES

The sequence of time-varying transition probability matrices is based on the estimates of the asymmetric Log-ACD model imposing that $\gamma^+ = \gamma^- = 1$. We impose it because it allows to compute analytically the transition probabilities (unconditional with respect to the current duration x_i). Using the constrained estimates, at the start of each price duration,

Table 4.5. Forecasting and trading results

Threshold	% Correct Decisions Model	Trend follower	Gain/Loss on Portfolio Managed	Unmanaged
DISNEY:				
\$1/8	53.54	48.12	2,039,625	6,131,344
\$1/4	57.77	55.25	1,534,375	2,080,809
IBM:				
\$1/8	53.55	56.17	−286,250	22,327,121
\$1/4	55.04	55.59	158,500	7,584,072
\$1/2	57.78	58.89	289,750	2,272,090
BOEING:				
\$1/8	53.47	57.91	−1,645,375	−350,173
\$1/4	52.30	55.05	−659,625	−77,328
\$1/2	56.27	54.60	−129,125	−7,785
EXXON:				
\$1/8	51.67	47.37	−1,940,875	12,932,551
\$1/4	50.49	44.99	−616,125	4,200,269
\$1/2	52.35	53.20	292,375	1,068,069

A correct decision is a correctly forecasted direction of price change. 'Model' is the asymmetric Log-ACD model. Resulting gain/loss after three month period is in \$. 'Managed' means that the portfolio is managed using the model, and 'unmanaged' means it follows the buy-and-hold strategy. The model is estimated on the September-November 1996 period for the Disney and IBM stocks, and on the January-May 1997 period for the Boeing and Exxon stocks.

we compute the (conditional) probability of a price increase. If this probability is greater (lower) than 1/2, we predict a price increase (decrease). At the end of each duration, the end state is observed and the realized outcome is compared to the predicted outcome. By repeating this procedure for all available durations, we can compute the percentage of correct decisions implied by the model. For the three stocks and for several possible price thresholds,[12] the results are given in column 2 of Table 4.5. For the IBM stock and for a threshold of \$1/4, we show in Figure 4.1 the evolution of the probability of a price increase, i.e. the conditional probability $P(y_i = 1|\mathcal{F}_{i-1})$, given by formula (4.A.6) specialized to the case $\gamma^+ = \gamma^- = 1$. When this probability is larger than 1/2, the next price movement is forecasted to be an increase. The dotted line in Figure 4.1 gives the realized states at the end of the price duration. As can be seen on Figure 4.1 and as expected from the structure of the model, the conditional probability $P(y_i = 1|\mathcal{F}_{i-1})$ is strongly influenced by the previous realized states.

As indicated in Table 4.5, the model delivers a percentage of correct decisions slightly greater than 50%, for all stocks and for all thresholds. As a first benchmark for the performance of the model, we also give

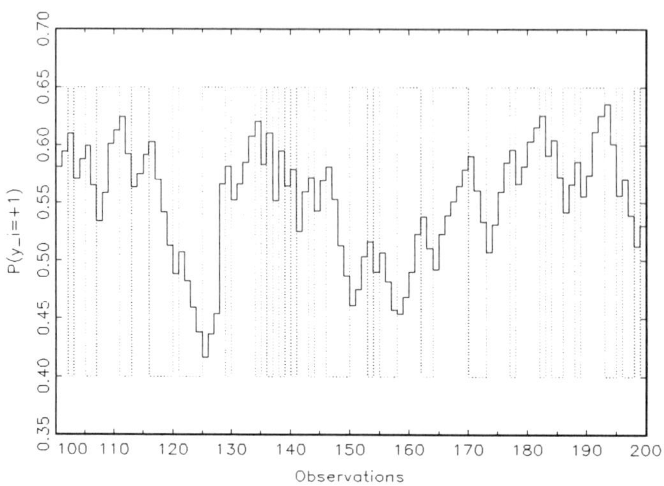

The solid line shows the evolution of the probability of a price increase computed from the asymmetric Log-ACD model for IBM price durations (threshold at \$1/4). The dotted line shows the evolution of the realized price, with the value 0.4 indicating a decrease and the value 0.65 an increase.

Figure 4.1. Conditional Probability of a Price Increase $P(y_i = 1|\mathcal{F}_{i-1})$

the percentage of correct decisions if a pure trend follower strategy is followed, i.e. when the predicted end state of duration x_i is set equal to the observed state at the start of the duration. In other words, if a price increase (decrease) has been observed, the next price movement is predicted to be a price increase (decrease) too. The results are given in the third column of Table 4.5. In the case of Disney, the asymmetric Log-ACD model performs better than the trend follower strategy, the opposite is true (sometimes marginally) for the IBM stock, while the results are mixed for Exxon and Boeing. Before drawing conclusions regarding the forecasting performance of the model, we conduct an evaluation that relies on trading strategies.

3.3.2 A TRADING STRATEGY

As a related application of the asymmetric ACD model, we now combine the computed transition probabilities with a possible trading strategy.[13] The latter is defined as follows:

- if a price increase is forecasted, n shares of the stock are bought and are added to the existing position; if the portfolio has an existing short position, it is settled at the prevailing ask price, prior to buying the n shares;

- if a price decrease is forecasted, n shares are short-sold and are added to the existing short position; if the portfolio has an existing long position, it is settled at the prevailing bid price, prior to short-selling the n shares.

We choose $n = 1000$, with a transaction cost equal to \$25. The first decision is taken at the start of the second duration and the game is ended at the end of the (three or five) month period. The portfolio is self-financed, i.e. it borrows money (at a 5% interest rate) if shares are to be bought. When shares are short-sold or when a trading profit is realized, the amount of money received is placed at a 5% rate too.

For the four stocks and for several thresholds, the outcome of this trading strategy (which we call the managed portfolio) after a three (or five month) period is given in column 4 of Table 4.5. Generally speaking, the results are not very good as the portfolio managed by the asymmetric ACD model loses money in most cases. Although the corresponding percentage of correct decisions is higher than 50% in all cases, the model often ends up with a loss due to very large transaction costs.[14]

It is also interesting to compare it with a benchmark strategy, which we take to be the buy-and-hold strategy in this case. The buy-and-hold strategy is one of the standard benchmark models in finance when actively managed portfolios have to be evaluated. See for example Campbell, Lo and MacKinlay (1997) or Sharpe, Alexander and Bailey (1999) for a general discussion regarding the performance of actively managed portfolios. Under the buy-and-hold strategy (which is equivalent to tracking an unmanaged portfolio), n shares are bought at the start of the period and they are sold at the end, resulting in a profit or loss. To conduct a fair comparison between the two strategies, n is chosen such that the financing cost of the buy-and-hold strategy is equal to the total cost of the managed portfolio, i.e. the available amount of money needed at the start of the period to buy the shares is equal to the amount that can be borrowed for an interest cost (at a 5% interest rate) equal to the total cost of the managed portfolio. The total cost of the managed portfolio is of course equal to the sum of the interest costs and transaction costs.

As indicated in Table 4.5, the portfolio based on the buy-and-hold rule easily outperforms the managed portfolio in all cases. With the exception of the Boeing stock, the buy-and-hold rule delivers a large gain for the three (or five) month period. Of course, the performance of the buy-and-hold strategy is strongly dependent on the start and end share prices of the stocks. With the exception of the share price of the Boeing stock, the other stocks witnessed a significant price increase during the corresponding time period. Further comments on the forecasted conditional probabilities and trading strategy are given in the next subsection.

3.3.3 COMMENTS

In the two preceding subsections, we have presented a possible practical application of the asymmetric Log-ACD model. However, we want to stress that the results are highly dependent on the stock we study and the period under review. In the finance literature dealing with the assessment of the performance of trading strategies and actively managed portfolios, studies are usually conducted on a large sample of stocks and for a much longer timespan. Thus we view these results as an interesting illustration of what the model can do, but considerable more work would be needed to evaluate the performance of the model by considering a wide variety of cases. Furthermore, the performance of an actively managed portfolio strongly depends on the transaction costs involved in the trading of the shares. Regarding the Disney stock for example, if the transaction costs are decreased from \$25 to \$10 per trade, then the buy-and-hold strategy becomes less profitable than the one based on the asymmetric Log-ACD model.

APPENDIX 4.A

We consider the joint density of the static two-state exponential transition model set in the competing risk framework, i.e. the function defined in (4.6). Several features of the model can be highlighted. First, this density integrates to one, as it should:

$$\begin{aligned}&\textstyle\sum_{y_i=-1,1} \int_0^\infty f(x_i, y_i|y_{i-1})dx_i \\ &= \textstyle\int_0^\infty \lambda_i^+ e^{-(\lambda_i^+ + \lambda_i^-)x_i}dx_i + \int_0^\infty \lambda_i^- e^{-(\lambda_i^+ + \lambda_i^-)x_i}dx_i = 1.\end{aligned} \tag{4.A.1}$$

Integrating x_i in (4.6) yields the transition probabilities

$$f(y_i|y_{i-1}) = (\lambda_i^+)^{I_i^+} (\lambda_i^-)^{I_i^-} \int_0^\infty e^{-(\lambda_i^+ + \lambda_i^-)x_i}dx_i = \frac{(\lambda_i^+)^{I_i^+} (\lambda_i^-)^{I_i^-}}{\lambda_i^+ + \lambda_i^-}, \tag{4.A.2}$$

so that $P(y_i = 1|y_{i-1}) = \lambda_i^+/(\lambda_i^+ + \lambda_i^-)$ and $P(y_i = -1|y_{i-1}) = \lambda_i^-/(\lambda_i^+ + \lambda_i^-)$, which are the results given in Table 4.3. Furthermore, as

$$f(y_i|x_i, y_{i-1}) = \frac{f(x_i, y_i|y_{i-1})}{f(x_i|y_{i-1})} \tag{4.A.3}$$

and

$$f(x_i|y_{i-1}) = \sum_{y_i=-1,1} f(x_i, y_i|y_{i-1}) = (\lambda_i^+ + \lambda_i^-)\, e^{-(\lambda_i^+ + \lambda_i^-)x_i} \tag{4.A.4}$$

(an exponential distribution), we have that

$$f(y_i|x_i, y_{i-1}) = \frac{(\lambda_i^+)^{I_i^+}\,(\lambda_i^-)^{I_i^-}}{\lambda_i^+ + \lambda_i^-}, \tag{4.A.5}$$

which does not depend on x_i. Thus y_i is independent of x_i, conditionally on y_{i-1}.

When the model is extended to the Weibull-ACD case, the joint density $f(x_i, y_i|\mathcal{F}_{i-1})$ is given by (4.11). Similar computations as above give

$$f(y_i|x_i, \mathcal{F}_{i-1}) = \frac{[\frac{\gamma^+}{\Psi_i^+}(\frac{x_i}{\Psi_i^+})^{\gamma^+-1}]^{I_i^+}\,[\frac{\gamma^-}{\Psi_i^-}(\frac{x_i}{\Psi_i^-})^{\gamma^--1}]^{I_i^-}}{\frac{\gamma^+}{\Psi_i^+}(\frac{x_i}{\Psi_i^+})^{\gamma^+-1} + \frac{\gamma^-}{\Psi_i^-}(\frac{x_i}{\Psi_i^-})^{\gamma^--1}}, \tag{4.A.6}$$

which implies that generally y_i is not independent of x_i, given the previous state and all the previous durations. However, it is obvious that when $\gamma^+ = \gamma^-$, $f(y_i|x_i, \mathcal{F}_{i-1})$ does not depend on x_i, meaning that in that case y_i is (conditionally) independent of x_i. It can be shown that when $\gamma^+ = \gamma^- = \gamma$,

$$f(x_i|y_{i-1}) = [(\Psi_i^+)^{-\gamma} + (\Psi_i^-)^{-\gamma}]\,\gamma\, x_i^{\gamma-1}\, e^{-x_i^\gamma[(\Psi_i^+)^{-\gamma}+(\Psi_i^-)^{-\gamma}]}, \tag{4.A.7}$$

i.e. a Weibull distribution with parameters γ and $[(\Psi_i^+)^{-\gamma} + (\Psi_i^-)^{-\gamma}]^{1/\gamma}$.

Notes

1 The main property of QMLE is its consistency even if the assumed error distribution is not the exponential (under usual regularity conditions). This robustness comes at the expense of efficiency, but in very large samples this drawback is not a big worry.

2 The unexpected volume is defined as the volume in excess of the normal volume or liquidity volume. The source of the unexpected volume is the arrival of informed traders in the market.

3 Published as Engle (2000).

4 In principle, a third end state is possible: the state where there is no price change in the mid-price over duration x_i. This state does not occur given that we use price durations. The model could easily be extended to a multi-state transition model. Another reason for considering more than two states arises if one wants to account for several levels of price increase or decrease. Notice, however, that a continuous price change is excluded because of the discreteness of price changes.

5 For example, in Lindeboom and Van den Berg (1994) and in Carling (1996), dependence between durations arises because the hazard rates depend on stochastically related unobserved components.

6 However, when γ^+ and γ^- are not equal, we cannot obtain the conditional (on the past) transition probabilities analytically.

7 Strictly speaking, there should be 12 estimation outcomes, but the Disney stock with $c_p = \$\frac{1}{2}$ gives too few price durations to be meaningfully estimated.

8 Student tests for the hypothesis that $\gamma^+ = 1$ give p-values of 0.04, 0.94, 0.23 and 0 for the Disney, IBM, Boeing and Exxon stocks, respectively; corresponding tests for the hypothesis that $\gamma^- = 1$ give p-values of 0.60, 0.94, 0 and 0 .

9 Student tests for the hypothesis that $\gamma^+ = \gamma^-$ give p-values of 0.07, very close to 1, 0, and 0.93 for the Disney, IBM, Boeing and Exxon stocks, respectively.

10 Student tests for the hypothesis that $\alpha_1 < \alpha_2$ give p-values of 0.40, 0, 0 and 0.04 for the Disney, IBM, Boeing and Exxon stocks, respectively.

11 Student tests for the hypothesis that $\alpha_3 > \alpha_4$ give p-values of 0.01, 0.09, 0.09 and 0.01 for the Disney, IBM, Boeing and Exxon stocks, respectively.

12 We have estimated the model for each set of price durations corresponding to a different threshold of the price change used to thin the quote process. Estimates are not reported since they are qualitatively similar to those reported in the previous subsection.

13 This strategy is only meant to be illustrative. In a 'real life' situation, other parameters have to be taken into account: risk analysis of the position, overnight positions, limited amount of short-selling, limit positions in trading ...

14 Under the given trading strategy, the model is required to trade at the end of every price durations, which explains the very high transaction costs.

Chapter 5

INTRADAY VOLATILITY AND VALUE-AT-RISK

1. INTRODUCTION

When intraday data are modelled, at least two different approaches can be used. As detailed in Chapter 3 and 4, a first possibility is to deal directly with the irregularly time-spaced data and thus use duration models, or joint models for durations and associated marks (such as the return over the duration). This approach fits well with the literature on market microstructure, which stresses the importance of the times between market events, since they supposedly convey important information.

An alternative approach is to apply 'standard' time series tools directly to the recorded intraday data. For example, with this kind of data, it is possible to define intraday returns from the prices and then use standard time series models to analyze these returns. This approach has to take care of the irregular spacing of the observations. One way to do this is to ignore plainly the issue. This is referred to as working in transaction time rather than in calendar time. Another way is to 're-sample' the intraday data so as to produce regularly time-spaced data. This is the approach we adopt in this chapter.

More precisely, in Section 3, we present estimates of GARCH models on regularly time-spaced intraday returns built from the intraday data of several stocks traded on the NYSE. This allows us to characterize the intraday volatility of these stocks. We stress the need of taking into account the intraday seasonality in the volatility prior to estimating the GARCH models. As an application of these models, we present in Section 4 a study on intraday Value-at-Risk. Before all this, we provide in Section 2 a brief review of ARCH models and of the issue of market efficiency.

The material presented in this chapter is based on Giot (2000a, 2000b) and is set in the general framework of the intraday volatility studies by Andersen and Bollerslev (1997, 1998, 1999) and of the work by the Olsen & Associates group on high-frequency FOREX data.

2. A REVIEW OF ARCH MODELS

Volatility models of the ARCH type were introduced by Engle (1982). In this section, we characterize the main properties of the ARCH model and present some extensions that were introduced later in the literature. Before focusing on these topics, we present a simple model of asset returns consistent with the so-called market efficiency hypothesis. This model is then set in the ARCH framework.

2.1 ASSET RETURNS AND MARKET EFFICIENCY

2.1.1 MARKET EFFICIENCY

Let P_t be the price of a financial asset (for example a stock, a bond, a foreign currency) at time t. The one-period return is usually defined as $r_t = \ln P_t - \ln P_{t-1}$.[1] Given the series of observed P_t, how can the corresponding asset returns r_t be characterized?

According to the theory of efficient markets, prices fully incorporate the information available to all market participants, which implies that the price changes (hence the returns) should not be forecastable (see Fama, 1970, 1991, Malkiel, 1996, Campbell, Lo and MacKinlay, 1997).[2] An important question is the proper definition of 'the information available to all market participants'. Usually, three forms of market efficiency are introduced, which depend on three possible information sets. If returns cannot be forecasted on the basis of the past history of returns (or prices), then market efficiency reduces to weak efficiency. If the information set includes the past history of returns and all publicly available information (such as the state of economic variables or characteristics of the firm), one speaks of semi-strong efficiency. Finally, if the information set includes public and private information, strong efficiency is introduced.

The fact that returns are not forecastable should also be qualified. When returns are said to be unforecastable, one usually speaks of the unforecastability of abnormal returns, i.e. returns in excess of the expected return as given by an appropriate model (assumed to be 'true' by the market participants). A famous example is given by the capital asset pricing model, where risky securities must yield a higher return than low-risk ones (so that the holder of the risky securities is compensated for the risk he takes).

After this brief discussion of market efficiency, we now introduce a model for the returns r_t defined above. Our goal in this chapter is to study intraday volatility, not to investigate market efficiency hypotheses. Thus, the available information set is assumed to be the past history of returns, which corresponds to the weak efficiency concept. Furthermore, we assume no risk-expected return trade-off and simply model the expected return as being equal to a constant.

2.1.2 A SIMPLE MODEL FOR ASSET RETURNS

According to the weak form of market efficiency, the returns r_t should be independent over time. If this was not true, agents, using the information available at time t, could act accordingly and lock in a profit. If the information is available to all agents, this should ensure that the market inefficiency is corrected as all market participants act in the same way. This translates into the following specification for the asset price P_t:

$$\ln P_t = \ln P_{t-1} + \mu + e_t \tag{5.1}$$

or

$$r_t = \mu + e_t, \tag{5.2}$$

where μ is the expected one-period return (assumed constant in this case) and e_t is an element of an independent white noise process. Then, $\ln P_t$ is said to follow a random walk, with drift if μ is not equal to zero.

For most classes of assets, the empirical studies indicate clearly that the hypothesis of serial independence of returns is too restrictive. However, these empirical studies point out that asset returns are usually uncorrelated over time, which suggests that in (5.2) e_t can be assumed to be a martingale difference sequence. Accordingly, we have that $\text{Cov}(r_t - \mu, r_{t-j} - \mu) = 0$ for all $j > 0$. Thus, the martingale hypothesis rules out any linear dependence between returns, but allows for nonlinear dependence. For example, $\text{Cov}((r_t - \mu)^2, (r_{t-1} - \mu)^2)$ could be different from 0. This allows for temporal dependence between the squares of the returns, which is a consequence of volatility clustering. Indeed, most series of asset returns do exhibit volatility clustering, which translates into periods of high volatility (a sequence of large positive or negative returns) followed by periods of low volatility (a sequence of small positive or negative returns). This issue is addressed in the next subsection.

2.2 THE ARCH MODEL

In the previous subsection, it has been argued that a suitable model for asset returns should include an uncorrelated error term, but should still allow for dependence. The ARCH model aims to address this issue by introducing temporal dependence between the squares of the error terms. The ARCH(1) model introduced by Engle (1982) can be written as

$$r_t = \mu + e_t \tag{5.3}$$

$$e_t = \epsilon_t \sqrt{h_t} \tag{5.4}$$

where μ is the expected one-period return, ϵ_t is an IID sequence based on the $N(0,1)$ distribution and h_t is defined as

$$h_t = \omega + \alpha e_{t-1}^2. \tag{5.5}$$

To guarantee the positivity of h_t, we assume that $\omega > 0$ and $\alpha \geq 0$.

2.2.1 CONDITIONAL AND UNCONDITIONAL MOMENTS

Let us denote by I_{t-1} the information set available at time $t-1$, $\mathrm{E}_{t-1}(.)$ the expectation given I_{t-1}, and $\mathrm{Var}_{t-1}(.)$ the corresponding conditional variance. By definition, ϵ_t is such that $\mathrm{E}(\epsilon_t) = 0$, $\mathrm{E}(\epsilon_t^2) = 1$, $\mathrm{E}(\epsilon_t^3) = 0$ and $\mathrm{E}(\epsilon_t^4) = 3$. Because the error term e_t of the return equation is defined as the product of ϵ_t and the square root of h_t, it follows that it is uncorrelated but not independent as there is autocorrelation in the squares of e_t. The conditional moments of r_t can be easily obtained: $\mathrm{E}_{t-1}(r_t) = \mu$ and $\mathrm{Var}_{t-1}(r_t) = h_t$. In other words, h_t is the conditional variance of the return process.

If $\alpha < 1$, the process defining r_t is weakly stationary.[3] It can be shown that $\mathrm{E}(r_t) = 0$, $\mathrm{E}(r_t^2) = \omega/(1-\alpha)$ and $\mathrm{E}(r_t^3) = 0$. The kurtosis coefficient of r_t, which is the ratio of the fourth moment to the square of the variance, is given by

$$KC = 3\frac{1-\alpha^2}{1-3\alpha^2} \text{ if } \alpha < \sqrt{1/3}. \tag{5.6}$$

This implies that the unconditional distribution of the returns has fatter tails than the normal distribution (which has $KC = 3$) whenever $\alpha > 0$. Moreover, the autocorrelation function of r_t^2 is given by $\rho_j = \alpha^j$. If α is close to 1 (but smaller than 1), the autocorrelation function is slowly decreasing (albeit at a geometric rate), and a large previous shock e_{t-1} (positive or negative) translates into a large conditional volatility h_t. Almost all empirical studies indicate that fat tails and volatility clustering are both stylized facts of return series for many assets. However, if α is close to 1, the kurtosis coefficient given in (5.6) does not exist.

The kurtosis coefficient given in (5.6) is based on the assumption that the distribution of ϵ_t is $N(0,1)$. Other distributions are possible. For example we can assume that ϵ_t follows a Student distribution with ν degrees of freedom, i.e. $\epsilon_t \sim t_\nu$. In that case, KC is equal to

$$KC = \lambda \frac{1-\alpha^2}{1-\lambda\alpha^2} \tag{5.7}$$

if $\alpha < \sqrt{1/\lambda}$, with $\lambda = 3(\nu-2)/(\nu-4)$, the kurtosis coefficient of the Student distribution, which exists if $\nu > 4$. Because of the additional parameter ν, the ARCH(1) model based on the Student distribution has fatter tails than the corresponding model based on the normal distribution.

2.2.2 ML AND QML ESTIMATION

Maximum likelihood estimation of the ARCH(1) model is easy to implement once the density function of ϵ_t is specified. Let θ denote the vector of the parameters to be estimated. If the ϵ_t are assumed to be normally distributed, then the conditional log-likelihood function for a sample of T observations is equal to

$$L_t(\theta) = \sum_{t=1}^{T} l_t(\theta) \tag{5.8}$$

where

$$l_t(\theta) = -0.5 \ln h_t - 0.5\epsilon_t^2 \tag{5.9}$$

with ϵ_t defined by (5.4) and h_t by (5.5).

The ML estimation is usually performed using the BHHH algorithm since it does not require the computation of second order derivatives of l_t with respect to the parameters. The ML estimates are conveniently considered to be consistent and asymptotically normally distributed, although these results are holding under some restrictive conditions and are not at all easily proved. A consistent estimate of the asymptotic variance-covariance is provided as a byproduct of the BHHH procedure. Procedures for estimating ARCH models are available in most econometric software packages.

Once the ML estimation has been performed, it is important to conduct specification tests on the estimated model. By assumption, the ϵ_t are IID $N(0,1)$, which implies that the standardized residuals

$$\widehat{\epsilon}_t = \frac{\widehat{r}_t - \widehat{\mu}}{\sqrt{\widehat{h}_t}} \tag{5.10}$$

should also be IID $N(0,1)$ if the model is correctly specified. Autocorrelation tests on squared standardized residuals provide a way of testing if the volatility clustering has been taken into account by the ARCH model. By computing the kurtosis coefficient of the $\widehat{\epsilon}_t$, it is possible to check if the excess kurtosis has been correctly captured. For example, with the normal distribution, KC should be equal to 3. If KC is larger than 3, this indicates the need for an underlying distribution exhibiting fatter tails, for example the Student distribution. Another approach to diagnostic checks is to use the density forecast method illustrated by Diebold, Gunther and Tay (1998) on ARCH models (see also subsection 3.4 of Chapter 3, where this method is applied to duration models).

If the Student distribution with ν degrees of freedom is chosen for the error term, then $l_t(\theta)$ to be used in (5.8) is defined as

$$l_t(\theta) = \ln\left(\frac{\Gamma((\nu+1)/2)}{\Gamma(\nu/2)}\right) - 0.5\ \ln(\nu h_t) - \frac{\nu+1}{2}\ \ln\left(1+\frac{\epsilon_t^2}{\nu h_t}\right). \quad (5.11)$$

In this case the conditional variance of r_t is equal to $h_t\,\nu/(\nu-2)$ if $\nu > 2$.

QML estimation of the ARCH model results from maximizing the likelihood function defined in (5.8)-(5.9), i.e. assuming normality. The asymptotic consistency and normality of the QML estimator has been proved under certain conditions by Lee and Hansen (1994) and by Lumsdaine (1996). The usual sandwich estimator applies to the variance-covariance matrix of the estimator (see subsection 3.3 of Chapter 3, where this formula is explained in the context of duration models).

2.3 EXTENSIONS

The ARCH(1) model presented in the previous subsection assumed a constant one-period expected return equal to μ. This hypothesis can be relaxed by introducing a conditional mean equation for the returns, like $r_t = \mu + x_t'\delta + e_t$, where x_t is a vector of regressors. For example, the returns could be autocorrelated, suggesting the specification

$$r_t = c + \delta r_{t-1} + e_t, \quad (5.12)$$

with e_t following the ARCH(1) specification given by equations (5.4) and (5.5). As discussed in Campbell, Lo and MacKinlay (1997) or in Lo and MacKinlay (1999), a small amount of autocorrelation in asset returns is not incompatible with the market efficiency hypothesis. Indeed, particular features of market structure, such as institutional settings, practical implementations of indexes and mutual funds, and 'friction' in the trading process, can account for the observed autocorrelation, which nevertheless remains small and usually does not allow for a trading profit. In the case of intraday data, stale quotes or bid-ask bounces for the trade process can produce autocorrelation.

An immediate extension of the ARCH(1) model is to allow for a multi-period dependence between the squared returns. The ARCH(p) model is

$$h_t = \omega + \alpha_1 e_{t-1}^2 + \alpha_2 e_{t-2}^2 + \ldots + \alpha_p e_{t-p}^2, \tag{5.13}$$

where $\omega > 0$ and all $\alpha_i \geq 0$. This allows for a more complex dynamic structure for the squared return process. The ARCH(p) model is detailed in Engle (1982).

A drawback of the ARCH(p) model is the relatively large number of coefficients that may be needed to accommodate the dynamics of the squared returns process. This can be cumbersome for estimation as positivity constraints have to be set on all α_i coefficients. Bollerslev (1986) introduced the GARCH(p,q) model as a generalization of the ARCH(p) model by adding a distributed lag structure on the conditional variance:

$$h_t = \omega + \alpha_1 e_{t-1}^2 + \ldots + \alpha_p e_{t-p}^2 + \beta_1 h_{t-1} + \ldots + \beta_q h_{t-q}, \tag{5.14}$$

where $\omega > 0$, all $\alpha_i \geq 0$ and all $\beta_i \geq 0$. The GARCH(1,1) model has been extremely popular in the empirical literature as it usually provides a good representation of the empirical data and is very parsimonious; see Bauwens, Lubrano and Richard (1999, Ch. 7) for details.

The GARCH(p,q) model was one of the first generalizations of the ARCH model following the publication of Engle (1982). In the subsequent years, many others followed, usually involving more complex specifications of the conditional variance. A complete review of all these models is beyond the scope of this chapter and more information can be found in Bollerslev, Engle and Nelson (1994), a book edited by Engle (1995), or Palm (1996). Many of these extensions are programmed in econometric packages. Among the possible models, let us mention the exponential GARCH (EGARCH) model of Nelson (1991) that we use in the sequel of this chapter. In the EGARCH(1,1) model, the logarithm of the conditional variance can be written as

$$\ln h_t = \omega + \theta\epsilon_{t-1} + \gamma(|\epsilon_{t-1}| - \mathrm{E}|\epsilon_{t-1}|) + \beta \ln h_{t-1}, \tag{5.15}$$

where $\beta < 1$. This model allows for an asymmetric response of h_t to volatility shocks in the innovation term ϵ_{t-1} when θ differs from zero. The derivative of $\ln h_t$ with respect to ϵ_{t-1} is equal to $\gamma - \theta$ when ϵ_{t-1} is negative and is equal to $\gamma + \theta$ when ϵ_{t-1} is positive. Empirical studies conducted on daily data using EGARCH specifications usually find that $\gamma + \theta$ is positive while θ is negative, so that negative shocks have a more pronounced impact on volatility than positive shocks. This leads to an asymmetric news impact curve (the graph of $\ln h_t$ on ϵ_{t-1}), with a larger slope when the innovation is negative than when it is positive (Engle and Ng, 1993).

3. ARCH MODELS FOR INTRADAY DATA

In the previous section, we briefly reviewed the class of ARCH models. As indicated by the surveys on this literature, the GARCH model and the subsequently introduced models have become extremely popular in the 90's. Indeed, with the growing volatility of many markets and the importance of volatility for the pricing of derivative contracts, there is an important need for volatility models. Furthermore, ARCH models are easy to understand and estimate, which certainly explains a part of their success.

ARCH models have been applied to monthly data, weekly data and daily data. With the availability of intraday databases, a new field of application is available for this class of models, namely the modelling of *intraday* volatility. At first glance, it might appear that the usual ARCH models could directly be applied to intraday data. However, the material given in the first three chapters of this book indicates that one must proceed carefully. Indeed, tick-by-tick data are not regularly time-spaced, and intraday data feature an important intraday seasonality, which should also affect volatility. Actually, these two issues are closely linked, as the irregular spacing of the data can partially be explained by an intraday seasonal effect: markets are more active at the start and the end of the day, which leads to shorter intervals between trades and quotes.

Standard volatility models assume that the data are regularly time-spaced, which is not the case of the tick-by-tick intraday data. In time-series modelling, one can estimate a model for seasonally unadjusted data by including a seasonal component in the model, or one can take care of seasonality before estimating a model designed for seasonally adjusted data.

For modelling intraday volatility, we follow the second approach. Thus, prior to estimating GARCH models, we process the data to take account of the irregular time spacing and of the intraday seasonality. The following subsection deals with the so-called time transformations, which take as input the original irregularly time-spaced data and give as output data on which the volatility models can be readily applied. The issue of intraday seasonality is also discussed.

3.1 TIME TRANSFORMATIONS AND INTRADAY SEASONALITY

In the context of intraday data, time transformation techniques are used to convert a given dataset into a new one, such that some features of the data are highlighted. For example, the problem of interest can involve the modelling of intraday returns on a 20 minute grid (i.e. we want to model intraday returns with a time horizon of 20 minutes). In this case, we need a data transformation that converts the original irregularly time-spaced data into regularly, 20 minute-spaced, data.

Data transformations bearing on irregularly time-spaced data were discussed in Chapter 2 when price and volume durations were introduced (based on the original trade and quote durations). In this chapter, we focus on transformations yielding regularly time-spaced data. Before introducing regularly time-spaced data, we first present a review of the existing literature on time transformations and intraday seasonality.

3.1.1 LITERATURE REVIEW

Time transformations that can be applied to intraday data have been recently studied in the literature. Le Fol and Mercier (1998) review most of the possible time transformations that can be used. They highlight the characteristics of several time scales (calendar time, volume time, volume time, ...), including the time transformations introduced by Olsen & Associates to take into account the intraday seasonality in high-frequency FOREX data.

Using the HFDF93 database (see Appendix A of Chapter 2), the Olsen & Associates research group conducted several studies (see Guillaume, Dacorogna, Davé, Muller, Olsen and Pictet, 1997; Guillaume, Pictet and Dacorogna, 1995) on the properties of returns in the FOREX market.[4] More particularly, they focused on the conditional volatility of these returns, which they modelled using GARCH specifications. Because trading in the FOREX market is decentralized with main trading locations in Asia, Europe and the U.S.A., it exhibits an important intraday seasonality, which can be ascribed to the opening and closing of trading in different time zones and to lunchtime of traders. To take into account the seasonal aspect of intraday volatility, Dacorogna, Muller, Nagler, Olsen and Pictet (1997) introduce the θ-time scale function $\theta(t)$, which can be viewed as a time integral of worldwide activity in the FOREX market and is defined as

$$\theta(t) = a_0(t - t_0) + \sum_{k=1}^{3} \int_{t'=t_0}^{t} a_k(t')\, dt' \tag{5.16}$$

where $k = 1 \ldots 3$ identifies the succession of the three geographical markets (see Chapter 1, subsection 3.3), $a_k(t')$ is an activity measure in market k at calendar time t', t_0 is the start time (time of opening of the first market), and a_0 is the activity at the start time. According to this equation, there is a one-to-one deterministic relationship between calendar time t' (recorded times for quotes in the original database) and operational θ-time, such that time intervals with high activity are enlarged and time intervals with small activity are shortened. The resulting θ-time is then scaled so that one full week in θ-time corresponds to one full week in the original calendar time, which gives the sampling times. Broadly speaking, the θ-time scale is a sampling scheme combined with a deseasonalization technique for the variance.

Comparing estimates of GARCH models in calendar time and θ-time, Guillaume, Pictet and Dacorogna (1995) highlight the importance of taking into account the intraday seasonality: in the original calendar time, GARCH estimates are not meaningful[5] and the aggregation properties[6] of the GARCH model break down completely. Using the same GARCH model on data based on θ-time yields consistent estimates. However, there are still some problems with the aggregation properties of the GARCH model. Guillaume, Pictet and Dacorogna (1995) conclude that the simple GARCH model cannot fully take into account the heterogeneity of traders who operate at different frequencies (i.e. traders who have different 'time horizons' for their trades).

Intraday volatility has been the focus of several papers by Andersen and Bollerslev. First, Andersen and Bollerslev (1997) provide a thorough description of the application of GARCH models to high-frequency data (for currency trading at the FOREX and futures trading at the Chicago Mercantile Exchange) and particularly insist on the need to take into account the intraday seasonal component prior to estimating the model. Using a primary dataset of 5 minute returns for the DM/$ exchange rate and S&P500 index futures, they estimate GARCH models at various frequencies (i.e. using sampling intervals multiple of the original 5 minute interval) with and without taking into account the intraday seasonality. Their results are relatively similar to those of Guillaume, Pictet and Dacorogna (1995): if the intraday volatility is not modelled, the parameter estimates are erroneous and the aggregation properties break down completely. However, they do not use the θ-time scale of Dacorogna, Muller, Nagler, Olsen and Pictet (1997) but model the intraday volatility pattern using flexible Fourier functional forms (which are applied to the data regularly sampled at 5 minute intervals).

Using the same database of high-frequency returns for the DM/$ exchange rate and in the framework of OLS regressions with dummy variables, Andersen and Bollerslev (1998) characterize and separately identify three key components of the intraday volatility: the GARCH effect (which stems from the daily or long-run heteroscedasticity, but also affects the intraday returns because of the aggregation properties of the GARCH model), the intraday pattern (opening and closing of trading centers around the world), and the short-term effects due to the macroeconomic news announcements by central banks and government agencies. They study the short-term and long-term impact of the announcements and conclude that these are responsible for important spikes in the intraday volatility. However, these spikes are short-lived and do not contribute in a major way to the cumulated daily volatility.

Andersen and Bollerslev (1999) use the notion of integrated volatility (defined as the cumulative sum of squared intraday returns) as a measure of volatility and show that standard volatility models of the GARCH type provide reasonably good forecasts of this volatility measure. Furthermore, they show that high-frequency returns should be favored when volatility is forecasted whatever the time horizon that is needed. For example, 5 minute returns (if properly modelled) help forecast better monthly volatility than daily returns.

Maillet and Michel (1998) focus on the distribution of stock returns in a volume time scale, i.e. a time scale where transaction volume is constant between observations (volume is considered to be a proxy of the information gathered by market participants, so that constant volume implies that the same amount of information is supposedly released between these newly defined returns). For the same dataset, they compare the empirical characteristics of returns both regularly sampled and sampled in a volume time scale. The distribution of returns defined in the volume time scale is different from the distribution of returns defined in calendar time: ARCH effects and the kurtosis coefficient are much stronger in calendar time than in volume time, which gives some support to the hypothesis that ARCH effects are induced by the rate of arrival of information (see also Lamoureux and Lastrapes, 1990, and subsection 3.3 in this chapter). ARCH effects and the kurtosis coefficient are also much stronger when the sampling frequency is increased (which can be related to the aggregation results of Drost and Nijman, 1993).

As outlined in this review of the literature, transforming the irregularly time-spaced data and taking into account the intraday seasonality are two closely related subjects. We now use techniques similar to those of Andersen and Bollerslev (1997) to deal with the TAQ data (which was described in Chapter 2) in an equidistantly time-spaced framework. Then we apply GARCH models to these new data. In the next subsection, we focus on equidistantly sampled data.[7]

3.1.2 EQUIDISTANT SAMPLING

To transform the original dataset into a new one featuring regularly time-spaced observations, we first define a sampling grid with an associated sampling time equal to s seconds. As we focus on data released by the NYSE, the sampling grid is defined over the market opening hours (9h30 to 16h). A new marked point process Q' is defined as (t'_i, b'_i, a'_i), where the t'_i define the grid over the period 9h30-16h with a s minute sampling interval, i.e. $t'_i - t'_{i-1}$ is equal to s for all i. Associated to t'_i are b'_i and a'_i, the sampled bid-ask quotes. For every t'_i, they are the most recently recorded bid-ask quotes (i.e. b_i and a_i in the notation of Chapter 2), except for the first observation of the day which consists of the first b_i and a_i. The return process is then defined on the mid-point of the equidistantly time-spaced bid-ask quotes, i.e. the return process consists of all $r_i = \ln p'_i - \ln p'_{i-1}$, where $p'_i = (a'_i + b'_i)/2$. Because we focus on the intraday returns, we delete the first return of the day as it is the overnight return, i.e. the return between the last recorded price before 16h on the previous market day and the first recorded price after 9h30.

In a second step, we include trade related information in the Q' dataset. Over each s minute sampling interval, we compute the traded volume, the number of trades and the average volume per trade (these variables are used in the volatility specifications in subsection 3.3). Merging the trade and bid-ask quote datasets, the marked point process for the equidistantly sampled bid-ask quotes becomes $(t'_i, b'_i, a'_i, v'_i, av'_i, n'_i)$, where v'_i is the traded volume, av'_i is the average volume per trade, and n'_i is the number of trades between t'_{i-1} and t'_i.

Descriptive statistics for the newly defined regularly time-spaced data are given in Table 5.1. We focus on two actively traded stocks on the NYSE, Boeing and Exxon. For both stocks, the period under review is January to May 1997 (21 weeks of intraday data) and the equidistant sampling is performed for several sampling intervals (s): 5 minutes, 10 minutes, 15 minutes, and 30 minutes. Although we consider several sampling intervals and two different stocks, the intraday returns exhibit similar characteristics that we comment hereafter.

Firstly, the returns are significantly autocorrelated at the 5% level for the Exxon stock: the $Q(10)$-statistics are larger than the critical value (equal to 18.3), especially when s is small. For the Boeing stock, $Q(10)$ is significant only for $s = 5$ minutes, but it is not much below the critical value for higher values of s. In subsection 3.2 below, we discuss this slightly negative or positive autocorrelation in the returns. Secondly, the distribution of the returns has fat tails, since the kurtosis of the returns exceeds the benchmark value of 3, being between 6.5 and 10.6 for

Table 5.1. Statistics on equidistantly sampled returns

	5 min	10 min	15 min	30 min
	Returns (Boeing)			
Sample size	8112	4056	2704	1352
Oversampling	0.78%	0.17%	0.14%	0.07%
$Q(10)$	20.5	16.6	17.3	14.2
Kurtosis	10.6	8.9	7.6	6.5
Kurtosis'	4.6	4.5	4.5	4.5
	Squared returns (Boeing)			
$Q(10)$	836.7	279.6	155.2	40.4
$Q(10)$'	1110.9	417.8	274.5	98.2
r_1'	0.20	0.19	0.20	0.21
r_2'	0.14	0.13	0.13	0.07
	Returns (Exxon)			
Sample size	8112	4056	2704	1352
Oversampling	0.41%	0%	0%	0%
$Q(10)$	51.1	37.1	34.3	24.4
Kurtosis	6.9	6.4	6.1	6.1
Kurtosis'	4.0	3.9	3.9	3.7
	Squared returns (Exxon)			
$Q(10)$	696.9	282.9	136.3	42.6
$Q(10)$'	644.5	272.3	147.5	78.9
r_1'	0.12	0.11	0.11	0.12
r_2'	0.11	0.08	0.07	0.14

Equidistantly sampled intraday returns and squared returns for the period January 97 - May 97, for the Boeing and Exxon stocks traded at the NYSE. The oversampling rate is the ratio of the number of identically sampled quotes to the number of all sampled quotes. $Q(10)$ denotes the Ljung-Box Q-statistic for the first ten autocorrelations of the returns (or squared returns). $Q(10)$' denotes the same statistic for the intraday seasonally adjusted data. Kurtosis denotes the kurtosis coefficient of the returns, while Kurtosis' denotes the kurtosis coefficient of the seasonally adjusted returns. r_1' and r_2' denote the first two autocorrelations on the square of the seasonally adjusted returns. The seasonally adjusted returns are defined by dividing the raw returns by the square root of the deterministic volatility function.

the Boeing stock and around 6 for the Exxon stock. When the returns are deseasonalized (see below), the kurtosis is reduced (it is around 4.5 for the Boeing stock and around 4 for the Exxon stock). Thirdly, the squared returns are very significantly autocorrelated (even after the intraday seasonality in the volatility has been removed) as evidenced by the large $Q(10)$-statistics computed for these squared returns. Furthermore, the autocorrelation in the squared returns strongly increases when s gets smaller. For the Boeing stock, the $Q(10)$-statistic for the squared returns increases 10 times (9 times for Exxon stock) when s is shortened

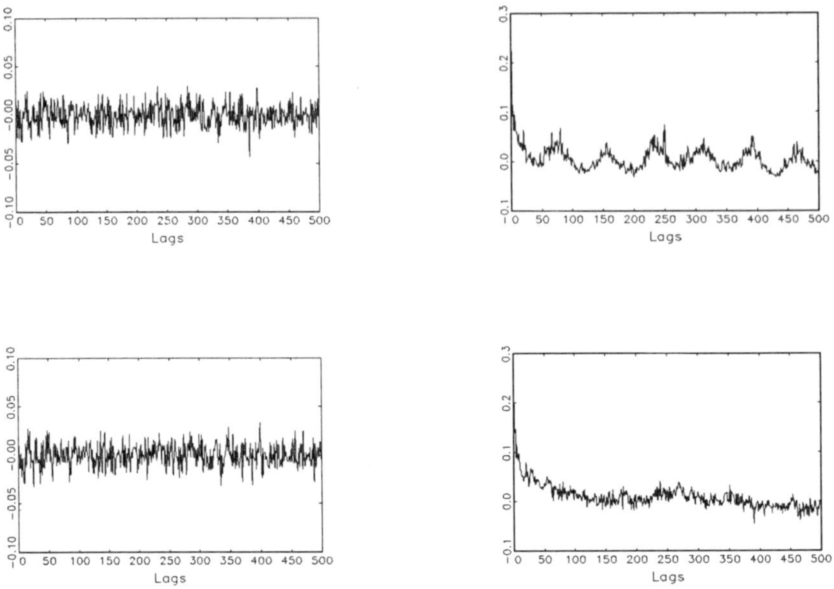

From left to right and up to down: returns, squared returns, returns after isa, squared returns after isa (isa=intraday seasonal adjustment)

Figure 5.1. Autocorrelation functions for the returns and squared returns of the Boeing stock ($s = 5$ minutes)

from 30 minutes to 5 minutes. Andersen and Bollerslev (1997) find similar results with FOREX and futures data (see Table 1 in their paper). Lastly, while there is a strong persistence in the squared returns, the first autocorrelation has a rather low value, around 0.2 for the Boeing stock and close to 0.1 for the Exxon stock. This implies that the autocorrelation function (ACF) is slowly decreasing. This is confirmed by the plots of the ACF of the squared returns given in Figures 5.1 and 5.2 (see below for details on the intraday seasonality).

3.1.3 INTRADAY SEASONALITY AND VOLATILITY

In the previous subsection, intraday returns were defined for a prespecified grid on the time scale ranging from 9h30 to 16h in s minute long increments. Several studies in the empirical market microstructure literature indicate that the volatility of these returns is not constant during the trading day. More precisely, an intraday pattern has been found, where returns are much more variable at the start and end of the

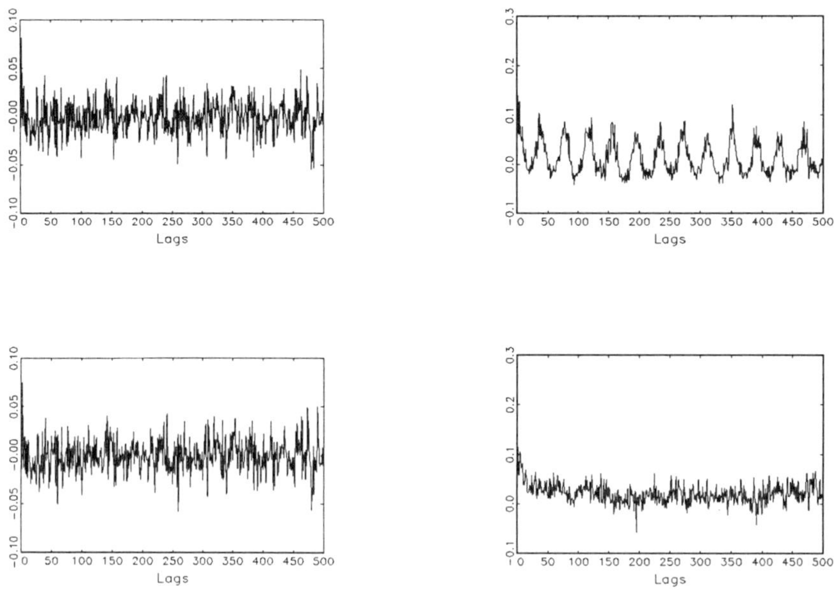

From left to right and up to down: returns, squared returns, returns after isa, squared returns after isa (isa=intraday seasonal adjustment)

Figure 5.2. Autocorrelation functions for the returns and squared returns of the Exxon stock ($s = 10$ minutes)

day than around lunch time. Thus, the variance of the returns follows a U-shaped function. If the pattern of intraday volatility is assumed to follow a deterministic function of time, it can be measured by computing averages (for example over 30 minute intervals) of the squared returns recorded during these intervals.

A second possibility is to assume that the intraday volatility is made up of two distinct components: firstly, an intraday deterministic pattern such as defined above; secondly, a stochastic function modelling the remaining part of the volatility, i.e. the part not captured by the deterministic function. This is the method used in Andersen and Bollerslev (1997, 1998, 1999) or in Giot (2000a), where the stochastic function belongs to the GARCH class. Three steps are needed to implement this procedure:

(1) A deterministic intraday pattern is computed, for example using the method outlined above. Thus, for all s minute long intervals, we compute the average squared returns (previously defined on the sampling

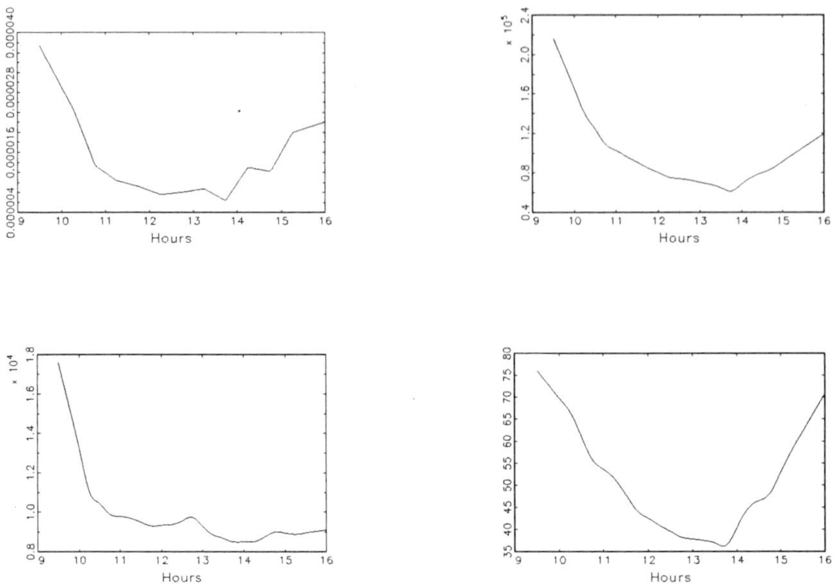

From left to right and up to down: volatility, traded volume, average volume per trade, number of trades

Figure 5.3. Intraday seasonal component (time-of-day functions) for the volatility, traded volume, average volume per trade and number of trades of the Boeing stock ($s = 5$ minutes)

grid) allowing for a time-of-week effect, i.e. that the average volatility depends on the time-of-day and day of the week. For example, with $s = 5$ minutes, the average volatility for returns defined on the [9h55,10h] interval can be different on Mondays and Tuesdays. This yields the deterministic intraday volatility function, called $\phi(t_i)$.[8]

For the Boeing stock for example, Figure 5.3 (upper left panel) gives the intraday volatility pattern for the returns sampled with $s = 5$ minutes. The importance of taking into account the intraday seasonal component of the volatility can be seen by plotting the autocorrelogram of the squared returns. Working with a 5 minute sampling interval for the Boeing stock and 10 minutes for the Exxon stock, Figures 5.1 and 5.2 (upper right panels) give the autocorrelograms of the squared intraday returns. With a 5 (10) minute long sampling interval, there are 78 (39) intervals during one trading day. In Figures 5.1 and 5.2, the volatility peaks at lags multiple of 78 and 39 are clearly visible. Similar graphs are given in Andersen and Bollerslev (1997, FOREX and futures data) and in Giot (2000a, IBM data).

(2) Deseasonalized returns rd_i are computed by dividing the returns by the square root of the deterministic intraday volatility function:

$$rd_i = r_i/\sqrt{\phi(t_i)}. \tag{5.17}$$

For the Boeing and Exxon stocks, Figures 5.1 and 5.2 (lower right panels) give the autocorrelogram of the squared deseasonalized returns. As can be checked on these autocorrelograms, the intraday seasonal peaks are no longer visible. However, the slowly decaying autocorrelation functions and the corresponding Q-statistics given in Table 5.1 indicate that taking into account the intraday seasonality has not removed the autocorrelation in the volatility. This leads to the last step.

(3) GARCH models are specified to capture the possible dependence in the deseasonalized returns. Results of estimation are provided in the following subsection.

Descriptive statistics for the deseasonalized returns rd_i of both stocks are given in Table 5.1 and were already discussed in the preceding subsection. To summarize, squared deseasonalized returns are significantly autocorrelated, which indicates volatility clustering not explained by a time-of-day effect. The strong cycles in the ACF have been completely removed, which bodes well for the application of standard volatility models on these data. The kurtosis of these returns is smaller than the kurtosis of the original returns.

3.2 GARCH AND EGARCH MODELS

In this section, we estimate GARCH models on the deseasonalized returns rd_i sampled at different intraday frequencies. We model the conditional volatility as being a GARCH(1,1) process and we introduce an asymmetric effect by using an EGARCH(1,1) model. As the results in Table 5.1 indicate that the returns are slightly autocorrelated, an AR(1) model is selected for the returns. The error term is assumed to be $N(0,1)$ for both models. For the GARCH(1,1) specification, we also estimate the model with an error term assumed to be distributed as t_ν. Thus the two specifications use the conditional mean equation

$$rd_i = c + \delta\, rd_{i-1} + e_i, \text{ with } e_i = \sqrt{h_i}\epsilon_i. \tag{5.18}$$

In the GARCH(1,1) model, the conditional variance equation is

$$h_i = \omega + \alpha e_{i-1}^2 + \beta h_{i-1}, \tag{5.19}$$

Table 5.2. GARCH and EGARCH estimation results (Boeing)

	5 min	10 min	15 min	30 min
	GARCH(1,1) with normal errors			
c	-0.016 (0.010)	-0.026 (0.014)	-0.023 (0.017)	-0.035 (0.025)
δ	0.014 (0.012)	-0.002 (0.017)	-0.007 (0.021)	-0.038 (0.030)
ω	0.026 (0.004)	0.047 (0.009)	0.081 (0.018)	0.137 (0.038)
α	0.071 (0.006)	0.088 (0.010)	0.112 (0.016)	0.125 (0.024)
β	0.904 (0.009)	0.866 (0.016)	0.809 (0.029)	0.741 (0.051)
$Q(10)$	**31.30**	12.66	6.40	5.95
	GARCH(1,1) with Student errors			
	5 min	10 min	15 min	30 min
c	-0.023 (0.008)	-0.036 (0.012)	-0.040 (0.016)	-0.046 (0.023)
δ	-0.016 (0.011)	-0.027 (0.016)	-0.031 (0.020)	-0.065 (0.029)
ω	0.007 (0.002)	0.019 (0.005)	0.046 (0.012)	0.100 (0.038)
α	0.056 (0.006)	0.068 (0.009)	0.095 (0.015)	0.110 (0.027)
β	0.888 (0.011)	0.863 (0.018)	0.795 (0.032)	0.681 (0.086)
ν	3.551 (0.198)	4.653 (0.396)	5.598 (0.641)	5.243 (0.785)
$Q(10)$	**28.46**	14.12	8.36	6.40
	EGARCH(1,1) with normal errors			
	5 min	10 min	15 min	30 min
c	-0.025 (0.010)	-0.037 (0.014)	-0.029 (0.018)	-0.048 (0.025)
δ	0.014 (0.012)	-0.003 (0.017)	-0.005 (0.021)	-0.054 (0.030)
ω	0.011 (0.002)	0.008 (0.004)	0.004 (0.006)	0.004 (0.011)
θ	-0.012 (0.006)	-0.018 (0.010)	-0.037 (0.016)	-0.052 (0.025)
γ	0.163 (0.012)	0.201 (0.020)	0.250 (0.030)	0.274 (0.044)
β	0.951 (0.006)	0.927 (0.012)	0.881 (0.023)	0.835 (0.042)
$Q(10)$	**37.36**	12.14	6.98	8.03

Estimation results for the GARCH model (5.18)-(5.19) and the EGARCH model (5.18)-(5.20). Both models are applied to 21 weeks of intraday data. $Q(10)$ denotes the Ljung-Box Q-statistic for the squared standardized residuals. It is typeset in bold when it exceeds the 5% critical value.

and ϵ_i is assumed to be either $N(0,1)$ or t_ν. In the EGARCH(1,1) model, the conditional variance equation is

$$\ln h_i = \omega + \theta\epsilon_{i-1} + \gamma(|\epsilon_{i-1}| - \sqrt{2/\pi}) + \beta \ln h_{i-1}, \tag{5.20}$$

and ϵ_i is assumed to be $N(0,1)$.[9]

Estimation results for both stocks and both specifications are given in Tables 5.2 and 5.3. In these tables, we give the estimated values of the parameters of the models and the corresponding standard errors.

Both the GARCH(1,1) and the EGARCH(1,1) models capture well the autocorrelation in the volatility of the deseasonalized returns. Ex-

Table 5.3. GARCH and EGARCH estimation results (Exxon)

	5 min	10 min	15 min	30 min
	GARCH(1,1) with normal errors			
c	-0.010 (0.010)	-0.005 (0.015)	-0.012 (0.018)	-0.016 (0.026)
δ	-0.051 (0.012)	-0.021 (0.017)	0.068 (0.021)	0.057 (0.029)
ω	0.042 (0.006)	0.039 (0.013)	0.102 (0.034)	0.096 (0.054)
α	0.075 (0.007)	0.058 (0.011)	0.094 (0.021)	0.079 (0.029)
β	0.884 (0.011)	0.903 (0.023)	0.804 (0.051)	0.824 (0.078)
$Q(10)$	7.39	7.13	5.01	11.17
	GARCH(1,1) with Student errors			
	5 min	10 min	15 min	30 min
c	-0.007 (0.008)	0 (0.014)	-0.006 (0.017)	-0.018 (0.025)
δ	-0.073 (0.010)	-0.034 (0.016)	0.050 (0.020)	0.040 (0.029)
ω	0.010 (0.003)	0.026 (0.009)	0.068 (0.023)	0.081 (0.049)
α	0.064 (0.006)	0.052 (0.010)	0.084 (0.018)	0.079 (0.029)
β	0.862 (0.013)	0.889 (0.025)	0.789 (0.050)	0.795 (0.094)
ν	3.230 (0.223)	6.144 (0.705)	6.465 (0.911)	8.549 (2.064)
$Q(10)$	**33.76**	6.49	7.06	12.07
	EGARCH(1,1) with normal errors			
	5 min	10 min	15 min	30 min
c	-0.018 (0.010)	0.006 (0.015)	-0.003 (0.018)	-0.012 (0.027)
δ	-0.059 (0.012)	-0.028 (0.016)	0.069 (0.020)	0.057 (0.029)
ω	0.011 (0.002)	0.006 (0.002)	0.006 (0.005)	0.002 (0.007)
θ	0.001 (0.006)	0.007 (0.008)	0.019 (0.014)	0.023 (0.021)
γ	0.143 (0.012)	0.110 (0.021)	0.176 (0.036)	0.157 (0.068)
β	0.936 (0.009)	0.954 (0.015)	0.897 (0.033)	0.894 (0.073)
$Q(10)$	15.12	13.99	6.41	12.01

See note of previous table.

cept for a part of the $s = 5$ results, for all models the $Q(10)$-statistics of the squared standardized residuals are not significant at the five percent level.[10] The persistence in volatility is quite large, with $\alpha+\beta$ larger than or close to 0.9 in the GARCH specification, and β larger than or close to 0.9 in the EGARCH model. When the Student GARCH model is estimated, $\alpha+\beta$ takes a somewhat lower value while ν is small (close to 5 for the Boeing stock, and around 7 for the Exxon stock): as expected, the distribution of the returns is fat-tailed. Persistence in volatility and kurtosis are increased when the sampling frequency is increased. For example (Boeing stock), $\alpha+\beta$ increases from 0.87 to 0.98 when going from 30 minute to 5 minute returns. In this case, the ν coefficient decreases from 5.2 to a value smaller than 4, which corresponds to an increase in kurtosis for higher frequency returns.

The asymmetric effect is small for both stocks. It is slightly negative and significant at the 5% level for the Boeing stock, and slightly positive but insignificant for the Exxon stock. For example, for the Boeing stock with $s = 15$ minutes, when ϵ_{i-1} is negative, the slope of the conditional variance is equal to 0.287; it is equal to 0.213 when the standardized innovation is positive. For the Exxon stock with $s = 10$ minutes, the slopes are equal to 0.117 and 0.103 respectively. Thus, the asymmetry in the news impact curve is rather weak (estimation results on daily data usually indicate a more pronounced asymmetric effect).

At short time intervals ($s = 5$ or 10 minutes) for the Exxon stock, the autoregressive coefficient δ of the mean equation is negative in all specifications, while it is positive for the other sampling frequencies. The slightly negative autocorrelation at the highest frequencies indicates a bouncing effect in the returns. For the Boeing stock, δ is not significant in most results. Broadly speaking, the estimation results for the Boeing and Exxon stocks do not differ much.

3.3 VOLUME AND NUMBER OF TRADES

In the literature on GARCH models, trade related variables such as the traded volume or the number of trades have been found to have a big impact on the estimates of the GARCH parameters when included in the specification of the conditional variance.

For the traded volume, using the theoretical framework provided by the so-called mixture of distribution hypothesis, Lamoureux and Lastrapes (1990) find that including volume as an additional variable in the conditional variance equation leads to a very important decrease in the autoregressive coefficient of the variance equation, so that $\alpha + \beta$ in the GARCH process is close to zero. In their study based on daily data for US stocks, the GARCH effect completely disappears once volume is included in the conditional variance equation.

Regarding the volatility-volume relationship, Jones, Kaul and Lipson (1994) suggest that it is the number of trades, and not the average volume per trade, that is the main driving force behind volatility. In the Lamoureux and Lastrapes framework, both effects are intertwined as the traded volume is the product of the number of trades and the average volume per trade. Jones, Kaul and Lipson (1994) split the traded volume into two components, the number of trades and the average volume per trade, which they use as additional variables in a volatility equation.[11] Using daily data for a large number of US stocks traded on the NASDAQ,

Table 5.4. Influence of trade related variables on EGARCH estimates (Boeing)

	5 min	10 min	15 min	30 min
		EGARCH(1,1)		
β	0.951 (0.006)	0.927 (0.012)	0.881 (0.023)	0.835 (0.042)
		EGARCH(1,1) with traded volume (ζ_1)		
β	0.055 (0.025)	0 (.)	0 (.)	0 (.)
ζ_1	0.645 (0.021)	0.699 (0.034)	0.723 (0.045)	0.836 (0.072)
		EGARCH(1,1) with number of trades (ζ_2)		
β	0 (.)	0 (.)	0 (.)	0 (.)
ζ_2	1.421 (0.034)	1.644 (0.058)	1.673 (0.076)	1.758 (0.119)
		EGARCH(1,1) with average volume per trade (ζ_3)		
β	0.938 (0.009)	0.917 (0.015)	0.859 (0.034)	0.782 (0.081)
ζ_3	0.023 (0.007)	0.024 (0.013)	0.043 (0.026)	0.102 (0.065)
		EGARCH(1,1) with average volume per trade (ζ_4) and number of trades (ζ_5)		
β	0 (.)	0 (.)	0 (.)	0 (.)
ζ_4	0.297 (0.022)	0.248 (0.038)	0.259 (0.055)	0.304 (0.098)
ζ_5	1.387 (0.035)	1.606 (0.058)	1.630 (0.077)	1.691 (0.121)

Estimation results for the EGARCH models given by (5.18)-(5.21) or (5.18)-(5.22) applied to 21 weeks of intraday data.

they show that the volatility-volume relationship disappears when the number of trades is included in the volatility equation.

To assess the link between volatility and the trade related variables (volume, number of trades, and average volume) on an intraday basis, we use the Q' datasets (see subsection 3.1.2) and we add these variables to the volatility equation of the AR(1) model (5.18). The specification of the conditional volatility h_i is taken of the EGARCH type and written

$$\ln h_i = \omega + \theta\epsilon_{i-1} + \gamma(|\epsilon_{i-1}| - \sqrt{2/\pi}) + \beta \ln h_{i-1} + \zeta_j z_i, \qquad (5.21)$$

where z_i is the added trade related variable. The latter can be the traded volume v_i' (coefficient ζ_1), the number of trades n_i' (ζ_2), and the average volume per trade av_i' (ζ_3). To test the Jones, Kaul and Lipson (1994) model, we use the following specification for h_i:

$$\ln h_i = \omega + \theta\epsilon_{i-1} + \gamma(|\epsilon_{i-1}| - \sqrt{2/\pi}) + \beta \ln h_{i-1} + \zeta_4 av_i' + \zeta_5 n_i'. \quad (5.22)$$

Because all three variables exhibit a strong intraday pattern (see Figure 5.3 for the Boeing stock), they were deseasonalized using the same tech-

Table 5.5. Influence of trade related variables on EGARCH estimates (Exxon)

	5 min	10 min	15 min	30 min
		EGARCH(1,1)		
β	0.936 (0.009)	0.954 (0.015)	0.897 (0.033)	0.894 (0.073)
		EGARCH(1,1) with traded volume (ζ_1)		
β	0.132 (0.027)	0.043 (0.040)	0.075 (0.049)	0 (.)
ζ_1	0.717 (0.023)	0.851 (0.039)	0.902 (0.053)	1.059 (0.080)
		EGARCH(1,1) with number of trades (ζ_2)		
β	0.045 (0.028)	0.031 (0.040)	0 (.)	0 (.)
ζ_2	1.380 (0.039)	1.555 (0.066)	1.823 (0.086)	2.135 (0.139)
		EGARCH(1,1) with average volume per trade (ζ_3)		
β	0.412 (0.049)	0.157 (0.070)	0.681 (0.084)	0.525 (0.109)
ζ_3	0.459 (0.033)	0.643 (0.052)	0.307 (0.078)	0.452 (0.112)
		EGARCH(1,1) with average volume per trade (ζ_4) and number of trades (ζ_5)		
β	0.079 (0.023)	0.027 (0.034)	0 (.)	0 (.)
ζ_4	0.464 (0.023)	0.550 (0.043)	0.548 (0.057)	0.526 (0.099)
ζ_5	1.308 (0.039)	1.482 (0.065)	1.767 (0.086)	2.011 (0.140)

See note of previous table.

nique as the one used for volatility. Estimation results for the Boeing and Exxon stocks are given in Tables 5.4 and 5.5.

As can be seen in Tables 5.4 and 5.5, the coefficient β decreases from a value larger than 0.9 to almost zero once the traded volume is included in the EGARCH specification for the conditional variance. Simultaneously, the coefficient of the traded volume (ζ_1) is positive and strongly significant. These results are in agreement with the evidence presented by Lamoureux and Lastrapes (1990) on daily data and Maillet and Michel (1998) on intraday data on Elf-Aquitaine (a large liquid stock traded at the Paris Bourse). Thus, the traded volume affects the conditional volatility of the price process in the same way with intradaily data as with daily data.

Including the number of trades in the specification of the conditional variance has a similar effect on the estimated coefficients of the EGARCH process: the autoregressive effect disappears almost completely. By contrast, the average volume per trade (coefficient ζ_3) has a smaller impact on the β coefficient in the volatility equations. The impact is very small with the Boeing data, while for the Exxon data, the impact is more important, since the β estimates are reduced from 0.9 to about 0.5, and even 0.15 in one case.

To disentangle the effects of the number of trades and of the average volume per trade on the volatility, equation (5.22) for $\ln h_i$ is used. The estimation results given in Tables 5.4 and 5.5 clearly show that, as soon as the number of trades is included as an additional variable, the coefficient β goes down to zero. We conclude from these results that it is the number of trades that is mostly responsible for the drop in the value of the β estimates. It seems that the volatility dynamics is captured by the dynamics of the number of trades rather than of the average volume per trade. In conclusion, our results support the Jones, Kaul and Lipson (1994) hypothesis. Similar results are obtained by Giot (2000a) for the IBM stock.

4. INTRADAY VALUE-AT-RISK

In the preceding section, volatility models of the GARCH type were estimated using intraday returns in order to characterize the intraday volatility of several stocks traded on the NYSE. We also analyzed the influence of trade related variables on the volatility specifications. In the finance literature, volatility models are often used to characterize trading risk. One of the foremost examples is the notion of Value-at-Risk (VaR), which is a way to quantify the possible loss of a trader or financial institution. In this section, we present an application of VaR to intraday data for several stocks traded on the NYSE. We use the methodology of Giot (2000b), although we do not use intraday duration models as an alternative to measuring VaR.

4.1 VALUE-AT-RISK

Intraday VaR is an application of VaR techniques to intraday data. Thus, we first need to introduce the VaR notion. Broadly speaking, VaR is a quantitative tool which aims to assess the possible loss that can be incurred by a trader or bank over a given time period and for a given portfolio of assets. Over the last ten years, this technique has been increasingly used by banks and regulators all over the world as a way to estimate possible losses related to the holding and trading of financial assets. While the VaR can be computed for a large class of assets (stocks, bonds, derivatives such as futures and options, ...), we focus on stocks. More information about VaR techniques can be found in Jorion (2000), Danielsson and de Vries (2000), and Danielsson, Hartmann and de Vries (1998).

From a statistical point of view, the VaR can be easily defined if a sample of past returns on the portfolio of assets is available. Indeed, once the time series y_i of the returns is known and the risk level α of the VaR is specified, the VaR at level α for the given sample is simply defined as the empirical α%-quantile of the distribution of the returns. Hereafter, this empirical quantile is denoted z_α. Because z_α is such that $F(z_\alpha) = \alpha$, where $F(x)$ is the cumulative distribution function (CDF) of returns, it is also the case that the probability area to the right of z_α is equal to $1 - \alpha$. This allows for an intuitive explanation of the VaR z_α: with probability $1 - \alpha$ the returns will be larger than the VaR. For example if $\alpha = 5\%$ and if $z_\alpha = -1.645$ (with daily returns measured in percent), returns larger than -1.645 will be observed 95% of the times. If a sum of W_0 is invested, the corresponding VaR is equal to $z_\alpha W_0$. For example if $W_0 = \$100,000$, in 95% of the cases the trader will lose less than \$1,645. Contrary to some widespread beliefs, the VaR does not specify the *maximum* amount that can be lost. In our example, a loss of \$5,000 cannot be ruled out, albeit it will occur with a very small probability. Because the VaR is tantamount to computing a quantile of the distribution of returns, it is of paramount importance that the returns be identically distributed if the VaR is to be forecasted based on past data. Indeed, if the distribution of returns is different at two dates, characteristics of the distribution (such as the quantiles) will be different. Hereafter we assume that this hypothesis is true.

From an empirical point of view, the computation of the VaR of a portfolio of assets thus requires the computation of the empirical α%-quantile of the distribution of the returns of the portfolio. Because the returns are assumed to be identically distributed, the predicted VaR (i.e. VaR for future returns) can be based on these past returns. Broadly speaking, the VaR can be computed using two kinds of models, parametric and non-parametric models (see van den Goorbergh and Vlaar, 1999, or Jorion, 2000). Both types of models are detailed in subsection 4.2.

Intraday VaR is an extension of VaR to intraday returns, i.e. returns defined on intraday prices. As mentioned earlier, the main goal of VaR is to assess the possible loss that can be incurred by a trader or financial institution over a given period of time. Due to regulatory reasons, the time horizon is usually a ten day period and the models are evaluated on daily returns.[12] However, for active market participants such as floor traders or market makers, the time horizon of their returns is much shorter and the corresponding trading risk must therefore be assessed on such short time intervals. Indeed, as detailed in Chapter 1, the specialist (at the NYSE) and the market makers (at the NASDAQ) trade almost continuously during the day, which implies that the time horizon of their trades is quite small. For example, a market maker can buy an asset from a trader and sell it one minute later to another market maker or trader.

4.2 VAR MODELS FOR INTRADAY DATA

As shown in subsections 3.1.3 and 3.2, modelling the volatility of intraday returns should take into account the intraday seasonality of the volatility and the stochastic behavior of the deseasonalized returns. This argument must be extended to VaR models as modelling VaR is tantamount to modelling characteristics of the returns closely linked to volatility. In this section we present some possible models for computing the VaR of the deseasonalized returns rd_i defined in subsection 3.1.3. Thus, all techniques are used on the resampled data where from the intraday seasonality has been removed and are direct applications of VaR techniques for daily data.

For all subsequent VaR models, we use the following notation. The original sample, which is denoted S, is the collection of sampled deseasonalized returns rd_i for $i = 1$ to N, N being the total number of observed returns. S is split in two subsamples, an estimation sample S_E and a forecast sample S_F. The estimation sample contains rd_i, for $i = 1$ to N_1. The forecast sample is the set of rd_i, for $i = N_1 + 1$ to N. The parameters of the parametric models used for the computation of the VaR, and the directly computed VaR in the case of the non-parametric models are based on the S_E dataset. The performance of the models is tested on the S_F dataset (see subsection 4.3).

4.2.1 PARAMETRIC MODELS

A parametric model is estimated on the returns of the S_E sample. The VaR for the forecast sample is then directly given by a deterministic function of the estimated parameters.

Normal distribution. This is the most simple model as it assumes that the returns rd_i, $i = 1 \ldots N_1$, are normally distributed: $rd_i \sim N(\mu, \sigma^2)$. If z_α is the quantile of the $N(0,1)$ distribution at the level α, then the VaR is equal to

$$VaR_N = \widehat{\mu} + z_\alpha \widehat{\sigma}, \tag{5.23}$$

where $\widehat{\mu}$ and $\widehat{\sigma}$ are the empirical counterparts of the theoretical moments. The one-step ahead $VaR_N(j)$ for $j = N_1 + 1$ is then equal to VaR_N.

Normal GARCH model. The normal GARCH model was introduced in subsection 2.3 and is given by a conditional mean equation for the returns, such as (5.18), and a conditional variance equation such as (5.19), or more generally (5.14). If an AR(1)-GARCH(1,1) model is estimated on the returns in the S_E sample, than the one-step ahead VaR for $j = N_1 + 1$ is equal to

$$VaR_G(j) = \widehat{c} + \widehat{\delta}\, rd_{N_1} + z_\alpha \sqrt{\widehat{h}_j}. \tag{5.24}$$

with the conditional variance specification (5.19).

RiskMetrics. The RiskMetrics version of VaR was introduced by JP Morgan in 1994 as a simple practical risk model which requires almost no empirical computations. In its most simple form, the basic RiskMetrics model is equivalent to an integrated GARCH(1,1) model where the constant term ω is set equal to 0, the parameter β is set at a prespecified value $1 - \lambda$, close to 1, and the coefficient of e_{i-1}^2 is set equal to λ.[13] Thus the volatility equation of RiskMetrics is written as

$$h_i = \lambda e_{i-1}^2 + (1 - \lambda) h_{i-1}. \tag{5.25}$$

Assuming an AR(1) model for the returns, once $\widehat{c}$ and $\widehat{\delta}$ are known, the one-step ahead VaR for $j = N_1 + 1$ is equal to

$$VaR_{RM}(j) = \widehat{c} + \widehat{\delta}\, rd_{N_1} + z_\alpha \sqrt{\widehat{h}_j}, \tag{5.26}$$

as in the GARCH(1,1) case.

Student GARCH model. The Student GARCH model was introduced as an extension of the normal GARCH model in subsection 2.2.3.[14] If this model is estimated on the S_E sample, than the one-step ahead VaR for $j = N_1 + 1$ is equal to

$$VaR_t(j) = \widehat{c} + \widehat{\delta} rd_{N_1} + t_{\widehat{\nu},\alpha} \sqrt{\widehat{h}_j}, \tag{5.27}$$

where $t_{\widehat{\nu},\alpha}$ is the α%-quantile of the $t_{\widehat{\nu}}$ distribution.

4.2.2 NON-PARAMETRIC MODELS

Empirical quantile. The empirical quantile method (also called historical simulation) is the simplest non-parametric approach. Given the returns in the S_E sample, the empirical α%-quantile rd_α is directly computable. Because the returns are assumed to be identically distributed, the one-step ahead VaR for $j = N_1 + 1$ is equal to rd_α.

Pareto tails. The method is semi-parametric as it assumes that the extreme returns follow a Pareto distribution, i.e. that the tails of the distribution of the returns can be approximated by a Pareto distribution. A distribution belongs to the class of Pareto distributions if $1 - F(y) \sim y^{-\gamma}L(y)$, where $F(y)$ is the CDF and $L(y)$ is a slowly varying function at infinity. Because $1 - F(y)$ is the probability area to the right of y, this implies that the probability mass in the right tail decreases as an inverse power of y. When financial returns are modelled, it is assumed that they follow a Pareto distribution only for 'large' returns, i.e. that $1 - F(y) \sim y^{-\gamma}L(y)$ is true when $y > c$, where c must be properly defined. The Hill estimator can be used to estimate $\widehat{\gamma}$ (see Gouriéroux and Jasiak, 2000), i.e.

$$1/\widehat{\gamma} = \frac{1}{k}\sum_{j=1}^{k} \ln(y_{(j)}) - \ln(c), \tag{5.28}$$

where c is the threshold above which the returns are assumed to follow a Pareto distribution, $y_{(j)}$ are the ordered returns, and k is the number of returns larger than c. The choice of c is not trivial as it directly determines $\widehat{\gamma}$. If c is large, few ordered returns $y_{(j)}$ are used in (5.28) and $\widehat{\gamma}$ has a large variance. If c is too small, too many $y_{(j)}$ are taken into account, many of which do not follow the Pareto distribution. Information on the determination of the threshold level c can be found in van den Goorbergh (1999).

As indicated by Gouriéroux and Jasiak (2001), the Pareto distribution is particularly useful for very low quantile VaRs. Indeed, if α is very small and one wishes to use the empirical quantile method, few returns will be available for the computation of the empirical quantile. However, if one assumes that the Pareto distribution holds for $y > c$, one has

$$1 - F(c) = \alpha_c \sim c^{-\gamma}, \tag{5.29}$$

and for a VaR_α larger than c,

$$1 - F(VaR_\alpha) = \alpha \sim VaR_\alpha^{-\gamma} \tag{5.30}$$

which leads to

$$VaR_\alpha = c\Big(\frac{\alpha_c}{\alpha}\Big)^{1/\gamma}. \tag{5.31}$$

Thus, once c and α_c are available (for example by using the empirical quantile method for a not too large VaR), VaR_α can be computed for extremely small α using equation (5.31), with γ estimated by $\widehat{\gamma}$.

The Pareto distribution is valid for large positive returns. In the application to VaR, one must consider large negative returns. The application of equation (5.28) to the left tail of the distribution of returns is immediate if y denotes the opposite of the returns rd_i.

4.3 EMPIRICAL APPLICATION

In this section, we apply the four parametric and two non-parametric VaR models introduced above to intraday data for two stocks traded on the NYSE, Boeing and Disney. We split the five month dataset (January-May 1997) in a three month long estimation sample S_E and a two month long forecast sample S_F. We deal with three sampling frequencies which yield 10, 15 and 30 minute returns respectively.

In Figures 5.4 and 5.5 we plot the non-parametric estimates of the density and cumulative distribution functions for the 15 minute returns of the Boeing and Disney stocks. The left panels of both figures correspond to the estimation sample (January-March 1997), and the right panels correspond to the forecast sample (April-May 1997). To make a comparison with hypothetical returns drawn from a normal distribution, we also plot the normal density and cumulative distribution functions fitted to these returns (i.e. with mean and variance estimated by the empirical mean and variance of the 15 minute returns). While the empirical density and cumulative distribution functions broadly resemble to the normal ones, fatter tails are immediately apparent as indicated by the larger probability mass in the tails of the empirical distribution (see the bottom figures which present a zoom of the left tails of the distribution).

The graphs intuitively show that the excess kurtosis is stronger for the Boeing stock than for Disney, especially in the forecast sample. It is also immediately obvious that the empirical distributions have more probability mass around 0 than the normal distribution. This can be easily explained by the fact that zero returns are frequently observed in high-frequency data. This corresponds to configurations where identical prices are recorded successively: because the prices must stick to the grid of prices defined by the tick size, this is a recurrent situation.

For each VaR model and each sample of returns, we compute the one-step ahead VaRs of the returns rd_i in S_F. All models are estimated using the returns rd_i in S_E. The GARCH models are estimated by maximum likelihood on the returns in S_E.[15] For the RiskMetrics method, c and δ are set at their estimated values in the normal GARCH model, and $1 - \lambda$ is set equal to 0.94. The starting value for the iterative computation of h_i is the sample unconditional variance of the returns in S_E. The normal distribution model is estimated on the returns with N_1

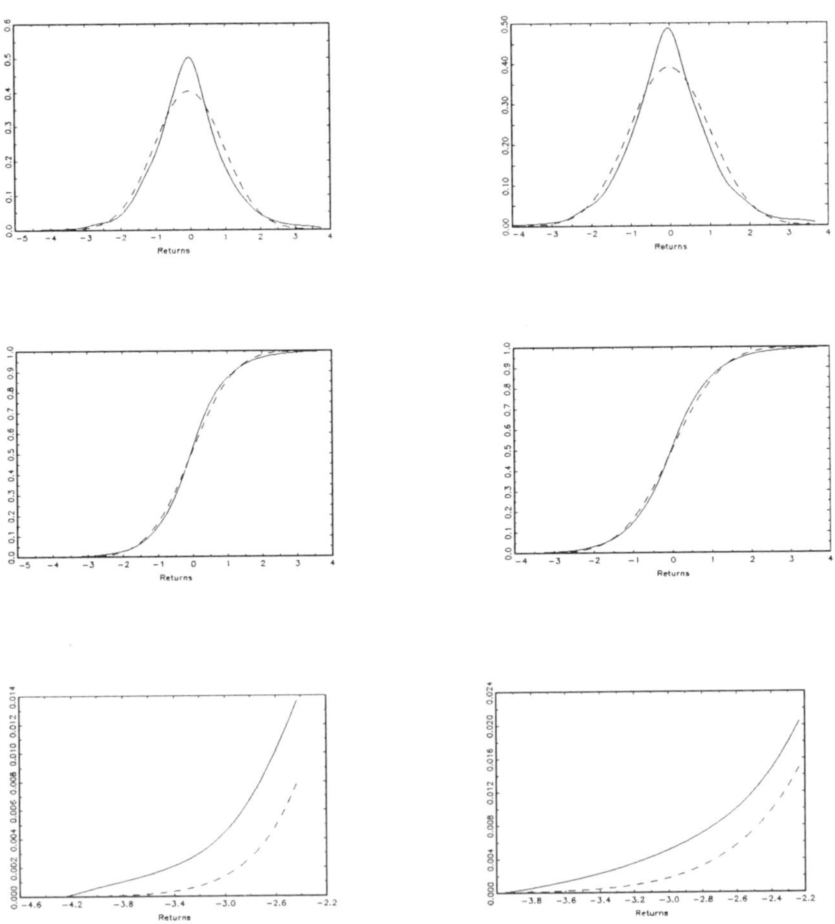

Figure 5.4. Empirical density (top), CDF (middle) and zoom of left tail of CDF (bottom) for 15 minute returns of the Boeing stock. The dashed lines correspond to a normal distribution with mean and variance given by the empirical estimates. The left panels correspond to the estimation sample (January-March 1997), the right panels to the forecast sample (April-May 1997).

increasing from its initial value after three months of data (e.g. 1,586 for Boeing 15 minute returns) to its final value N after five months (2,702 in the same example). In this way, new information is included in the estimation sample once it is available. This corresponds to the usual practice of using all information available to forecast the next one-step ahead VaR. The empirical quantile of the non-parametric methods

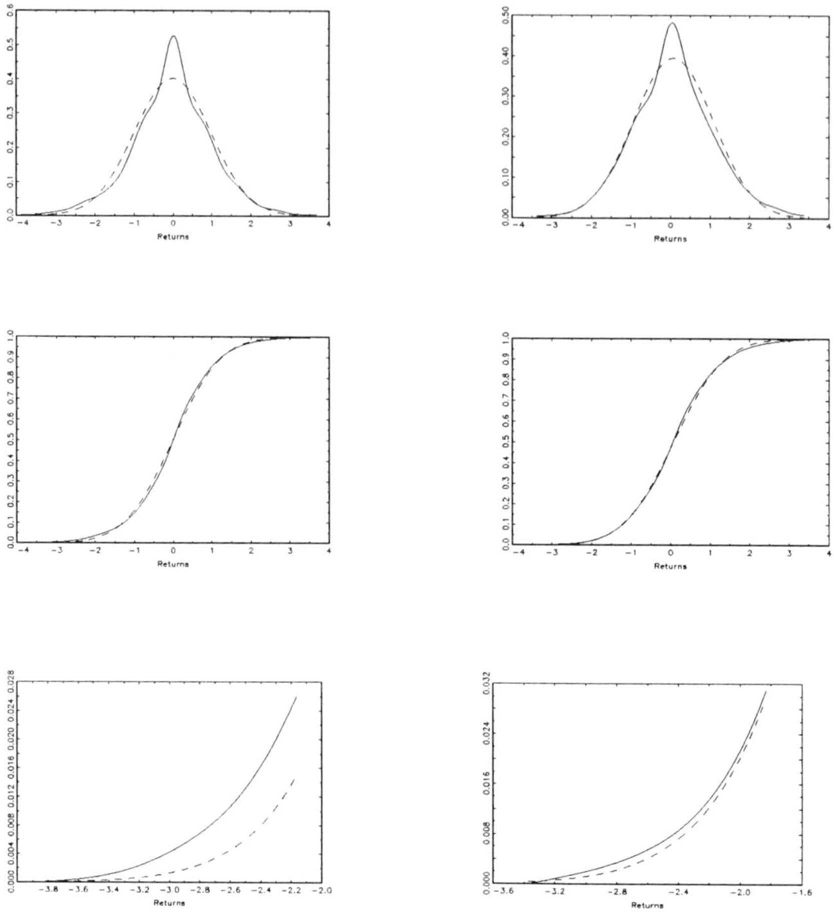

Figure 5.5. Empirical density (top), CDF (middle) and zoom of left tail of CDF (bottom) for 15 minute returns of the Disney stock. The dashed lines correspond to a normal distribution with mean and variance given by the empirical estimates. The left panels correspond to the estimation sample (January-March 1997), the right panels to the forecast sample (April-May 1997).

is directly computed from the returns in S_E with N_1 increasing like for the normal distribution model. The method based on the Pareto distribution for the tails uses equation (5.31) for small α, with $\alpha_c = 2.5\%$ and c computed using the empirical quantile method. This VaR is thus computed only for α smaller than 2.5%.

Table 5.6. Failure rates of VaR results (Boeing stock)

	10 minute returns				
	5%	2.5%	1%	0.5%	0.25%
Normal distribution	5.13	2.69	**1.97**	**1.07**	**0.84**
Normal GARCH	5.01	3.10	1.49	**1.16**	**0.89**
RiskMetrics	5.19	**3.52**	**1.91**	**1.25**	**0.66**
Student GARCH	4.72	2.27	0.66	0.24	0
Empirical quantile	4.60	2.39	0.96	0.30	0.18
Pareto tails	-	2.39	1.19	0.30	0
	15 minute returns				
	5%	2.5%	1%	0.5%	0.25%
Normal distribution	4.48	2.96	1.34	0.90	**0.72**
Normal GARCH	4.57	2.78	1.61	**1.16**	0.54
RiskMetrics	4.84	**3.49**	**1.97**	**1.43**	**0.81**
Student GARCH	4.84	2.69	1.08	0.36	0.27
Empirical quantile	5.02	2.78	0.90	0.54	0.18
Pareto tails	-	2.78	0.90	0.63	0.18
	30 minute returns				
	5%	2.5%	1%	0.5%	0.25%
Normal distribution	3.77	2.87	1.80	**1.44**	**0.90**
Normal GARCH	4.49	3.05	1.80	**1.44**	**1.08**
RiskMetrics	4.49	2.87	1.62	**1.44**	**1.26**
Student GARCH	5.75	3.05	1.44	0.72	0.36
Empirical quantile	3.77	1.97	1.26	0.72	0.18
Pareto tails	-	1.97	1.26	0.54	0.18

Failure rates for the models of intraday VaR. The estimation sample corresponds to the January-March 1997 period, and the forecast sample to the April-May 1997 period. A bold number indicates that the corresponding VaR is significantly different from the theoretical value at the 5% level.

The performance of each model is assessed by computing its failure rate for the returns rd_i in the forecast sample. The failure rate is the number of times the returns exceed the forecasted VaR. If the VaR model is correctly specified, the failure rate should be equal to the prespecified VaR level.

The failure rates for the two stocks are given in Table 5.6 (Boeing) and Table 5.7 (Disney). The results are quite good for the Boeing stock and almost perfect for the Disney stock as the empirical failure rates are close to their theoretical counterparts. This can be assessed using a statistical test. Indeed, because the computation of the empirical failure rate defines a sequence of yes/no observations, it is possible to test $H_0 : f = \alpha$ against $H_1 : f \neq \alpha$, where f is the failure rate (estimated by

Table 5.7. Failure rates of VaR models (Disney stock)

	10 minute returns				
	5%	2.5%	1%	0.5%	0.25%
Normal distr.	5.19	2.57	1.37	**1.01**	0.36
Normal GARCH	4.66	2.45	1.25	0.72	**0.54**
RiskMetrics	4.66	2.45	1.37	0.84	0.48
Student GARCH	5.91	2.69	0.84	0.42	0.12
Empirical quantile	5.19	2.03	**0.48**	**0.12**	0.06
Pareto tails	-	2.03	1.01	**0.18**	0.06
	15 minute returns				
	5%	2.5%	1%	0.5%	0.25%
Normal distr.	4.12	2.06	0.90	0.54	0.45
Normal GARCH	4.03	2.33	1.16	0.63	0.45
RiskMetrics	4.48	2.24	1.08	**0.99**	**0.63**
Student GARCH	4.21	1.88	0.63	0.36	0.09
Empirical quantile	**3.76**	**1.43**	0.54	0.27	0.18
Pareto tails	-	**1.43**	0.63	0.45	0.27
	30 minute returns				
	5%	2.5%	1%	0.5%	0.25%
Normal distribution	**3.05**	2.15	1.44	0.72	0.36
Normal GARCH	4.31	2.15	1.62	0.90	0.36
RiskMetrics	3.77	2.15	1.08	0.54	0.54
Student GARCH	5.39	1.97	1.08	0.18	0.18
Empirical quantile	3.59	1.79	0.54	0.18	0
Pareto tails	-	1.79	0.72	0.36	0

See note to previous table.

$\widehat{f}$, the empirical failure rate).[16] If T yes/no observations are available, the 95% confidence interval bounds for f are given by $\widehat{f} \pm 1.96\sqrt{\widehat{f}(1-\widehat{f})/T}$. In Tables 5.6 and 5.7, empirical failure rates are set in bold when the theoretical risk level (α) does not belong to the corresponding confidence interval: this denotes a failure of the VaR model.[17]

For the Boeing stock, the results indicate that there are no big differences between the models when α is large. When $\alpha \leq 1\%$, the normal, normal GARCH and RiskMetrics models clearly perform less well than the other models (Student GARCH, empirical quantile, and Pareto tails), which never fail. When $\alpha = 0.25\%$, the last three models never fail while the first three fail in all cases but one. Of course this was to be expected as the Student GARCH, empirical quantile and Pareto models all take into account the 'fat tails' feature of the distribution of returns. For the Disney stock, all models perform reasonably well because the distribution of the returns is sufficiently close to a normal distribution, see, in particular the bottom right panel of Figure 5.5. For both stocks, one must stress the remarkable performance of the Student GARCH model, which never fails!

Generally speaking, the empirical results are quite similar to those presented in Giot (2000b), who focused on three stocks (Boeing, Exxon and IBM) for 15 and 30 minute returns. However, the returns defined for these stocks feature a larger kurtosis, which implies that the normal, normal GARCH and RiskMetrics model perform rather poorly. This is one of the conclusions of Giot (2000b). In the examples presented in this section, the kurtosis of the 10, 15 and 30 minute returns is not very large, which explains that the methods based on the normal distribution are quite good at predicting the VaR.

Notes

1 Another possibility is to define the return as$(P_t/P_{t-1}) - 1$ (see Campbell, Lo and MacKinlay, 1997). In the case of stocks, we assume that there are no dividend payments between $t-1$ and t.

2 For a different and challenging view on the issue of market efficiency, see Shleifer (2000) and Shiller (2000). Another instructive reference is Lo and MacKinlay (1999).

3 Nelson (1990) shows that this process is strictly stationary if $\mathrm{E}[\ln(\alpha\epsilon_t^2)] < 0$, which is a milder condition that the one needed for weak stationarity. For example, with $\epsilon_t \sim N(0,1)$, strict stationarity requires that $\alpha < 3.56$.

4 A good deal of these results is synthesized in Guillaume (2000).

5 These estimates are not meaningful because there is a strong intraday seasonality in the variance and the 'simple' GARCH model cannot deal with this recurrent pattern in volatility. See also the discussion below on the Andersen and Bollerslev (1997) paper.

6 Drost and Nijman (1993) discuss the aggregation properties of the GARCH model, i.e. how the autoregressive parameter and moving average parameter evolve when returns are measured over finer intervals (which corresponds to a higher sampling frequency). They show theoretically that, when the sampling frequency increases, the autoregressive parameter tends to 1, while the moving average parameter tends to 0. They also provide formulas which link these parameters when the GARCH model is estimated at different frequencies. Empirical results confirm the adequacy of these formulas at daily and weekly frequencies.

7 We choose to use 'straightforward' equidistant sampling, i.e., we do not consider the different time scales introduced by Le Fol and Mercier (1998) before sampling our data.

8 Giot (2000a) uses the same method but all averages are computed on 30 minute intervals (instead of s minute long intervals). Cubic splines are then used to smooth the coarse volatility function.

9 $\sqrt{2/\pi}$ is the value of $\mathrm{E}(|\epsilon_{i-1}|)$ when $\epsilon_i \sim N(0,1)$, compare with (5.15).

10 For the Boeing stock when $s = 5$ minutes, and for the Exxon stock in one case, the $Q(10)$-statistics for the squared standardized residuals are significant at the 1% level. With respect to their values for the squared returns (1110.9 for Boeing and 644.5 for Exxon, see Table 5.1), the value of these statistics has nevertheless very much decreased.

11 While Lamoureux and Lastrapes (1990) use a GARCH model, Jones, Kaul and Lipson (1994) regress the daily volatility (measured by absolute daily returns) on the average volume per trade and the number of trades.

12 For an estimation of the ten day VaR not based on daily returns but on intraday returns, see Beltratti and Morana (1999).

13 The GARCH(1,1) model is said to be integrated if $\alpha + \beta = 1$, since this corresponds to a unit root in the autoregressive polynomial of the ARMA(1,1) representation of the squared return.

14 A more recent extension is the skewed Student APARCH model introduced by Giot and Laurent (2001) for modelling VaR for long and short trading positions, which is particularly useful when the distribution of the returns is skewed.

15 For the Boeing and Exxon stocks, $N_1 = 2,379$ for 10 minute returns, 1,586 for 15 minute returns, and 793 for 30 minute returns.

16 In the literature on VaR models, this test is also called the Kupiec LR test, if the hypothesis is tested using a likelihood ratio test. See Kupiec (1995).

17 Because this is a bilateral test, a model can fail if it underestimates or overestimates the true VaR. Thus, too conservative models are also rejected.

References

[1] Amihud, Y. and Mendelson, H. (1980). Dealership market: market making with inventory. *Journal of Financial Economics* 8, 31-53.

[2] Andersen, T.G. and Bollerslev, T. (1997). Intraday periodicity and volatility persistence in financial markets. *Journal of Empirical Finance* 4, 115-158.

[3] Andersen, T.G. and Bollerslev, T. (1998). DM-dollar volatility: intraday activity patterns, macroeconomic announcements, and longer-run dependencies. *Journal of Finance* 53, 219-265.

[4] Andersen, T.G. and Bollerslev, T. (1999). Forecasting financial market volatility: sample frequency vis-à-vis forecast horizon. *Journal of Empirical Finance* 6, 457-477.

[5] Bagehot, W. (1971). The only game in town. *Financial Analysts Journal* 27, 12-14.

[6] Baillie, R.T., Bollerslev, T. and Mikkelsen, H.O. (1996). Fractionally integrated generalized autoregressive conditional heteroskedasticity. *Journal of Econometrics* 74, 3-30.

[7] Bauwens, L. and Giot, P. (1998). Asymmetric ACD models: introducing price information in ACD models with a two state transition model. Discussion Paper 9844. CORE, Université catholique de Louvain.

[8] Bauwens, L. and Giot, P. (2000). The Logarithmic ACD model: an application to the bid-ask quote process of three NYSE stocks. *Annales d'Economie et de Statistique* 60, 117-149.

[9] Bauwens, L. and Giot, P. (2001). The moments of first-order Log-ACD models. Mimeo. CORE, Université catholique de Louvain.

[10] Bauwens, L. and Veredas, D. (1999). Stochastic conditional duration models. Discussion Paper 9958. CORE, Université catholique de Louvain.

[11] Bauwens, L., Lubrano, M. and Richard, J.-F. (1999). *Bayesian Inference in Dynamic Econometric Models.* Oxford: Oxford University Press.

[12] Bauwens, L., Giot, P., Grammig, J. and Veredas, D. (2000). A comparison of financial duration models with density forecasts. Discussion Paper 2000/60. CORE, Université catholique de Louvain.

[13] Beltratti, A. and Morana, C. (1999). Computing value at risk with high frequency data. *Journal of Empirical Finance* 6, 431-455.

[14] Bera, A.K. and Higgins, M.L. (1993). ARCH models: properties, estimation and testing. *Journal of Economic Surveys* 7, 305-366.

[15] Bernhardt, D., Dvoracek, V., Hughson, E. and Werner, I. (2000). Why do large orders receive discounts on the London Stock Exchange? Presented at the Western Finance Association meeting, Sun Valley, Idaho, June 2000.

[16] Biais, B., Foucault, T. and Hillion, P. (1997). *Microstructure des Marchés Financiers: Institutions, Modèles et Tests Empiriques.* Paris: Presses Universitaires de France.

[17] Biais, B., Hillion, P. and Spatt, C. (1995). An empirical analysis of the limit order book and the order flow in the Paris Bourse. *Journal of Finance* 50, 1655-1689.

[18] Biais, B., Hillion, P. and Spatt, C. (1999). Price discovery and learning during the preopening period in the Paris Bourse. *Journal of Political Economy* 107, 1218-1248.

[19] Bisière, C. and Kamionka, T. (2000). Timing of orders, orders aggressiveness and the order book at the Paris Bourse. *Annales d'Economie et de Statistique* 60, 43-72.

[20] Black, F. and Scholes, M. (1973). The pricing of options and corporate liabilities. *Journal of Political Economy* 81, 637-659.

[21] Bloomfield, R. and O'Hara, M. (1999). Market transparency: who wins and who loses? *Review of Financial Studies* 12, 5-35.

[22] Blume, L., Easley, D. and O'Hara, M. (1994). Market statistics and technical analysis: the role of volume. *Journal of Finance* 49, 153-181.

[23] Bollerslev, T. (1986). Generalized autoregressive conditional heteroskedasticity. *Journal of Econometrics* 31, 307-327.

[24] Bollerslev, T. and Domowitz, I. (1993). Trading patterns and prices in the interbank foreign exchange market. *Journal of Finance* 48, 1421-1443.

[25] Bollersev, T., Chou, R.C. and Kroner, K. (1992). ARCH modelling in finance: a review of the theory and empirical evidence. *Journal of Econometrics* 52, 5-59.

[26] Bollersev, T., Engle, R.F. and Nelson, D.B. (1994). ARCH models. In R.F. Engle and D.L. McFadden (eds.) *Handbook of Econometrics*, Vol. IV, 2961-3038. Amsterdam: Elsevier.

[27] Box, G. and Jenkins, G. (1976). *Time Series Analysis, Forecasting and Control.* San Fransisco: Holden Day.

[28] Brock, W.A. and Kleidon, A.W. (1992). Periodic market closure and trading volume: a model of intraday bids and asks. *Journal of Economic Dynamics and Control* 16, 451-489.

[29] Camacho, C. and Veredas, D. (2001). Random aggregation in ACD models when the stopping time is either endogenous or exogenous. Mimeo. CORE, Université catholique de Louvain.

[30] Cameron, A.C. and Trivedi, P.K. (1998). *Regression Analysis of Count Data.* Cambridge: Cambridge University Press.

[31] Campbell, J.Y., Lo, A.W. and MacKinlay, A.C. (1997). *The Econometrics of Financial Markets.* Princeton: Princeton University Press.

[32] Cao, C., Ghysels, E. and Hatheway, F. (2000). Why is the bid price greater than the ask? Price discovery during the NASDAQ preopening. *Journal of Finance* 55, 1339-1365.

[33] Carling, K. (1996). Testing for independence in a competing risks model. *Computational Statistics and Data Analysis* 22, 527-535.

[34] Chan, K.C., Christie, W.G. and Schultz, P.H. (1995). Market structure and the intraday pattern of bid-ask spreads for NASDAQ securities. *Journal of Business* 68, 35-60.

[35] Chen, S.X. (1998). Probability density function estimation using gamma kernels. Mimeo. School of Statistical Science, La Trobe University.

[36] Christie, W.G. and Schultz, P.H. (1994). Why do NASDAQ market makers avoid odd-eighth quotes? *Journal of Finance* 49, 1813-1840.

[37] Chung, K.H. and Van Ness, R.A. (2001). Order handling rules, tick size, and the intraday pattern of bid-ask spreads for NASDAQ stocks. *Journal of Financial Markets* 4, 143-161.

[38] Chung, K.H., Van Ness, B.F. and Van Ness, R.A. (1999). Limit orders and the bid-ask spread. *Journal of Financial Economics* 53, 255-287.

[39] Cox, D.R. and Isham, V. (1980). *Point Processes.* Reprinted in 1992 by Chapman and Hall.

[40] Cox, D.R. and Oakes, D. (1984). *Analysis of Survival Data.* Chapman and Hall.

[41] Dacorogna, M.M., Muller, U.A., Nagler, R.J., Olsen, R.B. and Pictet, O.V. (1997). A geographical model for the daily and weekly seasonal volatility in the Foreign Exchange market. *Journal of International Money and Finance* 12, 413-438.

[42] Danielsson, J. and de Vries, C.G. (2000). Value-at-Risk and extreme returns. *Annales d'Economie et de Statistique* 60, 239-270.

[43] Danielsson, J., Hartmann, P. and de Vries, C.G. (1998). The cost of conservativeness. *RISK*, January 1998.

[44] Darolles, S., Gouriéroux, C. and Le Fol, G. (2000). Intraday transaction price dynamics. *Annales d'Economie et de Statistique* 60, 207-238.

[45] Demarchi, M. and Foucault, T. (2000). Equity trading systems in Europe: a survey of recent changes.*Annales d'Economie et de Statistique* 60, 73-115.

[46] Diebold, F.X., Gunther, T.A. and Tay, A.S. (1998). Evaluating density forecasts, with applications to financial risk management. *International Economic Review* 39, 863-883.

[47] Domowitz, I. (1993). A taxonomy of automated trading systems. *Journal of International Money and Finance* 12, 607-631.

[48] Drost, F.C. and Nijman, T.E. (1993). Temporal aggregation of GARCH processes. *Econometrica* 61, 909-927.

[49] Dufour, A. and Engle, R. (2000). Time and the price impact of a trade. *Journal of Finance* 55, 2467-2498.

[50] Easley, D. and O'Hara, M. (1987). Price, trade size, and information in securities market. *Journal of Financial Economics* 19, 69-90.

[51] Easley, D. and O'Hara, M. (1992). Time and the process of security price adjustment. *Journal of Finance* 47, 576-605.

[52] Easley, D., Kiefer, N.M. and O'Hara, M. (1997). The information content of the trading process. *Journal of Empirical Finance* 4, 159-186.

[53] Engle, R.F. (1982). Autoregressive Conditional Heteroscedasticity with estimates of the variance of United Kingdom inflation. *Econometrica* 50, 987-1006.

[54] Engle, R.F. (1995). *ARCH. Selected Readings.* Oxford University Press.

[55] Engle, R.F. (2000). The econometrics of ultra-high frequency data. *Econometrica* 68, 1-22.

[56] Engle, R. and Lange, J. (2001). Predicting VNET: a model of the dynamics of market depth. *Journal of Financial Markets* 4, 113-142.

[57] Engle, R. and Lunde, A. (1998). Trades and quotes: a bivariate point process. Discussion Paper 98-07. Department of Economics, University of California, San Diego.

[58] Engle, R.F. and Ng, V.K. (1993). Measuring and testing the impact of news on volatility. *Journal of Finance* 48, 1749-1778.

[59] Engle, R. and Russell, J. (1997). Forecasting the frequency of changes in quoted foreign exchange prices with the autoregressive conditional duration model. *Journal of Empirical Finance* 4, 187-212.

[60] Engle, R. and Russell, J. (1998). Autoregressive conditional duration; a new model for irregularly spaced transaction data. *Econometrica* 66, 1127-1162.

[61] Escribano, A. and Pascual, R. (2000). Dynamic asymmetries in bid-ask responses to innovations in the trading places. Working Paper 00-47. Department of Economics, Universidad Carlos III Madrid.

[62] Fama, E. (1970). Efficient capital markets: a review of theory and empirical work. *Journal of Finance* 25, 383-417.

[63] Fama, E. (1991). Efficient capital markets: II. *Journal of Finance* 46, 1575-1618.

[64] Florens, J.-P., Fougère, D. and Mouchart, M. (1995). Duration models. In Matyas and Sevestre (eds.) *Econometrics of Panel Data*, 2nd. ed., 431-536. Dordrecht: Kluwer Academic Publishers.

[65] Garman, M. (1976). Market microstructure. *Journal of Financial Economics* 3, 257-275.

[66] Gerhard, F. and Hautsch, N. (1999). Volatility estimation on the basis of price intensity. An empirical analysis of Bund future intraday transaction data. Discussion Paper 99/19. Center of Finance and Econometrics, University of Konstanz.

[67] Gerhard, F. and Hautsch, N. (2000). Determinants of inter-trade durations and hazard rates using proportional hazard ARMA models. Discussion Paper 00/20. Center of Finance and Econometrics, University of Konstanz.

[68] Ghysels, E. and Jasiak, J. (1998). GARCH for irregularly spaced financial data: the ACD-GARCH model. *Studies in Nonlinear Dynamics and Econometrics* 2, 133-149.

[69] Ghysels, E., Gouriéroux, C. and Jasiak, J. (1997). Stochastic volatility duration models. Working Paper 9746. CREST, Paris.

[70] Giot, P. (2000a). Time transformations, intraday data, and volatility models. *Journal of Computational Finance*, 4, 31-62.

[71] Giot, P. (2000b). Intraday Value-at-Risk. Discussion Paper 2000/45. CORE, Université catholique de Louvain.

[72] Giot, P. and Laurent, S. (2001). Value-at-Risk for long and short trading positions. METEOR Research Memorandum RM/01/005. Maastricht University.

[73] Glosten, L. and Harris, L. (1988). Estimating the components of the bid/ask spread. *Journal of Financial Economics* 21, 123-142.

[74] Glosten, L. and Milgrom, P. (1985). Bid, ask, and the transaction prices in a specialist market with heterogeneously informed traders. *Journal of Financial Economics* 13, 71-100.

[75] Goodhart, C.A.E. and O'Hara, M. (1997). High frequency data in financial markets: issues and applications. *Journal of Empirical Finance* 4, 73-114.

[76] Gordon, J.S (1999). *The Great Game. The Emergence of Wall Street as a World Power 1653-2000.* New York: Scribner.

[77] Gouriéroux, C. and Jasiak, J. (2001). *Financial Econometrics*. Princeton: Princeton University Press.

[78] Gouriéroux, C., Le Fol, G. and Meyer, B. (1998). Analyse du carnet d'ordres. *Banque et Marchés* 36, 5-20.

[79] Gouriéroux, C., Jasiak, J. and Le Fol, G. (1999). Intraday market activity. *Journal of Financial Markets* 2, 193-226.

[80] Grammig, J. and Maurer, K.-O. (2000). Non-monotonic hazard functions and the autoregressive conditional duration model. *The Econometrics Journal* 3, 16-38.

[81] Grammig, J. and Wellner, M. (1999). Modeling the interdependence of volatility and inter-transaction duration processes. Discussion Paper 21. SFB 373, Humboldt University Berlin.

[82] Guillaume, D.M. (2000). *Intradaily Exchange Rate Movements*. Dordrecht: Kluwer Academic Publishers.

[83] Guillaume, D.M., Pictet, O.V. and Dacorogna, M.M. (1995). On the intra-daily performance of GARCH processes. Olsen & Associates Internal Document DMG 1994-07-31.

[84] Guillaume, D.M., Dacorogna, M.M., Davé, R.R., Muller, U.A., Olsen, R.B. and Pictet, O.V. (1997). From the bird's eye to the microscope: a survey of new stylized facts of the intraday foreign exchange markets. *Finance and Stochastics* 1, 95-129.

[85] Hafner, C. (1999). Durations, volume and the prediction of financial returns in transaction time. Mimeo. Presented at the Econometric Society World Congress in Seattle, August 2000.

[86] Handa, P., Schwartz, R.A. and Tiwari, A. (1997). L'écologie d'un marché dirigé par les ordres. In Biais, B., Davydoff, D. and Jacquillat, B. (eds.), *Organisation et Qualité des Marchés Financiers.*, 185-202. Paris: Presses Universitaires de France.

[87] Hasbrouck, J. (1988). Trades, quotes, inventories, and information. *Journal of Financial Economics* 22, 229-252.

[88] Hasbrouck, J. (1991). Measuring the information content of stock trades. *Journal of Finance* 46, 179-208.

[89] Hasbrouck, J. and Sofianos, G. (1993). The trades of market makers: an empirical analysis of NYSE specialists. *Journal of Finance* 48, 1565-1593.

[90] Hasbrouck, J., Sofianos, G. and Sosebee, D. (1993). New York Stock Exchange systems and trading procedures. Working Paper 93-01. New York Stock Exchange.

[91] Hausman, J., Lo, A.W. and MacKinlay, A.C. (1992). An ordered probit analysis of transaction stock prices. *Journal of Financial Economics* 31, 319-379.

[92] Heinen, A. (2000). Modeling time series count data: an autoregressive conditional Poisson model. Mimeo. Department of Economics. University of California, San Diego.

[93] Ho, T. and Stoll, H. (1981). Optimal dealer pricing under transactions and return uncertainty. *Journal of Financial Economics* 9, 47-73.

[94] Huang, R.D. and Stoll, H.R. (1996). Dealer versus auction markets: a paired comparison of execution costs on NASDAQ and the NYSE. *Journal of Financial Economics* 41, 313-357.

[95] Jasiak, J. (1998). Persistence in intertrade durations. *Finance* 19, 166-195.

[96] Jones, C.M., Kaul, G. and Lipson, M.L. (1994). Transactions, volume, and volatility. *Review of Financial Studies* 7, 631-651.

[97] Jorda, O. and Marcellino, M. (2000). Stochastic processes subject to time scale transformations: an application to high-frequency FX data. Mimeo. Department of Economics, University of California, Davis.

[98] Jorion, P. (2000). *Value-at-Risk* (second edition). McGraw-Hill.

[99] Kalbfleish, J. and Prentice, R. (1980). *The Statistical Analysis of Failure Time Data.* John Wiley and Sons.

[100] Kamionka, T. (2000). La modélisation des données haute fréquence. Mimeo. CREST. Paris.

[101] Kupiec, P. (1995). Techniques for verifying the accuracy of risk measurement models. *Journal of Derivatives* 2, 73-84.

[102] Kyle, A.S. (1985). Continuous auctions and insider trading. *Econometrica* 53, 1315-1335.

[103] Lamoureux, C.G. and Lastrapes, W.D. (1990). Heteroskedasticity in stock return data: volume versus GARCH effects. *Journal of Finance* 45, 220-229.

[104] Lancaster, T. (1990). *The Econometric Analysis of Transition Data.* Cambridge: Cambridge University Press.

[105] Lee, C.M. and Ready, M.J. (1991). Inferring trade direction from intraday data. *Journal of Finance* 46, 733-746.

[106] Lee, C.M., Mucklow, B. and Ready, M.J. (1993). Spreads, depths, and the impact of earnings information: an intraday analysis. *Review of Financial Studies* 6, 345-374.

[107] Lee, R. (1998). *What is an exchange?* Oxford: Oxford University Press.

[108] Lee, S. and Hansen, B. (1994). Asymptotic theory for the GARCH(1,1) quasi-maximum likelihood estimator. *Econometric Theory* 10, 29-52.

[109] Le Fol, G. and Mercier, L. (1998). Time deformation: definition and comparisons. *Journal of Computational Intelligence in Finance*, September/October 1998, 19-33.

[110] Lindeboom, M. and Van Den Berg, G.J. (1994). Heterogeneity in models for bivariate survival: the importance of the mixing distribution. *Journal of Royal Statistical Society B* 56, 49-60.

[111] Lo, A.W. and MacKinlay, A.C. (1999). *A Non-Random Walk Down Wall Street.* Princeton: Princeton University Press.

[112] Lumsdaine, R. (1996). Consistency and asymptotic normality for the quasi-maximum likelihood estimator in IGARCH(1,1) and covariance stationary GARCH(1,1) models. *Econometrica* 64, 575-596.

[113] Madhavan, A. (2000). Market microstructure: a survey. *Journal of Financial Markets* 3, 205-258.

[114] Madhavan, A. and Cheng, M. (1997). In search of liquidity: block trades in the upstairs and downstairs markets. *Review of Financial Studies* 10, 175-203.

[115] Madhavan, A. and Sofianos, G. (1998). An empirical analysis of NYSE specialist trading. *Journal of Financial Economics* 48, 189-210.

[116] Maillet, B. and Michel, T. (1998). Volume-time scale and intraday returns density. Document de travail 9801. Centre d'Economie Bancaire Internationale, Paris.

[117] Malkiel, B.G. (1996). *A Random Walk Down Wall Street.* New York: W.W. Norton & Company.

[118] Meddahi, N., Renault, E. and Werker, B. (1998). Modelling high-frequency data in continuous time. Mimeo.

[119] Mood, A.M., Graybill, F.A. and Boes, D.C. (1987). *Introduction to the Theory of Statistics* (3rd edition). McGraw-Hill International Editions.

[120] Nelson, D.B. (1990). Stationarity and persistence in the GARCH(1,1) model. *Econometric Theory* 6, 318-334.

[121] Nelson, D.B. (1991). Conditional heteroskedasticity in asset returns: a new approach. *Econometrica* 59, 349-370.

[122] O'Hara, M. (1995). *Market Microstructure Theory.* Oxford: Basil Blackwell.

[123] Pagano, M. (1998). The changing microstructure of European equity markets. In G. Ferrarini (ed.), *The European Securities Markets: The Investment Services Directive and Beyond.* Dordrecht: Kluwer Academic Publishers.

[124] Pagano, M. and Roell, A. (1992). Auction and dealership markets: what is the difference? *European Economic Review* 36, 613-623.

[125] Pagano, M. and Roell, A. (1996). Transparence and liquidity: a comparison of auction and dealer markets with informed trading. *Journal of Finance* 51, 579-611.

[126] Palm, F. (1996). GARCH models of volatility. In Maddala, G.S and Rao, C.R. (eds.), *Handbook of Statistics, Volume 14: Statistical Methods in Finance*, 209-240. Amsterdam: Elsevier.

[127] Pascual, R., Escribano, A. and Tapia, M. (1999). How does liquidity behave? A multidimensional analysis of NYSE stocks. Working Paper 99-64. Department of Economics, Universidad Carlos III Madrid.

[128] Pascual, R., Escribano, A. and Tapia, M. (2000). BLM: a bidimensional approach to measure liquidity. Working Paper 00-51. Department of Economics, Universidad Carlos III Madrid.

[129] Prigent, J.L., Renault, O. and Scaillet, O. (1999). An autoregressive conditional binomial option pricing model. Working Paper 9965. CREST, Paris.

[130] Roll, R. (1984). A simple implicit measure of the bid-ask spread in an efficient market. *Journal of Finance* 39, 1127-1139.

[131] Rosenblatt, M. (1952). Remarks on a multivariate transformation. *Annals of Mathematical Statistics*, 23, 470-472.

[132] Russell, J.R. (1999). Econometric modeling of multivariate irregularly-spaced high-frequency data. Mimeo. Graduate School of Business. University of Chicago.

[133] Russell, J.R. and Engle, R. (1998). Econometric analysis of discrete-valued, irregularly-spaced financial transactions data using a new autoregressive conditional multinomial model. Discussion Paper 98-10. Department of Economics, University of California, San Diego.

[134] Schwert, S.G. (1997). Symposium on market microstructure: focus on NASDAQ. *Journal of Financial Economics* 45, 3-8.

[135] Seppi, D. (1990). Equilibrium block trading and asymmetric information. *Journal of Finance* 45, 281-305.

[136] Sharpe, W.F., Alexander, G.J. and Bailey, J.V. (1999). *Investments* (sixth edition). Prentice-Hall.

[137] Shephard, N. (1999). BIN models for trade-by-trade data. Modelling the number of trades in a fixed interval of time. Mimeo. Presented at EC^2, Madrid, December 1999.

[138] Shiller, R.J. (2000). *Irrational Exubcrance.* Princeton: Princeton University Press.

[139] Shleifer, A. (2000). *Inefficient Markets: an Introduction to Behavioral Finance.* Oxford: Oxford University Press.

[140] Sofianos, G. and Werner, I.M. (2000). The trades of NYSE floor brokers. *Journal of Financial Markets* 3, 139-176.

[141] Stoll, H.R. (1978). The supply of dealer services in securities markets. *Journal of Finance* 33, 1133-1151.

[142] Stoll, H.R. (1989). Inferring the components of the bid-ask spread: theory and empirical tests. *Journal of Finance* 44, 115-134.

[143] Taylor, S.J. (1986). *Modelling Financial Time Series.* Chichester: John Wiley.

[144] van den Goorbergh, R. (1999). Value-at-Risk analysis and least squares tail index estimation. Research memorandum 578. De Nederlandsche Bank.

[145] van den Goorbergh, R. and Vlaar, P. (1999). Value-at-Risk analysis of stock returns. Historical simulation, variance techniques or tail index estimation? Staff Report 40. De Nederlandsche Bank.

[146] Veredas, D. (2001). Pointing out the main points of point processes. Chapter 2 of Ph. D. Thesis *Econometric Modelling of Financial Point Processes*. CORE, Université catholique de Louvain.

[147] Veredas, D., Rodriguez-Poo, J. and Espasa, A. (2001). On the (intradaily) seasonality, dynamics and durations zero of a financial point process. Mimeo. CORE, Université catholique de Louvain.

[148] Wahal, S. (1997). Entry, exit, market makers and the bid-ask spread. *Review of Financial Studies* 10, 871-901.

[149] Zhang, M.Y., Russell, J.R. and Tsay, R.S. (1999). A nonlinear autoregressive conditional duration model with applications to financial transaction data. Mimeo. Graduate School of Business. University of Chicago. Forthcoming in *Journal of Econometrics*.

About the Authors

Luc Bauwens is Professor of Economics at the 'Université catholique de Louvain' (Belgium) since 1991, and chairman of the Department of Economics since 2000. He is a member of the Center for Operations Research and Econometrics (CORE) and he was co-director of CORE from 1992 to 1998. He is also consultant for public agencies, utilities and financial institutions. He has published several books and papers in the fields of Bayesian inference, time series methods, simulation and numerical methods in econometrics, as well as empirical finance and international trade. He is associate editor of several journals. He obtained a Ph.D. in Economics at the Université catholique de Louvain in 1983 and he received the Leonard J. Savage Thesis Award in 1984.

Pierre Giot is Professor of Econometrics and Quantitative Finance at Maastricht University in The Netherlands and he is a member of CORE (Université catholique de Louvain). After graduating as a civil engineer (polytechnique) in electronics in 1993 and working for one year as a computer software consultant in Luxemburg, he completed a Ph.D. in Economics at the Université catholique de Louvain in 1999. His current research interests focus on quantitative finance, econometric models for intraday tick-by-tick data, empirical market microstructure and risk management. In addition to teaching and research, he has also been involved as a consultant in projects with financial institutions.

Email addresses of the authors:
bauwens@core.ucl.ac.be
giot@core.ucl.ac.be.

Index

Advanced Studies in Theoretical and Applied Econometrics

1. J.H.P. Paelinck (ed.): *Qualitative and Quantitative Mathematical Economics.* 1982 ISBN 90-247-2623-9
2. J.P. Ancot (ed.): *Analysing the Structure of Econometric Models.* 1984 ISBN 90-247-2894-0
3. A.J. Hughes Hallet (ed.): *Applied Decision Analysis and Economic Behaviour.* 1984 ISBN 90-247-2968-8
4. J.K. Sengupta: *Information and Efficiency in Economic Decision.* 1985 ISBN 90-247-3072-4
5. P. Artus and O. Guvenen (eds.), in collaboration with F. Gagey: *International Macroeconomic Modelling for Policy Decisions.* 1986 ISBN 90-247-3201-8
6. M.J. Vilares: *Structural Change in Macroeconomic Models.* Theory and Estimation. 1986 ISBN 90-247-3277-8
7. C. Carraro and D. Sartore (eds.): *Development of Control Theory for Economic Analysis.* 1987 ISBN 90-247-3345-6
8. D.P. Broer: *Neoclassical Theory and Empirical Models of Aggregate Firm Behaviour.* 1987 ISBN 90-247-3412-6
9. A. Italianer: *Theory and Practice of International Trade Linkage Models.* 1986 ISBN 90-247-3407-X
10. D.A. Kendrick: *Feedback.* A New Framework for Macroeconomic Policy. 1988 ISBN 90-247-3593-9; Pb: 90-247-3650-1
11. J.K. Sengupta and G.K. Kadekodi (eds.): *Econometrics of Planning and Efficiency.* 1988 ISBN 90-247-3602-1
12. D.A. Griffith: *Advanced Spatial Statistics.* Special Topics in the Exploration of Quantitative Spatial Data Series. 1988 ISBN 90-247-3627-7
13. O. Guvenen (ed.): *International Commodity Market Models and Policy Analysis.* 1988 ISBN 90-247-3768-0
14. G. Arbia: *Spatial Data Configuration in Statistical Analysis of Regional Economic and Related Problems.* 1989 ISBN 0-7923-0284-2
15. B. Raj (ed.): *Advances in Econometrics and Modelling.* 1989 ISBN 0-7923-0299-0
16. A. Aznar Grasa: *Econometric Model Selection.* A New Approach. 1989 ISBN 0-7923-0321-0
17. L.R. Klein and J. Marquez (eds.): *Economics in Theory and Practice.* An Eclectic Approach. Essays in Honor of F. G. Adams. 1989 ISBN 0-7923-0410-1
18. D.A. Kendrick: *Models for Analyzing Comparative Advantage.* 1990 ISBN 0-7923-0528-0
19. P. Artus and Y. Barroux (eds.): *Monetary Policy.* A Theoretical and Econometric Approach. 1990 ISBN 0-7923-0626-0
20. G. Duru and J.H.P. Paelinck (eds.): *Econometrics of Health Care.* 1990 ISBN 0-7923-0766-6
21. L. Phlips (ed.): *Commodity, Futures and Financial Markets.* 1991 ISBN 0-7923-1043-8

Kluwer Academic Publishers – Dordrecht / Boston / London

Advanced Studies in Theoretical and Applied Econometrics

22. H.M. Amman, D.A. Belsley and L.F. Pau (eds.): *Computational Economics and Econometrics.* 1992 ISBN 0-7923-1287-2
23. B. Raj and J. Koerts (eds.): *Henri Theil's Contributions to Economics and Econometrics.* Vol. I: Econometric Theory and Methodology. 1992 ISBN 0-7923-1548-0
24. B. Raj and J. Koerts (eds.): *Henri Theil's Contributions to Economics and Econometrics.* Vol. II: Consumer Demand Analysis and Information Theory. 1992 ISBN 0-7923-1664-9
25. B. Raj and J. Koerts (eds.): *Henri Theil's Contributions to Economics and Econometrics.* Vol. III: Economic Policy and Forecasts, and Management Science. 1992 ISBN 0-7923-1665-7
    Set (23–25) ISBN 0-7923-1666-5
26. P. Fisher: *Rational Expectations in Macroeconomic Models.* 1992 ISBN 0-7923-1903-6
27. L. Phlips and L.D. Taylor (eds.): *Aggregation, Consumption and Trade.* Essays in Honor of H.S. Houthakker. 1992. ISBN 0-7923-2001-8
28. L. Matyas and P. Sevestre (eds.): *The Econometrics of Panel Data.* Handbook of Theory and Applications. 1992 ISBN 0-7923-2043-3
29. S. Selvanathan: *A System-Wide Analysis of International Consumption Patterns.* 1993 ISBN 0-7923-2344-0
30. H. Theil in association with D. Chen, K. Clements and C. Moss: *Studies in Global Econometrics.* 1996 ISBN 0-7923-3660-7
31. P.J. Kehoe and T.J. Kehoe (eds.): *Modeling North American Economic Integration.* 1995 ISBN 0-7923-3751-4
32. C. Wells: *The Kalman Filter in Finance.* 1996 ISBN 0-7923-3771-9
33. L. Matyas and P. Sevestre (eds.): *The Econometrics of Panel Data.* A Handbook of the Theory with Applications. Second Revised Edition. 1996 ISBN 0-7923-3787-5
34. B. Assarsson, D. Edgerton, A. Hummelmose, I. Laurila, K. Rickertson and P.H. Vale: *The Econometrics of Demand Systems.* With Applications to Food Demand in the North Countries. 1996 ISBN 0-7923-4106-6
35. D.A. Griffith, C.G. Amrhein and J-M. Huriot (eds.): *Econometric Advances in Spatial Modelling and Methodology.* Essays in Honour of Jean Paelinck. 1998 ISBN 0-7923-4915-6
36. R.D.H. Heijmans, D.S. G. Pollock and A. Satorra (eds.): *Innovations in Multivariate Statistical Analysis.* 2000 ISBN 0-7923-8636-1
37. R. MacDonald and I. Marsh: *Exchange Rate Modelling.* 2000 ISBN 0-7923-8668-X
38. L. Bauwens and P. Giot: *Econometric Modelling of Stock Market Intraday Activity.* 2001 ISBN 0-7923-7424-X

Kluwer Academic Publishers – Dordrecht / Boston / London